Smart Talk

Contemporary Interviewing and Interrogation

Preliminary Edition

Denise Kindschi Gosselin
Western New England College

PEARSON
Custom
Publishing

PEARSON
Prentice
Hall

Taken from:

Smart Talk: Contemporary Interviewing and Investigation
by Denise Kindschi Gosselin
Copyright © 2006 by Pearson Education, Inc.
Published by Prentice Hall
Upper Saddle River, New Jersey 07458

This special edition published in cooperation with Pearson Custom Publishing.

Printed in the United States of America

20 19

ISBN 0-536-17383-4

2005340073

EM/MB

Please visit our web site at *www.pearsoncustom.com*

PEARSON CUSTOM PUBLISHING
75 Arlington Street, Suite 300, Boston, MA 02116
A Pearson Education Company

*To my husband, Robert,
with love and gratitude*

Contents

Preface

For eight years I served the Massachusetts State Police as a Trooper assigned to the Detective Unit of the Hampden and Hampshire County District Attorney's Offices. As a member of the unit my duties included the investigation of major crimes, including homicide, bank robbery, rape, fraud, embezzlement, larceny, as well as the investigation of suicides and unattended deaths. I specialized in the investigation of crimes against women and children, specifically in interviewing children. My additional duties included the rendition of fugitives, protection of state witnesses, as well as the preparation and execution of warrants. During those years I also participated in surveillance, undercover investigations, and narcotics raids. It was my practice in each case where I was the lead investigator to interrogate every suspected perpetrator, no matter how minor or significant the case appeared.

In all of the duties described as well as police work on the road, I found that communication was the most important ingredient for a successful case investigation. Professionalism is judged by others relative to the ability of an individual to communicate effectively within the discipline. Proficiency at interviewing and interrogation did not come naturally for me; it was not intuitive. I attended many seminars and training sessions on how to interview and interrogate. The process took years of purposeful attention on how to improve these skills and gain the necessary knowledge. It made a positive difference on the quality and quantity of information that was gathered from victims, witnesses, and perpetrators. The progression was an enjoyable challenge in learning human behavior. The information contained in this text is an introduction to the vast range of approaches to both interviewing and interrogation. It contains the information that I found most helpful throughout my career.

When my career changed direction into academia it became apparent that every discipline had its own course in the methods of improving communication skills. Competence in communication that is specific to each discipline is the hallmark of professionalism. Criminal justice was the exception to that rule; no colleges in my area offered a course on interviewing and interrogation. Although criminal justice professionals rely on their communication skills for every aspect of the job, there are a lack of educational tools to prepare for this discipline. This void brought about my desire to write this text. I hope that it will provide the basis for good communication for students in the criminal justice and related fields.

This book follows the course outline that I developed for my own classroom. It was tested and improved over a period of years. It contains a comprehensive introduction to the major interviewing and interrogation methods along with the legal considerations involved with these approaches. For students of different disciplines, each chapter begins with an introduction which forms the basis for the chapter to follow. For some of these chapters the introduction contains theoretical background. This is a radical departure from other interviewing and interrogation texts, and is purposefully not interwoven within the chapter itself. Some students will find it interesting and others will simply skip the theory! Its purpose is to satisfy those students and instructors who would like to know the theoretical background for the interviewing techniques. One focus of the book is interviewing special populations: children, the elderly, and persons having a disability or mental illness. To assist the learner there are short answer questions, fill-in questions, and appropriate exercises to practice the concepts for each chapter. An additional aid for teaching these concepts is a PowerPoint presentation for each chapter. The instructor's manual that accompanies this text will contain the answers along with suggested additional resources and exercises.

Acknowledgements

Thank you to Victoria Noble whose professionalism and caring made the writing of this book possible.

I owe a special debt of gratitude to Professor Dawna Komorosky from California State University at Hayward. Dawna, my friend and colleague, whose contribution in reading and editing this text provided consistency. Dawna has contributed significantly to this text and to the Instructor's Manual. Thank you to Patrick J. Faiella, Criminologist from Massasoit Community College in Massachusetts. Patrick tirelessly read this manuscript and provided his insight along with many of the end-of-chapter questions. To friend and husband, Robert Gosselin, thank you for your limitless ideas and non-waivering support. To my friends and colleagues at Western New England College, who encouraged and supported my efforts, thank you.

About the Author

A pioneer in law enforcement, the author became the first uniformed female officer for her hometown, Lunenburg, Massachusetts, and the first female campus police officer at the Community College she had attended.

The Massachusetts Senate honored her in 1978 as the first woman appointed constable for the City of Fitchburg. In 1979 she was named an Outstanding Young Woman of America.

Trooper Gosselin graduated in the 61st Recruit Training Troop of the Massachusetts State Police in January, 1980. During the years that followed she served as a uniformed officer performing route patrol activities; as an instructor at the Massachusetts State Police Academy; and as a major crime detective. Recognized as a local expert in Child Abuse Investigation, she spoke on cable television and on radio. She and Trooper Gibbons appeared on *America's Most Wanted* when John Walsh presented their fugitive case on the show. Additionally, she has made many presentations at professional meetings with the Department of Social Services, Department of Mental Health, and for the Office of the District Attorney. Trooper Gosselin has testified on numerous major crime cases, both in Criminal Court and in Civil Hearings.

Like many police officers, her education was fragmented, interrupted over the years by demanding work and family responsibilities. Denise holds an Associate Degree in Science in Law Enforcement from Mt. Wachusett Community College; her Bachelor and Masters Degrees in Criminal Justice were awarded from Westfield State College. At the University of Massachusetts she studied at the doctoral level in the Political Science department. Denise is currently a PH.D. candidate at Capella University. She was awarded a scholarship to attend the first Child Abuse and Exploitation Investigative Techniques Training Program at the Federal Law Enforcement Training Center. Denise has additional training in homicide, rape, and stalking investigation, and search and seizure. In 1995 she studied at the International Institute for the Sociology of Law in Onati, Spain.

From 1991 to the present the author has lectured at Greenfield Community College, Holyoke Community College, Springfield College, and Westfield State College. She has taught Domestic Abuse for the 74th Massachusetts State Police Recruit Training Troop and presented a professional workshop on Cognitive Interviewing Techniques at the Roger Williams Justice Institute, Rhode Island.

As a member of the Academy of Criminal Justice Sciences she has made numerous presentations and served as chair of the publications committee and program committee chair. Ms. Gosselin is a long-time member of the Northeastern Association of Criminal Justice Sciences. She has held the offices of President, Vice President, and Secretary.

Denise Kindschi Gosselin is now a faculty member of the Criminal Justice and Sociology Department at Western New England College. Her additional publications include *Heavy Hands: An Introduction to the Crimes of Family Violence,* currently in its third edition. She has contributed *Encyclopedia of Police Science, Encyclopedia of Juvenile Justice* and *Encyclopedia of Domestic Violence.* In edited texts Denise has published chapters entitled "Victim Interviewing in Cases of Domestic Violence: Techniques for Police" and "Intimate Partner Violence Against and by Women."

PART

I

Laying the Groundwork for Success

Smart Talk is about effective communication; it provides the guidelines for gathering information. Chapter One stresses the process of communication and required skills of the interviewer. Interviewing and interrogation are defined here. The difference between the two is critical to the fact-gathering approach. The nature of interviewing suggests a flexible process that may be dictated by the individual being interviewed. The nature of interrogation is persuasion that is accusatory. The chapter further addresses the personal qualities of an interviewer. The successful interviewer is one who has acquired a great deal of knowledge, about people being interviewed, the case that is being investigated, and the professionalism that is brought into the process. Rapport and its development are a critical component in successful interviewing; it is covered in this chapter. A brief introduction to various forms of non-verbal communication is included.

In Chapter Two the importance of the perspective and point of view of the interviewee is recognized through social systems theory. A three-phase approach to interviewing is suggested in this chapter; it provides a general framework for the process. Preparation, establishment of the psychological content, and the actual questioning are the categories presented. The suggestion here is that preparation prior to the interview is as important as the questioning itself. The options for determining when and where the interview takes place are covered. The potential problem of misinformation and its resulting contamination on the interview is outlined as it is a concern to modern investigators. In the final phase of interviewing, question types is given extensive coverage. An important aspect of successful interviewing comes with knowing which questions will elicit the desired responses, and which ones will facilitate answers.

Building on the previous chapters, Chapter Three suggests how the questioning is prepared. The goals of purposeful interviewing are met through examining the nature of the offense, determining if a crime was actually committed, and through identifying the perpetrator. Some general approaches to determining the nature of the offense and interviewing approaches for victims in specific crime situations is presented. Basic procedures of perpetrator identification options are outlined. This chapter also builds on the concept of rapport, which was introduced in Chapter One. The final section introduces the reader to methods of accessing statement accuracy.

Interviewing and Interrogation

KEY TERMS

Communication process	Elicit
Kinesics	Paralanguage
Persuade	Presumptive prosecution policy
Proxemics	Rapport

CHAPTER OBJECTIVES

After completing this chapter, you should be able to:

- Describe the communication process according to Berlo
- Define interview
- List the categories of persons that might be interviewed
- Define interrogation
- State the purpose of an interview
- State the purpose of an interrogation
- Compare and contrast an interview with an interrogation
- Describe the qualities for a good interviewer
- Explain how rapport affects the quality of the interview or interrogation process
- List numerous forms of nonverbal communications

Introduction

Crimes are solved when someone makes the decision to talk. Their level of cooperation is influenced by the communication skills of the interviewer. Enhancing these skills may improve the quality and quantity of creditable information made available during an interview or interrogation. The first lesson in communication involves an acknowledgement that the perceptions of both the interviewee and interviewer will influence the dialog. Communication itself involves the exchange of thoughts, messages, or information by speech, signals, writing, or behavior. In this first chapter, the processes of communication as envisioned by Berlo illustrate the complexity of communication. Communication is the core of all interviewing or interrogation. Theory may explain or expand the reasoning for the interviewing and interrogation practices. You will find the theoretical concepts only in the introduction of each chapter. Think about the theory presented as you read the rest of the chapter.

Courtesy of Corbis Images.

The Berlo SMCR model shows a *communication process* that is an interrelated scheme involving the four most important parts of communication: source, message, channels, and receiver (Berlo, 1960). For an interview to take place between two people, communication occurs back and forth between the person who initiates the interaction (the source) and the one who receives and interprets the meanings (the receiver). The message is made up of content, which is coded (stated) so that it will be received in the way that it is intended. The code is a system of agreed upon communication; it could be the English language, Morse code, sign language, film etc.

The substance of the communication is given meaning by an interpretation of the five senses through the channels which consist of seeing, hearing, touching, feeling, and tasting. Interest and prejudge affect the reception, rejection, or filtering of the transmission. The process of meaning is affected by the stimulus. A stimulus is anything that a person can receive through one of his or her senses, anything that can produce sensation in the human organism. The stimulus reaches your sense organs and is *decoded* by them. You set about *interpreting* this stimulus while determining what an appropriate *response* might be.

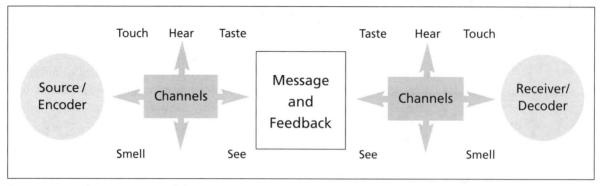

FIGURE 1-1. Berlo's S-M-C-R Model

Berlo stresses the role of relationship between the source and the receiver as an important variable (Wells et al., 2000). Four factors affect the transmission of the message: communication skills, knowledge level, socio-cultural system, and attitudes. The source will make assumptions about the receiver based on these variables; the receiver will do the same regarding the source. The messages back and forth will be dependent on the opinions formed of the other person according the senses, which determines how the messages are being received. If the source determines that the receiver is "stupid," questions are phrased with that opinion; the receiver senses "he thinks I am stupid," and forms the opinion that the source is arrogant!

The Nature of Interviewing

Interviewing is the practice of fact finding which produces information that can lead to conclusions about an event or incident. The core of interviewing is found in the process of communication. The methods of interviewing are as diverse as its many applications. During an interview a person is questioned about his or her knowledge of events which are under investigation. The purpose is to gather information. The person questioned during an interview is assessed by the interviewer for credibility through objective non-accusatory conversion. An interview typically is conducted during early stages of an investigation in a variety of environments. On the other hand, an interrogation is an exercise in persuasion. An interview may evolve into an interrogation if the interviewee is perceived as being unwilling to offer the truth.

The interviewing methods and concepts that are described in this text have broad professional applicability. Individuals that will use these skills include all government officials tasked with investigations, including but not limited to, corrections officers, parole officers, police officers, and probation officers. Interviewing proficiency will also benefit individuals in civilian employment such as human resources personnel, private investigators, school administrators, social service employees, and social workers. Criminal justice, sociology, and psychology students will find ideas for improved communication through the methods in interviewing. An estimated 80% of a police officer's investigative work consists of obtaining information through interviewing (Geffner & Rosenbaum, 2002). It makes sense that other professions have similarly high needs for the ability to obtain information through interviewing.

Before learning about the methods for interviewing it is important to understand the individuals that may be involved in the process. Keep in mind that these categories are not mutually exclusive; they sometimes overlap. For example, there are situations where the assumed victim turns out to be the perpetrator, or that the witness may also be a victim. Sometimes the suspect is identified as a victim. Further confusing the process is that the reported incident may not constitute a violation. The investigator makes the determination on whether the report does constitute an actionable incident. There are three categories of persons that may be interviewed: victims, witnesses, and suspects.

Victims

A victim is the person who is the object of an incident, crime, or other harm caused against them. The victim may be an individual, public or private corporation, government, partnership, or unincorporated association (Garner, 2004). For investigation purposes, it is important to establish if there is a relationship between the victim and the perpetrator. Knowledge of a relationship will direct questioning and affect the interpretation of information. A victim may be unwilling or unable to provide information that will be used against the perpetrator if there is a relationship; the victim may be uncooperative if they are intimates. Knowledge of the victim relationship may also shed light on the credibility of the statement should that become an issue.

The amount of cooperation will vary from person to person and depend greatly on the type of incident that is being investigated. It may also change during or after the interview; a second interview is not assured. Cooperation is among many issues of concern. The victim could have substantial injuries that put them into a coma or cause death. Investigators must be as thorough as possible when interviewing a victim in order to gain as much information as possible during the first interview.

Another reason for being thorough at the first interviewing opportunity is that in some jurisdictions a presumptive prosecution policy may be in place. A *presumptive prosecution* policy means that prosecution would continue regardless of the victim's participation whenever sufficient evidence exists that a crime was committed (Gosselin, 2005). There are two general approaches taken by the courts: no-drop and evidence-based prosecution policies. Under the no-drop approach the attempts at gathering evidence continues with encouragement for victim cooperation. Services such as counseling, housing assistance, and safety planning are among the ways that victim participation is encouraged. No-drop policies exist in order to remove the responsibility for prosecution from victims and ensure that that state proceeds where there is a compelling public safety interest (Davis, Smith, & Davies, 2001). The evidence-based approach assumes that victim will not be available and builds a case on physical evidence, medical records, and police testimony. Prosecution without victim participation can only occur when the investigator has taken the time to do a complete investigation and gathered all verbal and physical evidence at the time of initial access.

In all cases, the victim may fear that the person will return for purposes of retribution; the victim may feel prejudices against or from the one conducting the interview; the victim may feel tired, angry, or in pain at the time of the interview. It is likely that the person will be under immense stress while being interviewed; stress affects memory and recall (Artwohl, 2002). It is worthwhile to put the interviewee at ease through the establishment of rapport. A second interview may be warranted for taking photographs of bruising which may not appear visible at the initial interview. The victim may be a child or an elder with limited cognitive abilities, a person that is developmentally delayed, or simply someone with something to hide. The victim may be a professor or a student; a prostitute or a member of the clergy. All of these factors will influence the outcome.

Been There . . . Done That! 1–1

The impulse to always believe the victim is strong yet the interviewer must remember that not all allegations are true. One woman had reported being stalked and the investigation was ongoing for three years without success. At one point this 21-year-old female came into the police department with a bruise on her face, which was photographed. She received letters with sexually descriptive positions that the perpetrator threatened to do to the victim. She received flowers sent to her office. Despite this evidence of a serious stalking situation, a phone tape and discreet following by the police, no perpetrator was ever found. Eventually she was sent to me for interview. After complimenting her on the imaginative letters she could not hold back a slight smile. At that point she admitted to having written the letters, sent herself the flowers, and yes—she had hit herself in the face. The attention from the police had been a very positive point in her life. It ended and the case was closed.

Witnesses

A witness is someone who personally sees, hears, or otherwise observes something relating to the incident under investigation (Garner, 2004). Witnesses may also be called eyewitnesses. Eyewitnesses are notoriously inaccurate, incomplete, and unreliable. That having been said, the eyewitness is still of great value to the interviewer! The witness can provide important information that leads to the perpetrator and ultimately to the offender being held accountable. They can also give information that is misleading or inaccurate. Statements must be taken and critically analyzed for their truth, veracity, and relative importance to the case being investigated.

Techniques to enhance the recall of witnesses are an approach fast gaining credibility. Known as cognitive interviewing, these will be explored in depth later in the text. Kinesics and other behavioral approaches to statements are also frequently employed. The traditional interview technique of fact gathering is still valuable for many cases. A frequent complaint from investigators is that they lack the time to sufficiently interview. Case interviewing can be time consuming; following up the generated leads and corroborating the information is an essential aspect of investigating.

A witness interview is non-accusatory by the interviewer and may be conducted in a variety of places. The witness may be the person that is making accusations. At the scene of the crime, as many persons as possible that are present should be briefly interviewed. One method of handling a large of number of witnesses at a scene is for an investigator to take names and phone numbers first, and then interview as time permits. Witnesses may not want to get involved in the situation and have a way of disappearing; learning to access the crowd before that happens can be a challenge.

Witnesses may be reluctant to come forward with information. The reason may be that they simply are unaware that they possess information that would be helpful. So seeking out witnesses is often the case. Many reasons contribute to the withholding of information. Some reasons include a concern of not wanting to get involved, a fear the suspect will retaliate against them for having provided information to the police, a general fear of the suspect, and a relationship to the suspect or it may come from a distrust of the interviewer. Still others with information will think that it the incident is none their business! So while it is generally assumed that the witness will be a person that is cooperative, that is not always the case. Gentle persuasion may be employed when necessary to encourage witness cooperation.

Witnesses often struggle to provide accurate detail. Inconsistencies tend to reduce the value of a statement, but do not necessarily mean that it is fabricated. Children in particular may become confused on details of an incident. Receiving similar information from a variety of sources tends to fill in important voids and lend credibility to what is supplied through witness interviews. Perception has a lot to do with differences in reporting. When a manila folder is held up to any group of people, numerous colors will be suggested to describe it. During one study witnesses that were interviewed about a cruiser chase reported the speed of the car to be greater with the knowledge that it had crashed, versus those who did not know the cruiser had crashed (Abrams & Ramsey S. H., 2000).

Anonymous witness reports should always be regarded with suspicion. This holds particularly true when the reporter has experienced a personal problem with the accused, is a disgruntled neighbor, or when a previous relationship is found to have existed. Approach these complaints with caution and investigate them thoroughly since it is not unheard of that some complaints are filed in an attempt to get someone in trouble. Conversely, when relationships go sour the reporter may feel free to give information that they held back during a relationship. Either way, the investigator is best off to tread slowly and to be through.

We clearly cannot anticipate the effect that stress has on those being interviewed. Some research has suggested that witness accounts are more reliable when the person has been under stress (Abrams & Ramsey S. H., 2000). The opposite effect has also been noted. In highly negative emotional situations, such as witnessing a violent crime, eyewitness accounts may be more susceptible to misinformation (Porter, Spencer, & Birt, 2003). These basic principles about witness interviewing represent the characteristics of witnesses (Massachusetts Municipal Police Institute, 1981):

1. Witnesses usually see only part of what actually happens and usually recognize only part of what they see;

2. Witnesses usually remember only part of what they observe and usually describe only part of what they remember;

3. Witnesses who are angry, frightened or emotionally upset usually perceive only a fraction of what they might observe under normal circumstances;

4. Witnesses often see only what they expect, or want to see, and as a result provide a distorted version of what actually happened or an inaccurate physical description of the criminal offender;

5. Witnesses who are involved in violent incidents such as homicides, robberies, rapes, aggravated assaults or fatal accidents are often unable to immediately provide an adequate description of events or suspects;

6. Witnesses can be affected by a number of possible physical or emotional factors which may influence the validity of their information;

7. Emotional factors can cause a witness to lie, to become uncooperative or forgetful, or to give prejudicial information;

8. It is not unusual for a number of witnesses describing the same incident to furnish varying accounts of what happened or to provide a variety of descriptions for the criminal offender, as every witness see things differently and relates what he has seen in an individual manner;

9. An interviewer must recognize all these human limitations and individual differences in witness perception and be aware of the personal motives that can be involved in any particular case.

Been There . . . Done That! 1–2

During an investigation into an allegation of child sexual assault the mother of the child victim was being interviewed. She gave detailed information on what her daughter had told her. Frequently she cried during the interview. While her behavior was not unjustified, it was apparent that she had a high stake in the outcome of the case. More than half way into the interview I discovered that the perpetrator was her father, grandfather to the child victim. The mother confided that he had sexually abused her as a child also, a case that had never been reported. Among other things, she had suffered genital mutilation at the hands of her father. Don't assume that you know who the victim(s) are.

Suspects

For an initial response to the scene of an offense the responder should remove the suspect immediately if present. If the perpetrator is not present, interviews with the victim or witness should include attempts to identify the perpetrator. Along with a suspect description the interviewer should ask about locations where the suspect may be found. Any utterances made should be documented, including any alibi. Developing a strategy for a later interrogation begins at this stage.

An interview with a suspect should not take place until the interviewer has examined the facts of the case and spoken with the victim. The interviewer should not jump to conclusions during an initial meeting with a person thought to be the perpetrator. Nor should an interrogation take place until the interviewer is fairly certain that the person is guilty. Approaching the suspect should be similar to any witness unless it is a dangerous situation that compromises interviewer safety. This means that the approach is respectful, but not solicitous. A suspect may offer information that clears them immediately; be open to that possibility. An interview of a suspect takes on immense importance since it is often the only opportunity for a non-adversarial dialog. Once an interrogation is started the ability to freely gather information is over.

Been There . . . Done That! 1–3

A frantic call came in to the station by a woman claiming her child had been kidnapped and that she did not know the man who took the infant. Officers enroute to the scene saw a male walking with an infant in his arms and stopped to speak with him. As it turned out the "kidnapper" was the father of the child, with the legal right to have custody of her. His story was that his girlfriend, the mother, was an abusive drunk who was hitting the child. Without a car, he had left on foot to protect the infant. At the house the woman was found to be intoxicated and combatant. She admitted to hitting the child and was arrested for assault. In the cruiser she kept saying that she could not believe she had been arrested, she was the mother and after all . . . she was a woman; she had even made the call to the police! What was this world coming to?

The Nature of Interrogation

An interrogation is an exercise in persuasion with the goal of eliciting a truthful confession. This working definition is specific to gain a deeper understanding of the nature and purpose for conducting an interrogation. *Persuade* is defined as: To move by argument, entreaty, or expostulation, to a belief or position, or by course of action (Merriam-Webster's Collegiate Dictionary, 2004). *Elicit* means to draw out or entice forth; to bring to light; to bring out against the will; to deduce by reason or argument; as, to elicit truth by discussion (Merriam-Webster Online Dictionary, 2005).

The interrogation process is a give and take between the suspect and the interrogator, with the majority of the talking done by the interrogator. This back and forth may last as short as thirty minutes or it may take hours. It is structured and purposeful. The extent of cooperation will be determined early on; therefore the interrogator works within accepted boundaries with the suspect to elicit the information.

The interrogation is different from the interview in many ways. The primary difference between an interview and an interrogation is often in the perception of the interviewer. A change from interviewing to interrogation is evidenced by a change from the non-accusatory approach to one that is accusatory. Often occurring in a controlled environment, an interrogation involves eliciting information from a suspect that is perceived as unwilling to admit his or her role in a crime or it may involve an individual with a reason to hide the truth. Statements are sometimes asserted by the interrogator rather than the asking of questions. Mere persistence does not make the questioning unfair since there is no requirement that the first answer from a suspect be accepted as truthful (Williamson, 2004).

Concepts about human behavior and communication that are included in this text as interviewing techniques are applicable to interrogation practices also. Many professionals may be in a situation to interview suspects, yet relatively few will engage in interrogation. Legal interrogation guidelines limit the actions of the law enforcement officials. The reason for this narrowed application is that constitutional requirements generally govern state and federal action. The United States Supreme Court has defined interrogation as the questioning initiated by law enforcement officers after a person has been taken into custody or otherwise deprived of his freedom of action in any significant way (*Miranda* v. *Arizona,* 1966). The U.S. Constitution and the Bill of Rights protect citizens from actions of government officials and their agents and not from other citizens. Evidence that is obtained from the interrogation of one citizen by another citizen is not held to the same standard as an interrogation by a government officer. However, the government may not be able to accept evidence from civilians if it was obtained through egregious interrogation methods such as torture or vigilante action.

The law governing interrogation methods is not specified in any one place; criminal interrogations are guided by evolving standards of acceptable practices. Constitutional Law, Federal and State statutes, and Anglo-American tradition blend together with a current emphasis on the Fifth Amendment against self-incrimination, the Sixth Amendment guarantee of the right to counsel, and the Fourteenth Amendment guarantee of due process.

Interrogation Controversy

The controversy surrounding interrogation provides sufficient reason for students to study the process, regardless of any direct professional application. Debates over acceptable practices are not new to this generation. Interrogation methods have been controversial at least since the 1600's. Isolated attempts to prohibit torture as an interrogation method are documented in English jurisprudence as early as 1628 according to the United States Supreme Court (*Bram* v. *United States,* 1897). Early common law allowed an admission or confession as evidence of guilt regardless of it being the product of force or duress. Rather than conducting an investigation to establish guilt, enforcement officers resorted to torture to extract a confession from the accused during an interrogation.

The courts have alternatively used the unreliability of tortured confessions and the requirement for constitutional protections as reasons for rejecting their use against an individual to prove guilt. Psychologists tell us that some individuals will confess to a crime that they did not commit without exterior pressures and that others are susceptible to falsely confess in an interrogation environment (Kassin, 2005). This provides a dilemma for officials who are tasked with solving crimes. Interrogation information must be consistent with fact or reality; not false or erroneous, real, genuine, reliable, accurate, narrowly particularized, and highly specific (Webster, 1998).

While many veteran investigators felt that interrogations would become a lost art after the *Miranda* decision (1966) the Supreme Court has recognized the need for criminal justice investigators to conduct interrogations. It is in the best interest of society to identify correctly the individual whose transgression is illegal. When done properly the interrogation is still an important tool for an investigator to consider. Some evidence suggests that detectives are successful in obtaining confessions or admissions in 75% of the interrogations that are attempted (Leo, 1996).

It is against human nature to implicate oneself in wrongdoing; it is not necessarily in one's best interest. Why would someone confess to having committed an illegal act knowing that there will be consequences? That individual must be persuaded that it is in their best interest to admit. Persuasion can be accomplished through a variety of methods which will be described in future chapters.

Purpose of the Interrogation

The process of interrogation is one that is meant to encourage the suspect to provide evidence of guilt or involvement in an event. Sought by the interrogator is a confession or admission regarding participation or knowledge of wrongdoing. A confession is a statement made by a defendant disclosing his guilt of the crime with which he was charged and excluding the possibility of a reasonable inference to the contrary (*People*

v. *Anderson*, 1965). A confession is not limited to words, but may also include the demeanor, conduct and acts of the person charged with a crime. For example, the court has accepted situations where the defendant showed the interrogators how he had committed the murder of a young girl by acting out the manner in which he stabbed her (*People* v. *Baldi*, 1974).

In one of the few studies on the practice of interrogation, "success" was achieved when any amount of incriminating information was elicited from the suspect (Leo, 1996). While the goal is to entice a confession, eliciting an admission is considered a successful outcome of the interrogation. An admission is an acknowledgment of guilty conduct, containing only facts from which guilt may or may not be inferred (*Anderson*, 1965). The statement of admission may be a word, act, conduct or in any other way information that suggests guilt. Information about the suspect and his or her role or relationship to the crime, the victim, or the place of the offense may be part of the admission. Because the courts do not differentiate between degrees of incrimination, no distinction is drawn between confessions and admissions for purposes of their use as evidence against the individual in court.

Been There . . . Done That! 1–4

Rapport building is a process of developing a willingness to communicate. It can also be thought of as a getting-to-know-you phase. When interviewing a child or adult show empathy, concern, or interest as ways to build rapport. Rapport building can be an important phase for interrogations also. In one case I had just arrested a man who had been restrained by four officers in order to detain him. He was shocked at having been arrested and visibly shaken from the experience. I showed concern and asked if he was alright, making light of the four men having just pounced on him. From the look on his face I detected an immediate reaction of gratitude. Moments later I gave him his rights per Miranda, which he waived and agreed to give me a statement. Having sensed his willingness to communicate I wasted no time and did the interrogation in the cruiser on the way to the station. By the time we arrived I had a full confession and a thank-you from the perpetrator!

Personal Qualities of the Interviewer

The majority of contacts that occur between the investigator and citizen are face-to-face and typically one-on-one. The ability to communicate effectively may be the most desirable personal quality to achieve. Often it is assumed that the person who speaks or writes well comes by it naturally. Those that are reluctant to seek help towards improvement may be embarrassed about their lack of skill. Some individuals are oblivious to their deficiencies and may need encouragement from a supervisor in order to improve. From analysis of video and audio tape recordings police officers frequently appear inept, nervous, ill at ease, and lacking in confidence (Williamson, 2004). Most good oral and written communication skills are learned. It is therefore necessary to acquire the skills and then they must be practiced for these shortcomings to be addressed.

How things are said may be more important than what is being said. The way that a person communicates dictates the impression that is given about that person to others. It is how the individual's professionalism is judged. Those that sit in judgment are fellow professionals, the public, victims, and the perpetrator. The individual alone determines the impression that is given. People frequently state that an interviewer should, above all, be friendly. This author could not disagree more. If the victim or witness wanted to talk to a friend they would go out for coffee, not for an official interview! More appropriately the interviewer must be approachable, understanding, empathetic, patient, and nonjudgmental. In other words, being neutral and non-offensive without being distant are personal qualities that will benefit the communication process. Persons who are interviewed may be looking for help or direction; sometimes they are angry and confused. Confidence is therefore a necessary attribute of the interviewer—without arrogance, however. Learning the behaviors needed to be a successful interviewer begins with learning and understanding human nature.

Knowing yourself is the first part of that process. The ability to recognize that each one of us has a perspective that is unique carries with it the acknowledgment that you, the investigator, have prejudices and biases about someone or something. Some people can't stand stupid people or persons that come across as intellectuals. Others dislike certain physical characteristics or appearances. Some individuals are repulsed by those who commit criminal acts generally. The successful interviewer learns to put these aside in a conscious choice to be professional. Each is entitled to their own opinions, thoughts, and perspectives—but there is no room in the interview room for personal preferences. Learning to look past oneself to the case greatly enhances the value of the police interview. If one has difficulty in putting personal bias aside, a rethinking of job direction may be warranted.

Additionally, the individual who conducts frequent interviews should have a genuine curiosity. Curiosity is a term that refers to an emotional pressure to seek information, to explore, and to learn by observation. Wanting to find out everything possible about a case in this context refers to being open-minded about lifestyles and personal choices that may be different from those of the investigator. A positive attitude by the interviewer has a better chance to surface if interest is allowed to overtake bias.

A good interviewer is not necessarily an effective interrogator. Since interrogation is only a small part of the communication process, interview skills are of greater value. However, the skills for interrogation are an extension of the personal qualities for an interviewer, so they are addressed at this point. Training, experience, aptitude, and intelligence are prerequisites. The personal qualities for interrogation include all of the interview skills along with a high degree of confidence. That required confidence is achieved internally. The individual must possess self-confidence in his or her ability to face objection and overcome resistance through reason. It is not that different from taking a position on a debating team and arguing for one opinion over another. The debate is not a shouting match. It is an intellectual exchange that is based on the position of the interrogator without regard to their personal stake in the outcome of the debate. Once a position is taken by the interrogator, it must be backed up with evidence to strengthen that position. In addition, achieving absolute control over personal emotions is paramount for the interrogator. It is natural to feel embarrassment for the suspect when you catch him or her in a lie, or to feel pity for the subject because of the circumstance. Emotions can also drive an interrogator to vigorously proceed during an interrogation without regard for the suspect. An interrogation is not an exercise in humiliation, degradation, or physical or psychological torture.

Willingness to Develop Rapport

Central to any interview, and in some cases for interrogations, is an exchange called rapport. Frequently throughout this book there will be references to rapport, therefore the communication concept behind the process is introduced here. *Rapport* is the communication that results when two people agree on the means and willingness to communicate (Berlo, 1960). It is established by putting the interviewee at ease though mutual respect or understanding.

The social work interview has long embraced the importance of communication as presented through the theory of Berlo (Kadushin, 1972). To continue on that explanation from David Berlo, the nature of the communication involves not only what is said and heard—the message encoded, transmitted, received, processed, and decoded—but also the interpersonal context in which the process takes place. The recent reliance on rapport in policing interviews is evidenced in *Eyewitness Evidence,* a publication from the National Institute of Justice (U. S. Department of

Justice, 1999). If the context of the relationship is positive, then there is a comfortable, trustful and respectful feeling between the interviewer and person being interviewed. The positive relationship, which is another way to describe rapport, lowers barriers and brings a heightened willingness to participate in the interview. Both interviewer and interviewee are more likely to be receptive to messages being sent after rapport has been established. A good relationship is not necessarily a pleasant one, but one that is actively used to further the purpose of the interview (Kadushin, 1972).

The ability to develop rapport with another is a willingness to use words and behaviors to effectively impart information, with openness towards receiving back information from another person. Rapport is earned by the attitude and behavior of the interviewer. Without rapport the statement may lack completeness. At the beginning of any interview of any length or importance, the interviewer must first establish rapport with the person being interviewed. Rapport can be established through verbal or behavioral techniques. Later in this chapter the behavior approach to rapport building is discussed. Verbal methods for the development of rapport are covered in Chapter Three.

In painful communication situations of personal concern rapport is what brings a full and frank confession from a subject (Kadushin, 1972). The suspect is unlikely to talk about difficult situations that have hurt, frustrated, or been painful unless the investigator can convince the suspect that he or she is anxious to understand what the experience has meant to him.

Knowledgeable

Examination of recorded police interviews additionally indicate investigators had only a weak understanding of the legal requirements to prove an offense (Williamson, 2004). This deficiency is addressed by the knowledgeable investigator. He or she is one who keeps asking questions and continues to learn from each case that is investigated. The knowledgeable investigator researches the laws pertaining to the offences that are under investigation prior to conducting major interviews or interrogations. Gathering case facts is done during each investigation, no matter how many times a similar situation was faced or how routine the situation may appear.

The knowledgeable interviewer does not make judgments based on past encounters that were similar, or by race, gender, or age. Each situation represents the possibility that an unlikely person is at fault. We now know for example, that intimate violence occurs between persons of the same sex; that adolescents abuse their parents; that female elders are just as likely to perpetrate against an elderly husband as the man is against his elder wife. Rape is perpetrated against males and females; against persons in a courtship or a marriage relationship; within a same-sex relationship. The knowledgeable officer knows that the answers must be learned from the circumstances and will only come through listening and watching.

Professional

The interviewer must begin without case bias. Since the goal is to obtain information, the scene must be staged for the witness or victim to freely state their views of the situation. A preconceived notion about what the person may say inhibits conversation. Tolerating ambiguity refers to this skill of reacting positively to new, different, and at times unpredictable situations. This will call for patience as well as persistence. Both are firm requirements in dealing with people from other societies around the world.

The attitude of the interviewer or interrogator strongly impacts the extent of witness cooperation. A necessary ingredient of professionalism is respect, the capability of demonstrating respect in whichever way a specific culture requires: respect for age, respect in manner of speech, respect with eye contact, respect with hand or body gestures, respect for personal privacy, and so on.

Being nonjudgmental requires that the investigator learn to withhold judgment until all information is accumulated, while also taking into account cultural idiosyncrasies that could color judgment. Additionally, one must feel comfortable asking uncomfortable questions. Frequently the details of a statement being given will cause anxiety to the victim or witness. It may necessitate asking personal or probing questions to obtain completeness and accuracy.

Communicating

Communication is a process that includes sending and receiving both verbal and nonverbal messages. It is estimated that nonverbal communication often conveys a larger share of social information, approximately 65% or more; while verbal communication plays a less salient role, 35% or less (Lanning, 2002). So much information is communicated nonverbally that frequently the verbal aspect is negligible. Body language, facial expressions, gestures, personal spacing, and voice characteristics send out messages to the recipient individual.

These communications can be used to facilitate the building of rapport through matching techniques. Matching is a subtle form of the interviewer mimicking the nonverbal and paralanguage behaviors of the person being interviewed (Sandoval & Adams, 2001). The intent is to match the behavior or voice by making some form of movement in the same manner without attracting conscious attention to it. Nonverbal techniques for interviewing and interrogation are discussed in greater length in Chapter Six.

Kinesics

Kinesics is a form of nonverbal communication that includes body language, facial expressions, and gestures (Sandoval & Adams, 2001). How the body expresses itself to others is also referred to as body language. As one of the most effective media, it transmits feelings. The transmission of body language is usually more sub-conscious than conscious. Individuals who are deeply engaged in conversation demonstrate some similarities between them of which they probably are not consciously aware. For example, they are probably sitting in a similar fashion, they may make similar types and rhythms of hand gestures, they most likely speak in a similar tonality and tempo, and they probably breathe at a similar rate. Their body language will be aligned somehow. The participants will feel that they understand each other, but they might not be able to put their finger on the reason, except that the other person "makes sense." The practice of an interviewer matching the body language of the interviewee brings that feeling of making sense to the subject. It can facilitate a willingness to provide information during the interview.

Approval, agreement, acceptance, and continuing attention and understanding are indicated by a head nod from the interviewer (Wainwright, 2003). Agreement typically is indicated by the largest nods while feedback on understanding the interviewee is a slight nod. Wainwright (2003) suggests that men tend to use head nods more than women and that it may be useful for women to practice and purposefully use head nods more frequently.

Facial expressions include both conscious and unconscious movement of the nose, lips, eyebrows, tongue, and eyes (Ekman, 2001). In a persuasive communication environment, the value of facial expression, posture, body movement, and eye contact is about 50% of the overall message (Hogan, 2002). For example, lips may move into a grin to show happiness, grimace for fear, or pout to indicate sadness. When the individual has a lot at stake in a situation, and then lies about it, the emotions such as fear and disgust are evidenced through facial expressions (Wright, Boyd, & Tredoux, 2001). Eyebrows frown for anger or concentration and rise for intensity. The most frequent facial expressions according to Ekman (2001) are the lowering or rising of the eyebrow, often used to emphasize speech or to show disbelief and skepticism. Wide eyes typically indicate surprise or excitement with narrowed eyes indicating disagreement or a threat. One of the most reliable facial actions is the narrowing of the lips which signals anger. An interviewer may facilitate rapport by recognizing and addressing what the face reveals.

Gestures are woven inextricably in to our social lives and that vocabulary of gestures can be informative and entertaining . . . but also dangerous (Fisher & Geiselman, 1992). Gestures can be menacing (two drivers on a freeway), warm (an open-armed welcome), instructive (a police man giving road directions), or even sensuous (the liquid movement of a Hawaiian hula dancer); while verbal communication transmits words and thoughts. At times understanding the wants and feelings of others is far more important than understanding their words. Crossing of the arms for example, usually signals a defensive posture indicating that the person has become cautious (Hogan, 2002). When an interviewer attempts to develop rapport, defensive signals need to be overcome in order for the interview to proceed effectively.

Proxemics

Proxemics is the study of our use of space and how various differences in that use makes us feel more relaxed or more anxious. The term was coined by researcher Edward Hall during the 1950s (Wright & Loftus, 1998). Hall identified four bodily distances — *intimate* (0 to 18 inches), *personal-casual* (1.5 to 4 feet), *social-consultive* (4 to 10 feet), and *public* (10 feet and beyond) — as key points in human spacing behavior. Hall noted that different cultures set distinctive norms for closeness in, e.g., speaking, business, and courting, and that standing too close or too far away can lead to misunderstandings. Comfortable communication with someone that is not an intimate should take place outside of the intimate distance, or greater than 18 inches apart (Hogan, 2002).

Changing the distance between two people can convey a desire for intimacy, declare a lack of interest, or increase/decrease domination. Violation of personal space can nonverbally convey a message; for example, officers are encouraged to use the strategy of sitting close and crowding a suspect during an interrogation to gain the psychological advantage. When our personal bubble of space has been invaded we feel uncomfortable; tension and fear results. Most people will get up and leave rather than deal with the uncomfortable feeling of someone invading their space. Care should be taken that the interviewer does not violate individual space during the rapport establishment phase. If there are signals that the individual is uncomfortable, the interviewer should back off until he or she notices that the subject is willing to proceed.

According to Hogan (2002) communication spacing differs by gender. Men attempting to influence men should work within a 3 to 6 foot range. Women influencing women or men generally fall in the 1.5 to 4 feet range. The most complicated relationship exists when men attempt to persuade women—the successful distance may be between 2 to 8 feet and depends on feedback from the woman.

The distance between two people indicates their comfort with each other and their willingness to communicate.

Courtesy of Corbis Images.

Where we sit in relation to other people can aid or hinder communication. A comfortable and relaxed arrangement for two people at a table is to sit corner-to-corner (Hogan, 2002). This allows for maximum eye contact and other nonverbal signals, a good arrangement for cooperative work. In a side-by-side arrangement, body language is difficult to read and physical proximity is too close. This position works when both parties need to focus on the task at hand and not on each other. Unintentional conflict can develop between two people who sit across from each other.

Paralanguage

Paralanguage or the vocal part of speech and its nuances is communication that goes beyond the specific spoken words and may be the most effective method of establishing rapport (Sandoval & Adams, 2001). Language is only one of the ways that messages are sent; paralanguage includes the person's tone, pitch, and reflection, all of which expresses emotions. It includes pitch, amplitude, rate, and voice quality of speech. Paralanguage reminds us that people convey their feelings not only in *what* they say, but also in *how* they say it. Active emotions such as anger and fear are typically expressed by a fast rate of speech, loud volume, high pitch, and tone (Hogan, 2002). Passive emotions usually are relayed by a slower rate of speech, lower volume and lower pitch. In the interview setting, according to Sandoval & Adams (2001), the interviewer should try to match the pace of the witness to allow for enhanced recall and communication.

Conclusions

This chapter described communication as a process according to Berlo. This model provides a framework for future consideration of the interrogation and interviewing methods that will be described throughout this text. Interrogation and interview are defined in a way so as to compare and contrast the goals and methods employed in these approaches to eliciting information. Although this is not an exhaustive list of the personal qualities required for an interviewer, some qualities were set as a guideline to determine who should engage in the process. The different categories of persons that are to be interviewed, and their shifting capabilities, are stated. Since the establishment of rapport is such a critical aspect of interviewing, the nonverbal behavioral indicators that may be useful for rapport is covered in detail. The student can look forward to greater details of interviewing and interrogation methods in future chapters.

Chapter One Questions for Review

Short Answer Questions

1. How would you define a successful interviewer using the approach described in *Smart Talk?*

2. What is Berlo's model of communication?

3. Describe the qualities that make a good interviewer.

4. What is the definition and purpose of an interrogation?

5. Define interviewing and describe how it differs from interrogation.

6. What are the categories of individuals who may be interviewed?

7. What are some of the different types of nonverbal communication discussed in this chapter?

Fill-in Questions

1. _____ is the process of eliciting a confession from a suspect.

2. _____ is the process of gathering information.

3. The three categories of interviewees are _____ , _____ , and _____ .

4. Successful interviewers are _____ and _____ in order to obtain as much pertinent information possible.

5. _____ is the communication that results when two people agree on the means and willingness to communicate.

6. _____ communication often conveys a larger share of social information, approximately 65% or more.

7. The study of our use of space and how various differences in that space make us feel more relaxed or more anxious is called _____ .

8. The vocal part of speech and its nuances is referred to as _____ .

Exercises

1. Kinesics is an approach that has only recently been adapted for criminal justice interviewing. Go online and discover additional ways in which kinesics is used.

2. Test the principle of proxemics! Find someone on campus in the library or at the lunchroom who is sitting alone. Sit at the personal-casual distance (1.5 to 4 feet) next to someone. Observe what the person does. Next, sit facing someone else who is alone, without talking to them. Observe what the person does. Was the reaction different if the individual was male or female? Report your findings in a written report to the instructor.

Reference List

Abrams, D. E., & Ramsey S. H. (2000). *Children and the law: Doctrine, policy, and practice.* St. Paul, MN: West Group.

Artwohl, A. (2002). Perceptual and memory distortion during officer-involved shootings. *FBI Law Enforcement Bulletin,* 18–24.

Berlo, D. K. (1960). *The process of communication.* New York, NY: Holt, Rinehart, and Winston.

Bram v. *United States,* 168 U.S. 532 (1897).

Davis, R., Smith, B. E., & Davies, H. (2001). No-drop prosecution and domestic violence. *Justice Research and Policy,* 3(2), 1–13.

Ekman, P. (2001). *Telling lies: Clues to deceit in the marketplace, politics, and marriage.* New York, NY: W. W. Norton & Company.

Fisher, R. P., & Geiselman, R. E. (1992). *Memory-enhancing techniques for investigative interviewing: The cognitive interview.* Springfield, Il: Charles C. Thomas.

Garner, B. (2004). *Black's Law Dictionary* (8th ed.). St. Paul, MN: West Publishing Co.

Geffner, R., & Rosenbaum, A. (2002). *Domestic violence offenders: Current interventions, research, and implications for policies and standards.* Binghamton, NY: Haworth Press.

Gosselin, D. K. (2005). *Heavy hands: An introduction to the crimes of family violence* (3rd ed.). Upper Saddle River, NJ: Prentice Hall.

Hogan, K. (2002). *The psychology of persuasion.* Gretna, LA: Pelican Publishing.

Kadushin, A. (1972). *The social work interview.* New York, NY: Columbia University Press.

Kassin, S. M. (2005). True crimes false confessions. *Scientific American Mind,* 16(2), 24–32.

Lanning, K. (2002). Criminal investigation of sexual victimization of children. J. Myers, L. Berliner, J. Briere, C. T. Hendrix, C. Jenny, & T. Reid (editors), *The APSAC Handbook on Child Maltreatment* (2nd ed., pp. 329–348). Thousands Oaks, CA: Sage Publication.

Leo, R. A. (1996). Inside the interrogation room. *Journal of Criminal Law and Criminology.* 86, pgs. 266-303. Available: http://www.lexisnexis.com//universe.

Massachusetts Municipal Police Institute. (1981). Police and procedure: Interviewing witnesses. Unpublished.

Merriam-Webster Online Dictionary. (2005). Retrieved 2005, from http://www.m-w.com/

Merriam-Webster's Collegiate Dictionary. (2004). (11th ed.). Springfield, MA: Merriam-Webster, Inc.

Miranda v. *Arizona,* 384 U.S. 436 (1966).

People v. *Anderson,* 236 Cal. App. 2d 419 (1965).

People v. *Baldi,* 80 Misc. 2d 118 (1974).

Porter, S., Spencer, L., & Birt, A. (2003). Blinded by emotion: Effect of the emotionality of a scene on susceptibility to false memories. *Canadian Journal of Behavioural Science,* 35(3), 165–175.

Sandoval, V., & Adams, S. (2001). Subtle skills for building rapport using neuro-linguistic programming in the interview room. *FBI Law Enforcement Bulletin,* 1-5.

U. S. Department of Justice. (1999). *Eyewitness evidence: A guide for law enforcement.* (Report No. NCJ 178240). Washington, DC: U. S. Department of Justice.

Wainwright, G. (2003). *Teach yourself: Body language.* Chicago, IL: McGraw-Hill Companies.

Wells, G. L., Malpass, R. S., Lindsay, R. C. L., Fisher, R. P., Turtle, J. W., & Fulero, S. M. (2000). From the lab to the police station: A successful application of eyewitness research. *American Psychologist,* 55(6), 581.

Williamson, T. (2004). USA and UK responses to miscarriages of justice. J. R. Adler (editor), *Forensic Psychology: Concepts, debates and practice* (pp. 39–57). Portland, OR: Willan Publishing.

Wright, D. B., & Loftus, E. F. (1998). How misinformation alters memory. *Journal of Experimental Child Psychology,* 71(1), 155–164.

Wright, D. B., Boyd, C. E., & Tredoux, C. G. (2001). A field of study of own-race bias in South Africa and England. *Psychology, Public Policy, and Law,* 7(1), 119.

The Interview Process

KEY TERMS

Clarifying open-ended question	Closed-ended question
Confrontational question	Contamination
Initial open-ended question	Leading question
Postmodernism	Reinforcing behavior

CHAPTER OBJECTIVES

After completing this chapter you should be able to:

◆ Describe the three phases of the interview process
◆ Change a closed-ended question into the open-ended form
◆ Explain the difference between open and closed questioning
◆ Compare and contrast the methods of approaching the interview
◆ List the ways in which witnesses might make an identification of the suspect
◆ Describe the characteristics of a social systems approach to interviewing
◆ Explain the problem of misinformation and contamination
◆ List ways of minimizing the contamination of witness statements and identification

Introduction

In this chapter the procedures for conducting an interview are placed within the context of a social systems approach. This means that interviewing is made up of parts that are intertwined and interdependent on each other and inclusive of the perspectives of everyone involved. Each part influences the entire experience; things do do not happen in a vacuum. The extent to which the interviewer is prepared, where and when the interview takes place, and how the questions are phrased impacts the results. This way of thinking about the interview recognizes three modern themes in social systems theory; caring, self-development, and postmodernism (Anderson, Carter, & Lowe, 1999).

Courtesy of Corbis Images.

Caring must be a cultural characteristic, supported in the development and expression from the perspective of others. This means that during an interview the person relates the event from his or her unique point of view, colored by their past experiences, as well as physical and cognitive limitations. The perspective of the interviewee impacts the interview. For example, was their last encounter with a government official or police officer a negative one? How many have gone through an evening where "when I was stopped for speeding" stories seem endless? Assess whether the adult can read and write; determine if the child *really* understands your questions. Women do not recount incidents in the same way that men would; persons of ethnic background and those of color are similarly shaped by their view of the world and of the interviewer. People will develop the scenario from their own perspective. Let them do that!

Self-development encourages the interviewer to be constantly vigilant and self-aware. The openness to re-direction and change throughout the entire investigation is difficult to achieve without decisive action. If one remains flexible during an interview then objective observations are more readily apparent. Watching for the behavior indicators of deceit should direct the interview process; sensitivity to proximities allows the interviewer to strategically place themselves. Cognizance of nonverbal behavior improves the ability of the interviewer to retain control. This means that the interviewer must listen, watch, and be aware of what is going on during the interview. Do not keep asking questions; spend some time listening to what is being said—both verbally and physically.

The third ingredient to success in this approach is postmodernism which emphasizes the role of power that will be inherent in any interview conducted by government officials or police officers. Be aware that others view the interviewer not merely as an individual, but as a representative of a powerful organization of law and order. You will not be able to change the way an individual views the position that you hold. Many persons are in awe of this power, some are fearful of it. The effect of this assessment can be negated or supported depending on the goals of the interview. The postmodernist view suggests that all information is contextual. Reporting of information cannot be separated from authority and power; the credibility of the interviewer may be questionable from the perspective of the victim, witness, or suspect.

Phase I—Interview Preparation

Early research on the quality of interviews which had been videotaped, found that interviewing skills were generally poor, interviewers appeared inept, nervous, and ill at ease (Williamson, 2004). Concluding that police officers over-relied on confession evidence it meant that victims were frequently not interviewed thoroughly which resulted in the loss of potentially valuable evidence. Hence the movement for more experienced interviewers began in the early 1990's with the trend towards increased interviewing training for police officers.

One of the challenges for the interviewer is to control the events as much as possible, taking the time needed to do a through job while at the same time feeling at ease and comfortable with the process. In a perfect world the following steps would be taken to prepare for an interview; conducting a case review; and determining whether there is a prior record. The actual sequence of these steps is not as important as the completeness of them.

Case Review

The interviewer should not use the case review as a means of determining what the outcome is. This information should not influence or prejudice the interviewer. The purpose is to gather as much information as possible to compare and contrast when making a determination on the validity of the case and the creditability of the individuals involved. It identifies possible problems with the case and areas that need to be thoroughly explored during an interview. The interviewer must look critically at all case material and determine what part is made up of fact and what statements are investigator conclusions. Disregard the conclusions and scrutinize the facts. Things may not be what they seem!

Been There . . . Done That! 2–1

In the middle of the night I received a call that a woman was at the station telling a crazy story about having been kidnapped, strangled to unconsciousness, driven around in the trunk of a car, and then returned to her house by the offender. Admittedly the report was odd, particularly since this victim stated she knew the man! Truth is sometimes stranger than fiction though, and this one proved to be rich in details that could not be dismissed. I interrogated the offender after a thorough statement from the victim. He admitted that he wanted sex and she refused; angry, he choked her until she passed out. Frightened he thought he had killed her, so he put her in the trunk of his car to figure out what to do with the body. When he opened the trunk of the car to throw the body over a bridge he was amazed that she was not dead, but pleading for her life. After she convinced him to take her home and that she would not report anything, He did. The victim statement and confession were not enough, however, so I obtained a search warrant for his car. In the trunk was one blonde hair identified as having come from the victim.

The dispatcher or other person who takes the emergency call must collect complete and accurate information from the caller. This information becomes the case that will be reviewed by the responding officer(s). Asking open-ended questions followed by closed-ended questions, the 911 or emergency operator avoids suggestive or leading questions. The information is transmitted to the responding officer(s) and updated when more information becomes available. In addition to informing the caller that the police are on their way, the dispatcher becomes the eyes and ears of the responding officer.

The first responder case review therefore takes place after the initial call for service, typically while an officer is in route to the incident. Just as important as any other case preparation, review the specifics of the case such as the numbers of people involved, gender, approximate ages, and physical descriptions. Find out if a weapon was displayed or used. Request a records check on both the suspect and the victim for outstanding warrants and prior offenses. Obtain as much information about the incident as possible, including the location of the perpetrator if he or she is no longer at the scene. From this information determine the level of danger or injury of persons at the scene.

When the interview does not involve an emergency response, obtain and read any prior reports that were generated regarding the incident. If another police department or social service agency did a preliminary investigation to determine jurisdiction or child in need of services, for example, contact that department for any notes that had been taken. At least speak with the other investigators involved; ask him or her to share information about what they did, who they spoke with, how and why they came to the conclusion that the case should be handled by another department. This information may be very revealing, but should not influence the interviewer regarding the case or the persons involved.

Determine if there were other agencies that interviewed relative to the complaint. This would not be unusual if the victim is a child, an elder, or a person with a disability. Investigative powers are vested in specific state agencies for the protection of each of these special populations.

Conduct a background check on the suspect prior to the interview or interrogation.

Obtain copies of the statements taken. Determine the appropriate avenue to obtain these documents in the event the statements are not readily available or are withheld due to confidentiality. It may be necessary to seek the advice of your local district attorney and request that the documents be made available through court order. The investigator must assume that prior statements would jeopardize the case, particularly if they were taken through a non-forensic approach.

Thoroughly examine the evidence, if any has been collected regarding the crime, as well as its status. Determine the relevance that the collected evidence has to the case, the person who collected it, and its initial location at the scene.

Determine Prior Criminal Record

When responding to the scene of a crime where the perpetrator is known, have the dispatcher or desk officer run the name of the offender to determine if a prior record or outstanding warrants exist. In cases of domestic crimes the name of the victim should also be checked for prior offenses. This is done because it is sometimes difficult to determine in cases of domestic violence who is the victim and who is the perpetrator. The existence of a prior record for a similar crime may be helpful in making that difficult decision at the scene.

For interviews scheduled after the initial response the existence of a prior record will expose weaknesses of the individual as possible biases that exist. Use that information to determine the best approach and method of interviewing.

Viewing the Scene

Whenever the investigation involves a major crime, the scene should be viewed and personally documented by the interviewer. In cases where the officer was not dispatched to the scene, review any photographs and sketches that were made by the first responder. It is preferable to return as soon as possible.

Returning to the scene may also be useful after the interview with the victim. Obtain a court order if the scene is in a home rather than a public place; remember that there is no exception to the Fourth Amendment requirement for a search warrant even with a murder scene! Obtain a Mincey warrant (1978) prior to re-entering the scene of a murder. Use this visit to corroborate the statements of the victim with the actual scene. If the victim had never been to the scene prior to the incident or if the victim has no reason to have known the particulars about the scene yet is able to describe it to you, then that scene becomes evidence.

Been There . . . Done That! 2-2

A young girl of ten reported to me that she had been raped by her mother's boyfriend. She described in detail the assault and how it had happened. Additionally, she was able to describe the bedroom where it had occurred. The man was arrested and denied the allegations, stating that the girl was trying to break up the adults' relationship. The jury might have believed that—but in her statement I had asked her to describe the things that had been used during the rape and where they might be found. This is information that the girl could not have known. She described where he kept the Vaseline, the rags that were used after the rape, and the place that he hid the magazines he forced her to look at which portrayed child sex. On a search warrant I had confirmed these items and their locations. She was more creditable than the adult and he was convicted.

Misinformation

Preparing for an interview includes a conscious effort in reducing witness and victim misinformation. Misinformation refers to internal and external sources of information that produce variation in the answers given by an interviewee. Internal misinformation includes the cognitive and developmental factors of the individual being interviewed (Holliday, 2003), and the relative judgment of that person (Collins, 2004). The relative judgment process is evidenced when the person most like the suspect is selected from a lineup regardless of whether the actual perpetrator is among the group (U. S. Department of Justice, 1999). False eyewitness identification is the largest single factor contributing to the conviction of individuals who were later exonerated through DNA testing (Wells & Olson, 2003).

Misinformation from external sources includes any information of an event that is acquired by the interviewee after the event occurred. One of the most common sources of eyewitness error is when witnesses' memories become contaminated by information that they have acquired since they witnessed the event (Wright & Loftus, 1998). Interviewers using suggestive techniques or questions provide a common source of external change. External influences through suggestive questions from the interviewer are believed to have the strongest impact on victim and witness statements, particularly with vulnerable populations such as children (Finnila, Mahlberg, Santtila, Sandnabba, & Niemi, 2003).

When a person's memory of events is changed due to the introduction of misinformation it is referred to as *contamination*. Contamination can occur at different stages during an investigation. The interviewer has the ability to influence the statements of victims, witnesses, and suspects through the questions that are asked and the way in which they are phrased. Contamination results if the interview process is obstructed or negatively influenced by the interviewer with the result of causing the person being interviewed to provide inaccurate information (Sandoval, 2004). Participants exposed to misinformation who experience contamination later misinform about some aspect of the crime. Cognitive interviewing techniques have been shown to reduce the reporting of internal and external misinformation (Finnila et al., 2003; Holliday, 2003; U. S. Department of Justice, 1999).

The effects of external misinformation can be reduced by decreasing suggestive influences during questioning. The interviewer through leading questions, even the tone or pitch of voice that is used, can distort memories. A *leading question* is a question that contains a possible answer. Leading questions or suggestions on what you want to hear are potential contaminants. An example of misinformation would be the following leading question posed by an interviewer: "Please describe the car, it was red wasn't it?" This leading question suggests that a "red" car was already identified and the interviewer is seeking confirmation. The witness that is contaminated by this information may then report that the car was red, thinking he or she did in fact see that red car. Contamination can occur when lineups are not conducted properly, such as exposing a witness to a person or photo that is later used in a lineup (U. S. Department of Justice, 1999). Contamination to a witness memory can occur when investigators use the same photo in more than one lineup.

The effect of internal misinformation may be reduced through the use of age and intellect appropriate language and methods of questioning. Research indicates that older adults are more vulnerable to misinformation than young adults, reporting that they saw something that was actually only suggested to them (Memon, Gabbert, & Hope, 2004). Be particularly careful with elders aged 60 to 80 when seeking a face identification; in one study eighty-seven percent of the senior citizens falsely identified a face from a line-up (Memon et al., 2004).

Detecting Contamination. We cannot know when someone else has contaminated a witness prior to your contact. The problem it presents is that it is impeding our search for the truth. In order to minimize the effects of misinformation each person that conducts interviews, either at the scene or later, needs to be personally aware of the possibility and avoid playing a part in this. Secondly, investigators must attempt to corroborate all information through interviewing additional subjects and the collection of physical evidence.

Courtesy of Corbis Images.

Avoid misinformation and be vigilant about the possibility of contaminated evidence. To guard against its effects, collaborate all eyewitness information through physical evidence.

Phase II—Establishment of the Psychological Content

The most common situation is the on-the-scene interview, although criminal justice and social service officials conduct interviews in a variety of settings. The investigator who responds to the scene must seek out and identify those who may have knowledge of the event and whose information may contribute to the investigation. Numerous individuals may have to be questioned to obtain the needed information.

Individuals who are thought to have information about the case are identified and interviewed. The difficulty for an investigator is that a variety of emotions could interfere with the fact-gathering process. Some of the people will be willing to give information but will be nervous or anxious. Others may not be willing to give information because they feel intimidated or threatened by questioning from government officials. Some people may not want to give out information due to bias, fear, or concern of retaliation. Make the person as emotionally comfortable as possible.

Whether the questioning takes place at the scene or elsewhere, all persons being interviewed should be separated. Keeping the individuals apart will minimize the tainting of information due to overhearing another person give details of the offense and prevent individuals from comparing stories prior to being interviewed. Separating the individuals also provides the privacy that is needed to assure that an interested person or perpetrator will not hear the information that is being given.

When Should the Questioning Occur?

The officer should not hesitate to request that witnesses remain at the scene until they have been interviewed. Yet consideration must be given to the physical and emotional needs of the witnesses and the victim. If the person to be interviewed is emotionally upset, take the time to calm that excited person, even if it means a delay of the interview until the witness or victim has regained composure. Avoiding the temptation to rush an interview at the scene, the officers should create a favorable atmosphere for the witness to talk freely by selecting a quiet area in which to conduct the interview. Always maintain the privacy of the interviewee to the greatest possible degree. Individuals that are comfortable will likely provide more information. This principle applies to the timing of the interview as well as its setting.

The nature of the offense may dictate the timing of the interviews. When this is not the case, interviewers should retain control over the interviewing timing. Witnesses and victims should be interviewed as soon as possible after the incident under investigation has occurred in order to obtain an identification of the offender. Do this while their memory is still fresh. If the circumstances do not allow for an in-depth interview, such as when the identification is being sought for the perpetrator, do not hesitate to inform that witness that they may be contacted for a more thorough interview in the future.

Special populations such as children, elders, and persons with a disability should be interviewed at a time when they are likely to be most alert and responsive to questioning (Baladerian, 1998). Evening or early morning interviews are not likely to result in quality information from special population individuals. Prior to scheduling an interview find out from a caretaker when the best interview time for that individual would be.

Where Should the Questioning Occur?

At all times the needs and desires of the person being interviewed is paramount. Questioning must take place in an area that is free of distractions. Note if someone appears nervous or reluctant to speak with you; the individual may prefer a more private place to talk. The place where the interview occurs is selected for one of these three reasons:

◆ Convenience
◆ For a desired effect
◆ Due to available resources

Convenience. For short interviews or to gather preliminary information it is often more convenient to interview people at the scene of the crime. The primary benefit to the at-the-scene interview is the freshness of the information. Another benefit is that victim and witness cooperation tends to be highest when the crisis is being resolved and the police officer represents protection. When potential witnesses are not identified at the scene there is the risk that they will not be located at a later date.

The downside of conducting a short interview at the scene is that people may be reluctant to speak freely to the police in the presence of others. Be aware of this reluctance to speak with the officer and offer another meeting place if he or she prefers. Look for an overall nervous appearance, glancing around, or extreme hesitation on the part of the person being questioned. Also, an individual may be injured or otherwise unable to give a full and accurate accounting at the scene. Respect the needs of your victims and witnesses in order to obtain maximum truthful information.

For a Desired Effect. Another method used to determine the place for an interview would be when there is a calculated determination for a desired effect on the interviewee. For intimidation or control, interviewing at the police station may provide the best choice. An office can be preset with the order of chairs and designed for minimizing distractions. Interviewing someone in their home, with consent, provides a false sense of control to the interviewee that can be used to the advantage of the interviewer. Typically an individual has his guard down when in a familiar and comfortable location.

Due to Available Resources. Interview special populations in the place where there are the resources available to facilitate the communication. Be aware that the Americans with Disabilities Act (DOJ, 2003) requires accommodations be made for interviewing victims with a disability. Special rooms may be designed for interviewing of children and elders. Videotaping of interviews is most appropriately conducted in areas that are designed for this purpose. Documenting the interview through audiotaping can free the interviewer to concentrate on the phrasing of questions.

When in the
Police Station
or an Office

The greatest control over the environment is achieved when the interview takes place in a designated room of the police station or in an office. The location should be quiet and free of distractions, preferably within a 10' x 12' room (Yeschke, 2003). No phone, beepers, clocks or other electronic devices are in the room unless they are specifically used for the interview purpose. There should not be any windows and limited wall hangings, if any.

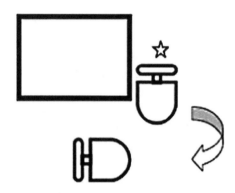

Yeschke (2003) suggests that the chair of the interviewer should be at a 45-degree angle to the interviewee to avoid presenting as a threat at the beginning of the interview. This practical use of proxemics recognizes the tension that is inherent when the position is changed to face-to-face interrogation seating. The moderate location straddles the social space and personal space where the participants are within four feet of each other. This distance allows for questioning that respects the personal territory without creating undue stress on the interviewee. Another advantage to this placement is the ease with which the interviewer can lean forward purposefully in order to cause anxiety in the persuasive interview approach. If there is a third person in the interviewing room he or she would be sitting out of the direct sight of the person being interviewed. If the placement from Figure 2-1 were used, the third person would sit to the left of the table, which is behind the interviewee.

FIGURE 2-1. Use proxemics in this interview position with the chairs placed at a 45°angle. The interviewer can lean forward or move his chair to face the interviewee to change the level of comfort.

Phase III — Actual Questioning

Plan to conduct an in-depth interview with the victim as soon as he or she is emotionally and physically able to do so. With the passing of time an individual may become confused and statements may lose detail. Avoid asking more than one question at a time, giving the person ample opportunity to provide an answer.

The trained interviewer knows that environmental and personal factors can influence what people hear and see. The lack of sleep, illness, weather, and light conditions are all potential distorters. During an interview attempt to determine if any extreme influences are involved. Consider the location and distance from the event when questioning witnesses. The ability to accurately observe and interpret things is also affected by pain, hunger, and distress. Emotions such as fear, anger, or worry impair perception. On the other hand, special interests may enable a witness to provide details that seem remarkable, such as a young boy that is interested in cars. What people see can be influenced by smells and sounds. Weave into questioning the five senses of smell, taste, and touch in addition to sight and hearing.

Typically an interview should be one-on-one. If two interviewers were in the room one would be the most obvious lead and do most of the talking. The second investigator would be helpful to take notes and assessing the witness's verbal and nonverbal behavior (Sandoval, 2004). When a second interviewer is included, it is preferable for that person to stay off to the side and out of the vision of the person being interviewed so as not to cause a distraction. At the end of the questioning the lead can be purposefully given to the second interviewer to fill in any gaps that were noted.

The Order of Interviews

The first officer at a scene should attempt to verify the identity of the suspect if he or she is known, as well as his location if he is not at the scene. All witnesses should be separated and asked not to discuss the details of the incident with others. The area should be canvassed to identify additional witnesses for questioning.

The type of crime and the availability of personnel to assist with the investigation may dictate the order of the interviews. If there is a victim, he or she should be interviewed by the first responder to obtain an identification of the suspect and the nature of any injuries. The suspect may be interviewed at the scene for determining culpability prior to making an arrest. When no person is placed in danger and an arrest is not mandated it may be helpful to conduct a preliminary interview of the suspect. Generally the witnesses are questioned second.

Types of Questions

No specific information or opinion about the case should be offered prior to the taking of statements. An open-ended question is a question asked in a way that encourages a narrative by giving direction to the interviewee because it does not limit the answer, it is broad and nonspecific. An open-ended question is asked in order to get as much information as possible about the person or the event. Open-ended questions would be used initially and as clarifiers through out the interview whenever narrative statements are expected. Closed-ended questions serve to limit the information that the person might give, to augment information already received, and to fill a specific need of the interviewer. A good balanced interview contains both question types used purposefully. Avoid using emotional or suggestive words. Do not rapid-fire questions at a person; give them time to answer completely.

Open-ended questions. An open-ended question is one that does not limit or direct the answer; therefore the phrasing of each open-ended question is important. An *initial open-ended question* seeks a full-undirected narrative response. A *clarifying open-ended question* seeks to complete or expand on the information already given. In order to elicit a full response don't interrupt the account by asking another question. Not interrupting indicates to the interviewee that you are willing to listen to their perspective, that you respect what they have to say. Interrupting the initial narrative gives an impression that what they have to say is of little importance. The way in which the question is phrased can increase or decrease the willingness of the person to respond. Good initial open-ended questions include:

- Please tell me what happened to you . . .
- Would you tell me everything that you know about . . .
- Please tell me everything that you did this past Saturday . . .

Initial open-ended questions avoid asking something that involves an imaginative answer or conclusion. Examples of bad initial open-ended questions include:

- Why did he do that to you?
- So what did you do to get her so angry?
- What was your involvement in the Saturday incident?

Encourage the person to continue their narrative through forced silence and reinforcing behaviors. A *reinforcing behavior* does not indicate approval or disapproval of what is being said. The behavior to encourage narratives can be verbal or nonverbal. Investigators must be aware that both verbal and nonverbal behavior will influence the statement being taken. Care must be taken to appear objective and nonjudgmental at all times. Good reinforcing narrative behaviors include:

- Saying "okay" in a matter of fact manner
- Please continue . . .
- I'm listening . . .

Negative reinforcing behaviors during an initial narrative include:

- Wincing (in response to a painful recollection of the victim)
- Knitting of the brow or pursing of one's lips (as if angry)
- Saying, "you have to be kidding" (as in disbelief)

The non-directed quality of open-ended questions allow for the interviewee to say what ever he or she wants without having preconceived expectations on what the interviewer wants to hear, so the questions are necessarily non-leading. Good questions include:

- Describe your assailant please
- What did the car look like?
- Tell me what you saw (heard, felt, did, etc.)

Bad open-ended questions that limit the answer and suggest an expected response include:

- Why don't you start off by telling me what your husband did to you?
- Describe that red car that was used during the incident
- Did it hurt when he did that to you?

When the person is being truthful the initial open-ended narrative should contain segments that are relatively equal in importance. These segments include what happened prior to the event, the event itself, and what she or he did after the event.

Been There . . . Done That! 2–3

During an interview with a rape victim she appeared to be withholding information. Requests for details of the assault were met with obvious resistance. At first I thought she was lying about having been raped. It then became apparent that she was hesitating because the details included things that were extremely difficult for her to talk about. He had done things to her that she did not want to admit had happened. The interview was made easier after I told her why it was necessary for me to know everything, including the things that were embarrassing. She did go on to give details although it was not easy for her to do that. Keep in mind that hesitation may be due to embarrassment or shame.

It may be helpful for the interviewer to encourage a narrative response at some additional time during the questioning or at the end. It can be used to explain events in greater detail, to develop information about subjective feelings, or to wrap things up. Examples of the clarifying open-ended question include:

- What did you do . . .
- What was your first reaction . . .
- Has anything like this ever happened to you before?

♦ Is there anything else you think I should know (or that you want to tell me)?

Closed-ended questions. Closed ended questions require a "yes" or "no" or otherwise brief response. They are the most common type of question and are useful for verifying information, filling in gaps of the interview, and obtaining specific factual information. Examples of good closed-ended questions include:

♦ What time did you go to bed on Saturday?
♦ Do you know the name of the person who did this to you?
♦ What is your age?

Care must be taken not to carelessly lead the witness through suggestive closed-ended questions.

♦ Was the car a blue Ford?
♦ Did you go to bed at 10 PM on Saturday?
♦ Did your father do this to you?

Follow-up questions. When the narrative is complete, asking follow-up questions probes deeper into the issues presented. Follow-up questions can be either the open or closed type, and seek to elaborate or to clarify what has already been said. Examples of follow-up questions include:

♦ You said that you "had sex"; please tell me what that means and explain in detail what happened.
♦ Where exactly did he touch you?
♦ What time had you gone to bed that night?

Direct or forced choice questions. These closed-ended questions are reserved for when you suspect that the person being interviewed knows more than they are telling you. They are asked in a non-accusatory tone of voice and without emotion. The purpose for using a direct or forced choice question would be to pin someone down for later impeachment.

♦ After you tripped and dropped the baby, was he still breathing?
♦ What did you trip on?
♦ Was your boyfriend angry when the baby would not stop crying that night?

Control questions. The person who asks the questions is in control of the interview. When sensing that you have lost that control, bring it back with a statement that requires the attention of the person being interviewed. The control question firmly establishes that the interview is not over. Examples of the question used to take back control would be:

♦ I understand that you are upset about this. Please take a deep breath and prepare yourself to answer these questions.

♦ These questions are difficult, I understand, but I am unable to help you without the details of what happened.

♦ We are almost finished; there are a few things that I am not clear on that need to be answered before we are done.

Leading Questions. Use leading questions when you want to guide the interviewee through a particular line of reasoning in a persuasive interview. By their nature, leading questions suggest an answer and should be avoided except for intentional use. These tend to distort the memory or perception of the person being questioned and the responses seldom reflect the thoughts of the interviewee. The following are examples:

♦ According to your neighbor . . .

♦ As you know . . .

♦ Your wife said . . .

Confrontational questions. A *confrontational question* is a question that is accusatory, typically involving a show of anger or disgust. When confrontational questions are introduced into the interview you can no longer go back to being friendly and helpful. Be sure that it is time to leave the relationship behind before bridging the interview with the interrogation. The decision to nudge towards an interrogation may begin with this manner of questioning. It is typically firm, but not necessarily loud. For example:

♦ John, I have interviewed your son — he tells me that you were the one who touched him. Can you tell me why you did that to him?

♦ You are real good, Pete; if I didn't know better I would think these signatures were done by someone else.

♦ So why did you pick her for your victim?

Determining an Approach

Behavior and personalities can affect your ability to obtain information during an interview. Prior to determining who will conduct the interview, each witness or suspect should be evaluated. Consider the personality that may influence what she or he sees, what might be remembered, and obvious likes or dislikes. Do not attempt the interview if there is obvious distain towards the potential interviewer and another other option is available.

Oblique Approach. This approach is suited for the interview where the interviewee will tell their story without prompting. As an avid listener you ask questions only to clarify points and avoid asking leading questions.

Regardless of the setting that is chosen for the interview, at the scene or at a designated place, the voluntariness of the statement is of great importance. If the person is willing to give information AND the person is not in custody then Miranda warnings are not required.

Been There . . . Done That! 2–4

Armed with an arrest warrant, my male partner and I picked up a man as he came out of work. He snarled at me in a way that a man under arrest should not be doing, as if he thought he would try to intimate me. So I took the upper hand and passed this one on to my partner. On the way to the station I said two words to the suspect: YOU STINK! It hurt his pride and he quickly started explaining that he was a working man and had just gotten out without having the chance to shower. Having gotten a reaction, I said it again: YOU STINK! Again he went on that he was not a bad man, just dirty. We arrived at the station and the two men went into the interrogation room. My partner (quite amused knowing he was the good guy—again) said, "She's a real bitch, ha?" In their common alliance, rapport had been established. The arrestee said he would answer any questions . . . as long as I was not in the room. Mission accomplished—a full confession resulted. Never underestimate the value of a good partner!

Formal Approach. The formal interview is conducted in a controlled environment such as a police department or detective office. This is best used to manage the individual who appears overly confident or condescending towards the interviewer. As a home court advantage, the formal setting is usually intimating enough to free the interviewer to think about more important considerations.

Informal Approach. Taking the informal route takes a lot of confidence! It works well for low-key interrogations that are conducted in the home of the perpetrator. It requires the willingness to sit and have conversation and the ability to persuade the person to invite you in. This is non-adversarial and no custody occurs with this approach. Asking questions and encouraging the suspect to talk, you become the gatherer of incriminating evidence that may be used to apply for an arrest warrant.

Conclusions

This chapter brings the student through the process of interviewing. The three phases represent the progression rather than the methods for being a successful interviewer. Each phase should be given equal weight towards the goal of obtaining the truth from witnesses and victims. It should be noted that interviewing is not just about talking. Of equal importance is listening. The process involves knowledge and planning. What is said becomes just as important as how and why it is said. Saying the wrong thing can cause contamination. Failure to ask the right questions can leave the interviewer empty handed. The bottom line is that interviewing is a learned skill.

Chapter Two Questions for Review

Short Answer Questions

1. What is the social system approach to interviewing and what modern themes are found in social systems theory?

2. Phase I of the interview process entails preparation for the interview. What happens during the case review step and what is the purpose?

3. What information does the first responder want to collect upon arriving at the scene of a crime?

4. What is contamination and when can it occur?

5. When should the interview take place and where should questioning occur?

6. What is the difference between open-ended and close-ended questions?

7. Briefly explain the other types of questions used in an interview.

8. Preparing for an interview takes a lot of work. There are many variables to consider and interview approach is one of them. Briefly describe each approach and when it is most useful.

Fill-in Questions

1. The approach to interviewing used in this chapter focuses on caring, self-development, and _____ , which emphasizes the role of power that is inherent in any interview.

2. The focus of Phase I is _____ .

3. The purpose of _____ is to gather as much information possible to determine the validity of the case.

4. _____ is when witnesses or victims give misinformation either through leading questions, when lineups are not conducted properly, or when memories are distorted.

5. Short interviews done at the scene of the crime are usually done out of _____ .

6. When interviewers are seeking a full narrative response they will ask _____ questions.

7. _____ are used to verify information.

8. When _____ are introduced into the interview the interviewer can no longer go back to being friendly or helpful.

9. The best approach of interviewees who are willing to talk is the _____ .

10. _____ is the most desirable physical arrangement between the interviewer and the interviewee.

Exercises

1. Instruct students to find at least one article in the library containing an interview. Suggest that news articles on controversial issues or political candidates often contain interviews. From the written interviews, the student must identify the type of questioning mostly used, i.e. open-ended or close-ended. The student must evaluate the article and the quality of responses as well as the type of question that elicited the response. Require that the student write a short paper citing the source used and the evaluation.

2. Play the PowerPoint presentation with audio interviews from *Eyewitness Evidence: A Trainers Manual for Law Enforcement.* Use only Part 1: Interviewing Procedures — Initial Response to the Crime. During the PowerPoint closed-ended questions are provided with the request that students convert these to open-ended questions. Instruct students to convert the questions in writing and pass them in to the instructor.

Reference List

Mincey v. *Arizona,* 437 U.S. 385 (1978).

Anderson, R. E., Carter, I., & Lowe, G. R. (1999). *Human behavior in the social environment: A social systems approach* (5th ed.). New York, NY: Aldine De Gruyter.

Baladerian, N. J. (1998). *Interviewing skills to use with abuse victims who have developmental disabilities.* Washington, DC: National Center on Elder Abuse.

Collins, W. (2004). Looks can be deceiving: Safeguards for eyewitness identification. Retrieved December 29, 2005, from http://www.wisbar.org/AM/Template.cfm?Section=Wisconsin_Lawyer& TEMPLATE=/CM/ContentDisplay.cfm&CONTENTID=47654

DOJ. (2003). *Enforcing the ADA: A Status Report from the Department of Justice.* (Report No. 1). Washington, DC: U.S. Department of Justice.

Finnila, K., Mahlberg, N., Santtila, P., Sandnabba, K., & Niemi, P. (2003). Validity of a test of children's suggestibility for predicting responses to two interview situations differing in their degree of suggestiveness. *Journal of Experimental Child Psychology,* 85(1), 32–50.

Holliday, R. (2003). Reducing misinformation effects in children with cognitive interviews: Dissociating recollection and familiarity. *Child Development,* 74(3), 728–752.

Memon, A., Gabbert, F., & Hope, L. (2004). The ageing eyewitness. J. R. Adler (editor), *Forensic Psychology: Concepts, debates and practice* (pp. 96–112). Devon, UK: Willan Publishing.

Sandoval, V. (2004). Strategies to avoid interview contamination. *Crime & Justice International,* 20(79), 29–37.

U. S. Department of Justice. (1999). *Eyewitness evidence: A guide for law enforcement.* (Report No. NCJ 178240). Washington, DC: U. S. Department of Justice.

Wells, G., & Olson, E. (2003). Eyewitness testimony. *Annual Review of Psychology,* 54(277), 277–295.

Williamson, T. (2004). USA and UK responses to miscarriages of justice. J. R. Adler (editor), *Forensic Psychology: Concepts, debates and practices* (pp. 36–57). Devon, UK: Willan Publishing.

Wright, D. B., & Loftus, E. F. (1998). How misinformation alters memory. *Journal of Experimental Child Psychology,* 71(1), 155–164.

Yeschke, C. (2003). *The art of investigative interviewing* (2nd ed.). Boston, MA: Butterworth-Heinemann.

Purposeful Interviewing and Processes

KEY TERMS

Active listening	Comprehensive questioning
Hate crime	Incendiary
Morphostasis	Purposeful interviewing
Primary aggressor	Testamentary evidence

CHAPTER OBJECTIVES

After completing this chapter you should be able to:

- ◆ Explain *morphostasis*
- ◆ Explain the primary objectives of *purposeful interviewing*
- ◆ Define the term *hate crime* along with its suggested interviewing approach
- ◆ Compare and contrast the terms *technique* and *method*
- ◆ List the ways in which comprehensive questioning would be useful for interviewing
- ◆ Describe the characteristics of active listening
- ◆ Explain the statement analysis approach
- ◆ List ways of developing rapport

Introduction

Social systems theory has three general characteristics that assist in framing the purposeful interview. First, it implies a comprehensive approach to interviewing. The bigger picture looms over each statement and personal contact that takes place. Tying them together presents a greater potential for description and integration of seemingly unrelated events into a single situation. *Comprehensive questioning* means getting as much information as possible. At a car stop with more than one person in the vehicle, does one of them appear upset? Have that person step out of the car away from earshot and ask, "Are you ok?" At the domestic disturbance, speak with the children in that house. When interrogating a sexual offender, ask, "Who did this to you?"

Suggestive leads are another aspect of social systems theory. Human behavior is thought to be multi-faceted yet somewhat predictable. Take for example the concept of continuation. Also called *morphostasis*, it is the understanding that the continuation of a system or family relationship may take priority due to the fear of the anticipated consequences of change. When a family is in danger of being destroyed or radically changed, the individuals may pool energies. By pulling together and forgetting past differences they combine against the thing that threatens continued existence. Families are considered organization units; the natural response is one of conserving energy to maintain the system and further its purposes. Saying to a domestic violence victim, "When you going to leave this creep?" is counterproductive. A different approach would be, "If you are going to stay in this relationship, perhaps you should think of safety planning in the event things get out of hand." The first statement creates an enemy. The second recognizes that you don't understand the reasons for staying, but that you are there to help when the victim *is* ready to leave.

A common language is also suggested by social systems theory. It allows criminal justice to borrow from other disciplines the concepts of human behavior. It provides the interviewer with *technique,* the devices whose application enables us to accomplish our purposes, to carry out our professional responsibilities. While the term suggests a cold, mechanical, or manipulative approach, it is the tool for generalizing that makes possible a common response. Although every person is different, everyone is similar in some respects.

Characteristics of Purposeful Interviewing

Purposeful interviewing refers to the realization that statements are sought for specific reasons (Gosselin, 2002). Purposeful interviewing is not a method but a broad approach to the process. Active listening and rapport development are useful in developing a technique which will be used in accomplishing the interview goal, regardless of the situation.

Active Listening

Active listening is a skill that makes evident to the person being interviewed that you are attentive to what is being said. It requires the interviewer to mentally relax and draw on their self-esteem and confidence. Express a willingness to commiserate and listen by exhibiting patience. It is important to not only listen to what is said, but also to know how it is said. Emotional outbursts and inflections of the voice may give a clue to sensitive areas of the interview. Sudden silence, uncertainty or confusion, or the shifting of conversation to an unrelated subject may indicate that information is being withheld. Nervous bodily reaction or facial reactions may signal that a sensitive area has been reached.

Understand their frame of reference in order to understand what is being told. Listen to the tone, voice inflection, and level of excitement from the subject during the interview. Watch for body language and facial expressions to see if they match what is being said.

The interviewer must remember what has been heard. Notes should be taken in a manner that does not interrupt the interviewing process. Some witnesses are reluctant to talk if they notice that the officer is taking down every word they say. Brief notes can be made without deterring or distracting witnesses. In some situations a room that has recording equipment can be set up in advance of the interview. Alternatively, a microphone can transmit information to another room where a note taker is making a full report.

Active listening may be demonstrated verbally and through non-verbal attentiveness. Examples of ways to show that you are actively listening include:

- ◆ Body language—nod your head, look curious, smile, vary your eye contact, lean slightly forward
- ◆ Body posture—face squarely or at a 45 degree angle, lean forward, shift as they do, be careful not to shift to show displeasure
- ◆ Concentrate and listen carefully
- ◆ Detachment—be cool and calm without showing emotion
- ◆ Do not roll your eyes in response to a statement

♦ Gestures — keep arms open and palms extended

♦ Patience — do not rush the interviewee

♦ Positive silence — silence can indicate acceptance or can be used to signal your control

Rapport Development

In Chapter One the reader was introduced to the concept of rapport. Rapport should be considered the first step in any interview. Although it is difficult to describe, it is basically a two-way communication. The concept represents a working relationship between the interviewer and the subject being interviewed. Whatever the individual may be feeling, the interviewer is not responsible for what has happened to him or her, but is responsible for the interviewer's own reaction. The victim may be feeling pain or confusion, and anger is directed at the interviewer. When interviewing an angry person talk slowly and softer than normal. Anger is a sign of weakness, which indicates a lack of self-control. Don't ever become visibly angry at a victim. Once it has occurred, the ability to negotiate rapport is gone.

If the interviewee is acting superior to the interviewer, maintain an emotional detachment. The successful interviewer should not take the interviewee personally or feel offended. Never apologize for asking questions. Be careful about changing behavior to one of arrogance. To establish a cooperative relationship the interviewer should:

1. Display a sincere interest;

2. Be patient and tactful;

3. Be respectful;

4. Control personal feelings;

5. Provide reassurance;

6. Encourage an untalkative witness by asking appropriate questions.

Objectives of Purposeful Interviewing

In the previous chapter, preparation was the first phase in the process of interviewing. Central to preparing for the interview is recognizing why police officers conduct interviews. The primary objectives are (Gosselin, 2002):

♦ To examine the nature of the offense;

♦ To determine if a crime was actually committed;

♦ For the purpose of identifying the perpetrator.

Been There . . . Done That! 3–1

For some reason we tend to think of victims as being nice people and offenders as monsters. When the pattern does not fit it makes it difficult to access the creditability of the victims. The key is active listening—get past the anger and hear what has happened. During one interview a female had been yelling at the police, shouting obscenities, and was extremely obnoxious. Sitting down in a quiet place, however, she explained to me how she had been beaten and raped by two men who then left her without clothes to die in the woods. She had been fortunate to find her way out for help, but thought that the police would not do anything for her because she was a prostitute. After a while she calmed down and gave descriptions on her assailants and told about it having happened to others on the street. As it turned out I was able to identify five women who had been severely beaten by these two men. Both had extensive violent felony records. They selected prostitutes as their victims because they thought the women could be intimidated into keeping quiet. The assaults by these men had nothing to do with sex-for-pay; they were vicious attacks where the perpetrators enjoyed beating and torturing women. They were both arrested and found guilty, and were sent back to prison where they belonged.

The Nature of the Offense

Earlier it was stated that individuals are all different, yet there are some identifiable similarities. That concept comes into play when generalizing about an approach to interviewing based on the nature of the offense. Remain calm and tactful with contradicting or antagonistic witnesses. Remember that witnesses who are angry, frightened or emotionally upset usually perceive only a fraction of what they might observe under normal circumstances. Emotional factors can cause a witness to lie, to become uncooperative or forgetful. Purposeful interviewing means that modifying an approach to meet the unique challenges of the crime results in a slightly different interviewing approach in order to elicit complete and truthful information.

Being purposeful in your interviewing also requires attention to the nonverbal communication that tells us something about the validity of the message, its urgency, whether it is being made humorously, seriously, or sarcastically (Kadushin & Kadushin, 1997). Nonverbal behaviors may communicate what interviewees cannot bring themselves to state openly. Feelings and attitudes of which interviewees are only vaguely aware of may be clear to the observant interviewer.

Purposeful interviewing also suggests that the nature of offense will dictate different questioning approaches. The following examples illustrate how the nature of the crime dictates the questioning.

Arson. It is desirable to interview as many witnesses as possible at the fire scene (Federal Emergency Management Agency, 1988). The reasoning behind this position is that some witnesses may be reluctant to talk later, the information is fresher, and that suspects have less opportunity to plan possible alibis. Moving through the crowd the investigators may identify a suspect to interview based on the strong odor of smoke. Who do you interview? Key interviewing witnesses include firefighters on the scene, eyewitnesses, property owners, spectators at the fire, victims, neighbors and business associates. Firefighters are first on the scene and need to be interviewed before others. They can tell what they saw and where the damage on the building was located. Second, interview the patrol officers. Third to be interviewed are the owners/occupants and the witnesses. It is not necessary to establish motive for arson prosecution . . . but juries like to hear it! Questions to answer include:

- Who will profit?
- Is this for spite/revenge?
- Is it juvenile fire setting?

Hate Crimes. Showing concern for the victim's safety, note and document all injuries. Only one person should conduct this interview, any other involved persons should remain unobtrusive during this questioning (McLaughlin & Walley, 2001). Be careful not to minimize the crime; display genuine concern for the victim's feelings. Note that it would be difficult for someone not targeted in this way to fully understand the emotional impact it has on the individual. There may be a heightened distrust on the part of the victim towards anyone who resembles the attacker; this obstacle to interviewing is important to anticipate and overcome. Document the financial damages if any and photograph both the victim and the scene. Record spontaneous utterances made by the victim.

Active listening is the most important interviewing skill you can learn!

Use an open-ended initial question format with follow-up questions. Using closed questions, ask for exact wording of what the suspect said before, during, and after the incident and how often. Describe the suspect with as much detail as possible, including tattoos or clothing.

It is the task of the resourceful police officer to overcome witness reluctance to being involved. Ethnic and racial minorities will likely need to be persuaded to cooperate. Examples of helpful statements include:

- It is important to stop this individual(s) from doing this to anyone else in your community.
- There is nothing to stop this from happening to your friends and family, we need your help.
- I know this is difficult for you, but there is something that can be done about this.

Partner Violence. There are often strong emotional ties between the victim and the offender in these cases. The victim may even be financially dependent on the assailant. In some cases the perpetrator faces loss of employment if convicted of domestic violence. A victim may therefore be unwilling or unable to provide information that will be used against the partner; hence purposeful interviews aim to verify and give credibility to the victim without expecting a high level of cooperation. Make sure you get all of the available evidence and victim statements regarding the violence at the scene; do not count on victim cooperation at a later date. Questions that will help to establish the seriousness include:

- How often has this happened in the past?
- Have you ever been hospitalized due to these attacks?
- Has he (she) ever threatened to kill you?

Sexual Assault. The initial questioning of the acquaintance sexual assault victim should be limited to issues concerning injury assessment, identification and location of the perpetrator, and collection of physical evidence. In other words, don't ask for information that you don't need to know. It is difficult to discuss any sexual experience with a stranger, even more so when it was an unpleasant experience. Typically the victim will give only partial information when he or she is faced with this uncomfortable situation; additionally, the incompleteness of the statement may be used later to impeach the victim credibility. The responding officer should be more concerned with reassuring the victim of her immediate safety. According to research, victims may be confused and upset after a sexual assault which requires police reassurance of her immediate safety (NCWP, 2001). Statements from the responding officer that would be appropriate include:

- You are safe *now.*
- I don't need to ask a lot of questions right now, but I have to know if there was penetration involved?
- I know that this is a lot to ask, but please do not smoke or have anything to drink until you have been examined by the doctor. (Briefly explain the forensic procedure that will follow.)

Do not ask leading or accusatory questions of the victim or witnesses:

- Did he have a gun?
- Why didn't you fight him off?
- Did you let him do this?

A detailed statement would likely follow after the victim is examined at a medical facility, when appropriate. If the victim directs anger at the police interviewer it is important to understand that this is misdirected. Patience and compassion are the ingredients needed to establish the necessary rapport for a more detailed interview at the appropriate time. The hospital examination room should be avoided as a place for that full interview. There are conflicting thoughts on allowing a support person in the room with the victim during the interview (NCWP, 2001). This decision may ultimately depend on the gender of the interviewer and their ability to persuade the victim to give a statement in private. Things that would be helpful to express empathy to the victim during the interview might include:

- How are you feeling?
- Would you feel more comfortable if I called you by your last name?
- Do you have any questions?

As with any interview, establishing rapport is an important first step in obtaining a complete statement. When interviewing the acquaintance sexual assault victim there are comments that would impede efforts to build rapport through a lack of respect for the victim. Examples include:

- DO NOT ASK: Will you take a polygraph?
- DO NOT STATE: It could have been worse.
- DO NOT COMMENT: Why were you out so late?

Open-ended questions should be asked to allow for the victim to describe the assault in her or his own words. Clarifying questions to establish specific facts should be asked after the victim has completed the narrative. The interviewer should be specifically aware of the victim's body language that indicates embarrassment or discomfort. Reassuring the victim that they are doing a good job at explaining as well as acknowledge that the questions are embarrassing will help to normalize the conversation.

White-Collar Crimes. The negative treatment that victims of white-collar crime receive when they seek help leaves them feeling guilty and ashamed (Burnley, Edmunds, Gaboury, & Seymour, 1996). Interviewers must overcome the victim's self-blame for having been duped by the con; assure the victim that the perpetrator is experienced at gaining confidence from individuals. Emphasis needs to be on the psychological needs of these victims in order to gain full cooperation and overcome the unwillingness

---

Been There . . . Done That! 3–2

An older gentleman came in with the complaint of his car having been stolen. With great difficulty he explained that he was a professor at a prestigious university with a lot to lose by making the complaint. As it turns out he was being blackmailed by a male prostitute that he had picked up in the city a few nights before. Although he had been a homosexual for years, he was in a marriage of conve-nience. His reputation in the commu-nity was at stake, but he could not bring himself to pay off the demand in order to get his vehicle returned. Without the right environment this information would not have been forth-coming. Time would have been wasted and likely the theft would not have been solved. A successful "sting" resulted in the arrest and prosecution of the blackmailer.

---

to admit to their full losses. Jim Ahrens, a police officer from Virginia, suggests that these victims experience anger and fear which become emo-tional barriers to communication that need to be eliminated (Burnley et al., 1996). Allow the victim to vent their feelings and be willing to vali-date them with statements like:

♦ Are you ok?

♦ I would be angry too.

♦ You have every right to feel like that.

Was a crime committed?

Research has indicated that during interviews police officers have only a tenuous understanding of the legal points needed to prove an offense under investigation (Williamson, 2004). It is not enough for the inter-viewer to *think* that a crime has been committed. These legal points that must be proved by the prosecution in order to sustain a conviction are the parts of the crime called its "elements." The interviewer must *know* what information is needed to prove that a crime has been committed. To determine the appropriate questions that need to be asked, taking the time to become familiar with the specific elements of the crimes that are being investigated is well worth it. This preparation provides the inter-viewer the opportunity to mentally prepare the questions that need to be asked in order to prove that the crime was committed. The confidence of knowing what you are looking for in the interview will also help you to be at ease. For example if the crime being investigated involves an elder, the age that constitutes elder becomes an element that must be shown. Whether or not the perpetrator knew that the person was an elder may also be an element. Know beforehand the exact age that con-stitutes an elder in your state, any requirement for knowledge of that fact. If the allegation is of stalking, determine the level of fear or threat that is required by your jurisdiction. For rape there must be penetration; be sure to document penetration versus attempted penetration.

Collecting evidence that a crime was committed provides the basis for a successful prosecution. Interviews are an integral part of determining if a crime was committed and if so, the type of crime. *Testamentary evidence* is what the witness says in a court of law; typically this form of evidence is collected through interviewing. It is evidence that is required to prove any contested fact. Physical evidence is something that may be seen, heard, touched, smelled, or tasted. Evidence may prove or disprove the involvement of a particular person or cast doubt on whether the crime was even committed.

Arson. The major role of the investigator is to rule out accidental causes of the fire such as heaters, appliances, fuses, or electrical outlets. Interviewing is the most important tool of the arson investigator! The goal is to determine if the fire is incendiary or accidental. *Incendiary* refers to "the criminal setting on fire of buildings or other property." This determination is based on the physical evidence at the scene and through interviewing.

Hate Crimes. The FBI defines a *hate crime* as a criminal offense committed against a person or property which is motivated, in whole or in part, by the offender's bias against a race, religion, disability, ethnicity/ national origin, or sexual orientation (West & Wiley-Cordone, 1999). An overt criminal act must be attempted, threatened or completed along with the requisite motivation. Bias, bigotry, or prejudice might be indicated through speech or written words from the perpetrator, or inferred from the racial, religious, ethnic, handicap, gender or sexual orientation of the victim. It may be inferred from the presence of one or more bias indicators.

Partner Violence. For a crime to be one of domestic violence there must be a legally recognized domestic relationship between the victim and the perpetrator. Frequently acknowledged categories include married and previously married persons; those that live together as husband and wife; persons that have a child in common; partners of same-sex relationships; parents and their children or grandchildren; siblings; and extended family members through blood or marriage. Some states expand on traditional meanings of domestic through the recognition of persons that live under the same roof, regardless of affiliation. Substantial dating relationships may also meet the definitional standard. If the perpetrator is within one of the domestic categories in relation to the victim, a special legal category exists. Victimization within a domestic relationship provides additional criminal and civil protections and increased sanctions that are not accessible to persons whose perpetrator is a stranger or non-domestic. Siblings, in-laws, and extended family though blood or marriage may also fall under the classification. Your State's definition will likely differ from others. Without a legally recognized relationship, there is no crime of domestic violence, although the act may constitute a different criminal category.

Sexual Assault. Sexual assault means any unwanted, forced sexual contact. This can take many different forms. It can be:

♦ Sexual harassment
♦ Exposing or flashing
♦ Forcing a person to pose for sexual pictures
♦ Forcing a person to look at pornography
♦ Fondling—an unwanted sexual touching
♦ Rape

Rape is defined as forced penetration with any object against the will of the victim. Penetration may be by a finger, the male sex organ, or any object. Any penetration, no matter how slight, is sufficient to constitute sexual intercourse. The majority of states legally recognize only females as rape victims while a few state laws are gender neutral. Those states that do not legally recognize the crime of rape with respect to male victims offer alternative legal protections. Experts believe that 10% of all rape victims are men.

White Collar. Although there has been some debate as to what qualifies as a white-collar crime, the term today generally encompasses a variety of nonviolent crimes usually committed in commercial situations for financial gain. Both federal and state legislation define the activities known collectively as "white-collar crimes." According to the Legal Institute, the most common white-collar offenses include antitrust violations, computer/internet fraud, credit card fraud, phone/telemarketing fraud, bankruptcy fraud, healthcare fraud, environmental law violations, insurance fraud, mail fraud, government fraud, tax evasion, financial fraud, securities fraud, insider trading, bribery, kickbacks, counterfeiting, public corruption, money laundering, embezzlement, economic espionage, and trade secret theft (Legal Information Institute, 2004). White-collar crime is estimated to cost the United States more than $300 billion annually.

Identify a Perpetrator

A primary justification for interviewing concerns the identification of the perpetrator and recognition of the victim. Obtaining and accurately recording the physical description of a criminal suspect is a basic requirement of the interview function. A good physical description can hasten the apprehension of the criminal offender and assist in obtaining a successful conviction. It is the responsibility of the investigating officer to secure the most accurate and complete description possible from those witnesses who had the best opportunity to observe the suspect or who have personal knowledge of his identity.

A victim may not be identified in situations where one is reluctant to come forward. Whether it is real or imagined, this occurs where the victim lacks confidence in the willingness of the criminal justice system to act on his or her behalf. Prostitutes, drug addicts, migrant workers, and other disenfranchised individuals frequently underreport victimization. Child victims, the elderly, and persons with a disability may not be aware of the criminal nature of an act committed against them. When interviewing, the determination of additional victims may increase the creditability of the prosecutions' case. Don't be afraid to ask, "Has this happened to anyone else that you know of?" The answer may surprise you.

Determining the victim from the perpetrator may be a challenging task. Most literature on domestic violence leads to the conclusion that battering is a male-on-female phenomenon, which occurs exclusively in heterosexual relationships. However, battering occurs with similar frequency and severity in lesbian and gay male relationships as compared to heterosexual relationships (Leventhal & Lundy, 1999). Most experts accept the rate of male victimization to be approximately 15% of domestic violence.

Primary Aggressor. Experts are now accepting the dilemma faced by criminal justice. Both the courts and the legislature discourage the practice of arresting both parties in situations that appear to be mutually combative. Approximately half of the states have laws that require police officers to make a primary aggressor determination rather than arrest both individuals (Hirschel & Buzawa, 2002). Dual arrests should be the last option used by law enforcement. The *primary aggressor* in a domestic relationship is the person who is exercising power and control over the other. Neither gender nor the size of the individual provides enough information to make that primary aggressor determination. Separating the parties and interviewing them provides the best available option. First, the situation should be examined to find out if violence was used by one person only. Absent evidence of self-defense, it would be a single arrest situation. If violence was used by both individuals questions must be asked about prior assaults to find out if one person was acting in self-defense. Without a history of violence the next step would be to see who is the most fearful and who is in control.

Healey et al. suggests the following guidelines to help in determining the primary aggressor (Healey, Smith, & O'Sullivan, 1999):

1. Question the couple and any witnesses closely before coming to a conclusion and making an arrest. Do not assume that the physically larger partner is always the primary aggressor.

2. Question the partners separately and determine how the visible marks were made and why. Did the victim bite an arm that was holding him or her down for example?

3. Ask if there has been a recent escalation in the violence and why. Determine if there has been a history of abuse.

4. Do not mistake anger for primary aggressive behavior. An angry victim's conduct is not a justification for arresting.

5. When signs of injury are exhibited by both parties, consider the possibility of self-defense and examine the relative level of injury or force involved. Determine who the initial aggressor was.

Been There . . . Done That! 3–3

Just prior to Christmas a call came in at 10 AM from a crying child that daddy was hitting mommy and had pushed her into the Christmas tree. By the time we arrived at the scene the tree was upright and there was no evidence of domestic abuse. The wife was interviewed apart from her husband and children, refusing to give any information and denying that she had been hit. There were no marks or bruises evident. The husband also denied any battering. There was no probable cause to make an arrest, even though I was sure that the man had hit his wife. The child who had called said she made up the story. No probable cause meant that no arrest could be made.

I next interviewed the three children and asked if they were ok, conducting an assessment on the level of risk for harm to the children if we were to leave them. Asking if there were any guns in the house the children told me that there was rifle in their bedroom closet! It was fully loaded and did not have a trigger guard attached. Following up these claims, evidence surfaced that the weapon belonged to the husband. Since the failure to secure a weapon in a locked container or with a safety lock is a felony crime, the guns in the house were confiscated and the husband was arrested.

Risk Assessment. Today's police officer has an obligation to make an assessment of the situation and form an opinion on the level of risk for harm. This principle applies in a variety of crime situations. If the crime scene is the home of the victim, or a place known to the perpetrator, basic security measures could be suggested. Does the perpetrator have a key?

Change the locks. Is the house alarmed? Alarms are fairly inexpensive. Are the doors and windows locked at all times? Does the victim keep the car locked? Does the victim carry a cell phone to call during an emergency? Is a restraining or no-contact order needed to increase the measure of security? These and many other questions related to safety can easily be discussed during an interview. What may seem like common sense to the average cynical police officer may be insightful to someone more trusting. Taking the time to discuss with the victim, methods of increasing their potential for safety will afford a greater peace of mind for that person and it also has the benefit of increasing future cooperation.

Making an Identification

It should be noted that eyewitness identification is not considered the most reliable form of evidence and will be closely scrutinized by the court. Mistaken identifications are not uncommon occurrences. Eyewitness identifications are made under strict legal requirements and must avoid any suggestiveness by the police. Contamination is a real problem when witnesses and victims are making identifications and investigators must be alert to its possibility.

Composites, photographs, or sketches may be used to help identify persons. Composites are developed from separate photographs or sketches of facial features. Do not show a witness a photo or live lineup prior to developing a composite; it may influence his memory of the suspect and cause contamination.

Field Identification

A showup is a lineup with only one participant, which occurs a short time after the commission of a crime. The showup method of witness identification is inherently suggestive, requiring the careful use of procedural safeguards (Technical Working Group for Eyewitness Evidence, 1999). When one or more witnesses interviewed at the scene indicate they are able to make an identification of the perpetrator, document that description prior to conducting the field identification showup. If possible bring the witnesses to the place that the suspect is being detained, cautioning that the perpetrator may not be at the location. Fully document both positive identifications and non-identification outcomes that occur, the time of the procedure, and its location.

Lineups

During an interview the witness or victim may indicate a willingness to identify the suspect from a lineup. Careful instructions to the witness prior to the viewing of either a photo or physical lineup are imperative.

Been There . . . Done That! 3–4

A photo line-up may or may not result in the identification of the perpetrator during an investigation. Care must be taken to make sure that the victim understands that the perpetrator may not be in the photo array, and that they must look at all photos before commenting out loud about any of the pictures. In one case the victim told me that she thought the number three picture was the man who had assaulted her, then went on to say that she was mistaken—he was number five. This identification was worthless and therefore discarded. It was later learned that none of the men in the photo array had been the attacker.

Explain that the purpose of the procedure is not only to identify the perpetrator but also to exonerate the innocent (Technical Working Group for Eyewitness Evidence, 1999).

Photo Lineup. The array should consist of at least six photos, including only one suspect. The non-suspect photos should be consistent for unique features such as scars or tattoos, but do not need to closely resemble each other in all features. Avoid using the same photos in a lineup of a new suspect to the same witness. Document the photo lineup order and the witness responses.

Live Lineup. One suspect is included with a minimum of four non-suspects. General resemblances are all that is needed, with the suspect significant features being similar. Avoid using individuals that are so similar as to make identification difficult. Be sure that the suspect does not stand out. Document the instructions that were made to the witness and the responses, the time and place of the lineup, and the identities of its participants.

Assessing the Statement Accuracy

Always consider the possibility of false reporting. The job of the interviewer is to discover the truth if that is possible; therefore the interviewer should adopt a neutral position to conduct interviews. A full investigation is still necessary even if it is suspected that the person is lying, distorting the facts, or withholding important information. Do not initially accuse the individual of falsely reporting or treat the person as if they were lying. Obtain as much information as possible and follow the leads that are provided. The facts of the case will speak louder than the accusation. It is not necessary to make judgments and unwise to jump to conclusions.

When a claim appears to be exaggerated consider if the victim who reports having been assaulted has any motivations for exaggeration. Look at the repercussions of the act. Is the victim a juvenile, married, or ashamed? Do not judge the reliability of the statement based solely on a moral evaluation of the person providing the information. Reality is stranger than fiction. To dismiss a complaint based on an initial statement because the individual does not fit the profile of a victim exposes the person to further violation and potentially allows a perpetrator to go free. Instead, take the position of corroborating the victim statement to increase its creditability when ever possible.

A witness may provide information that is correct in some ways and incorrect in others. The entire statement does not have to be ignored if it is discovered that part of the statement is inaccurate. It is not unusual for eyewitness accounts to vary on specifics of the situation. One person may remember a vehicle as red and another report the vehicle as blue. This does not mean that one or the other is lying; just note the inconsistencies for further evaluation. Review the statement for inconsistencies to other statements or known evidence in the case.

There are many reasons why contemporary interviewers need to be observant when taking statements from victims, witnesses, and perpetrators. Concerns over the reliability of interviews taken with child victims have caused convictions to be overturned (*State* v. *Michaels*, 1994). False allegations and witness misidentifications have caused imprisoned men to be freed after many years in prison (Death Penalty Information Center, 2004). Since 1973, 117 people in 25 states have been released from death row with evidence of their innocence. Finding the truth demands the evaluation of all evidence, including that obtained during an interview.

Conclusions

In this chapter you were introduced to the concept of purposeful interviewing. This is not a method, but a general approach to conducting interviews. This approach brings with it a determination to conduct interviewing with the goal in mind of obtaining as much accurate information as possible. Different crimes may require a different interviewing approach. Consider this information as an invitation to develop your interviewing technique. Be flexible and responsive — the reward will be an improved quality in your interview and the development of new skills. Develop active listening skills and rapport development to enhance the communication within the interview.

Implicit in this chapter is the idea that each phase of the interview leaves nothing to chance; you are in control. Looking at the allegation and making the determination of whether a crime was actually committed, taking the sometimes more difficult way to figure out who the perpetrator is, and questioning with a purpose has its rewards. All the information that brings you to your objective is useful for explaining the crime and justifying the response.

Chapter Three Questions for Review

Short Answer Questions

1. What are the three general characteristics that assist in framing the purposeful interview?

2. Why is understanding nonverbal cues received from interviewees important to the interviewer?

3. Why is it so important to interview the first arriving firefighters in a suspected arson?

4. What are some of the main reasons victims of domestic violence may be reluctant to provide details associated to their assault?

5. What are some of the requirements necessary for a crime to be one of domestic violence?

6. How accurate are eyewitnesses? What are some of the issues affecting eyewitness testimony?

7. What are the main characteristics of Purposeful Interviewing?

Fill-in Questions

1. Two types of lineups that are often used to identify the suspect include _____ and _____ .

2. _____ refers to the realization that statements are sought for specific reasons.

3. _____ may communicate what interviewees cannot bring themselves to state openly.

4. When interviewing the victim of a hate crime there may be a _____ on the part of the victim towards anyone who resembles the attacker. This obstacle to interviewing is import to anticipate and overcome.

5. When interviewing illegal aliens a false name may be given due to the fear of _____ .

6. When interviewing the victim of a sexual assault _____ questions should be asked allowing the victim to describe the events in his or her own words.

7. _____ are developed from separate photographs or sketches of facial features.

8. Sudden silence, uncertainty or confusion, or the shifting of conversation to an unrelated subject may indicate that _____ .

9. The interviewer should listen to the _____ , _____ , and _____ from the subject during the interview.

10. Psycholinguistics is a recently emerged discipline combining _____ and _____ .

Exercises

1. The New York State Defenders Association has an interesting site that provides information and links on police line-ups and identification techniques. Choose one problem that has been linked to police identification techniques and find a proposed method to change it. The web site is located at: http://www.nysda.org/Hot_Topics/Eyewitness_Evidence/eyewitness_evidence.html

2. Take ten minutes to have a conversion with someone in the class that you do not know and have never spoken with before. Ask them to explain something that they enjoy doing in their spare time. Listen intently on the words that they use. What can you tell about where this person comes from based on the way he or she speaks?

Reference List

Burnley, J., Edmunds, C., Gaboury, M., & Seymour, A. (1996). *National Victim Assistance Academy Textbook*. Washington, DC: Office for Victims of Crime.

Death Penalty Information Center. (2004). Innocence and the Death Penalty. Retrieved 2005, from http://deathpenaltyinfo.org/article.php?did=412&scid=6

Federal Emergency Management Agency. (1988). *Arson prosecution: Issues and strategies.* (Report No. FA-78). Washington, DC: United States Fire Administration.

Gosselin, D. K. (2002). Victim interviewing in cases of domestic violence: Techniques for police. L. J. Moriarty (editor), *Policing and Victims* (pp. 87–107). Upper Saddle River, NJ: Prentice Hall.

Healey, K., Smith, C., & O'Sullivan, C. (1999). *Batterer intervention: Program approaches and criminal justice strategies.* Collingdale, NY: Diane Publishing.

Hirschel, D., & Buzawa, E. (2002). Understanding the context of dual arrest with directions for future research. *Violence Against Women,* 8(12), 1449–1473.

Kadushin, A., & Kadushin, G. (1997). *The social work interview.* New York, NY: Columbia University Press.

Legal Information Institute. (nd). White-Collar Crime: An Overview. Retrieved January 13, 2004, from http://www.law.cornell.edu/topics/white_collar.html

Leventhal, B., & Lundy, S. E. (1999). *Same-sex domestic violence.* Thousand Oaks, CA: Sage Publications, Inc.

McLaughlin, K., & Walley, A. (2001). *Responding to hate crimes: A multidisciplinary curriculum for law enforcement and victim assistance professionals.* (Report No. NCJ 182290). Newton, MA: National Center for Hate Crime Prevention Education Development Center.

NCWP. (2001). *Successfully investigating acquaintance sexual assault: A national training manual for law enforcement.* Beverly Hills, CA: The National Center for Women and Policing.

State v. *Michaels,* 136 N.J. 299, 311–12, 642 A.2d 1372. (1994).

Technical Working Group for Eyewitness Evidence. (1999). *Eyewitness evidence: A guide for law enforcement.* (Report No. NCJ 178240). Washington, DC: US Department of Justice.

West, K., & Wiley-Cordone, J. (1999). *Toward a national voice: Maximizing our effectiveness.* Newton, MA: National Center for Hate Crime Prevention.

Williamson, T. (2004). USA and UK responses to miscarriages of justice. J. R. Adler (editor), *Forensic Psychology: Concepts, debates and practices* (pp. 36–57). Devon, UK: Willan Publishing

PART

II

Methods and Techniques

This second section of *Smart Talk* includes information on the most common methods and techniques of criminal justice interviewing. Chapter Four discusses typical approaches to the criminal justice interview. These may be used with the cooperative or uncooperative victim and witness. The traditional interviewing approach is based on answering the 5 W's and How! The approach is simplistic and without cumbersome procedures. Traditional interviewing is useful in determining the level of cooperation that can be expected from a witness, gathering emergency and crisis information, and for field operations. The structured interview is a three-step method of interviewing. Adding rapport building, narrative descriptions, and ample interviewing opportunity to the traditional approach, it is considered a valuable tool for interviewers. A third approach in this chapter is inferential interviewing. Inferential interviewing is a deception-detection approach. Promising a high rate of accuracy, it is a question-by-question analysis of the statement for statement coherence, response length, type-token ratio, and verbal hedges. Statement analysis is the next approach covered. It contains a word-by-word examination of the grammar within a statement. The approach looks at the parts of speech, extraneous information, lack of convictions, and balance of the statement in a four-part process. Each one of these methods is adaptable to the situations in which questioning might occur. Finally, the field statement analysis is a shortened version of statement analysis for field application.

Chapter Five covers forensic hypnosis and cognitive interviewing. These are two major forms of interviewing that use memory jogging techniques to facilitate recall. Both are recommended as interviewing approaches for cooperative witnesses and victims. The approach used in forensic hypnotic interviewing is different from cognitive interviewing however. The techniques of hypnosis are introduced in this chapter with the understanding that proficiency in this method should be obtained through continued study before its use in criminal investigation. The complexity of hypnosis and the regulation of its use for investigative purposes suggest that this is an introduction to the approach. Cognitive interviewing is a memory jogging approach that can be mastered by even the novice interviewer! This approach is easily learned and its use adapted to a variety of situations that require information retrieval. The foundation of the cognitive interview is the use of four mnemonics that are the memory jogging techniques. These should be learned and practiced for use in any interviewing situation.

The behavioral interviewing techniques in Chapter Six provide valuable tools for investigative interviewing and interrogation. The behavior indicators that are covered include nonverbal posturing, sensatory verbal communication, and eye movement. The techniques provide situations for interviewer interpretation. There are no step-by-step methods in this chapter. The techniques, once learned, are applicable in any interview or interrogation as additional tools when determining truthfulness versus deceit. Kinesics, a nonverbal communication form, was introduced in the first chapter. Here its practical application is illustrated. Founded in the late 1940's kinesics is a common approach to behavioral interviewing. A second approach covered in this chapter is neuro-linguistic programming (NPL). Still developing for interviewing use, facial expression and coding, in addition to eye movement, provide interesting insights to learning and communication.

Interviewing with Statement Analysis Techniques

KEY TERMS

Actus reus	Complainant
Extraneous information	Inferential interview
Lack of conviction	*Mens rea*
Side-tracker	Statement analysis
Traditional interviewing	Verbal leakage

CHAPTER OBJECTIVES

After completing this chapter you should be able to:

- ◆ Identify the sources of information
- ◆ State the motivations of a side-tracker
- ◆ Explain the traditional approach to interviewing
- ◆ Define *actus reus*
- ◆ Explain the structural approach to interviewing
- ◆ Compare and contrast traditional interviewing to structural interviewing
- ◆ Describe the characteristics of inferential interviewing
- ◆ List the four parts of statement analysis
- ◆ Explain the concept of the field statement analysis.
- ◆ List ways of detecting deceit

Introduction

The chapter starts out by identifying the sources for information that may be encountered. Included in this section are methods of traditional interviewing, structured interviewing, and statement analysis. *Traditional interviewing* is a straightforward asking of questions to obtain information about a case. The approach is typically referred to as a "just-the-facts" way to get answers to the questions that describe an incident. It is a neutral process during which the interviewer attempts to distinguish the truths through the statement from the subject (Hand, 2003). Hand (2003) describes this perspective as one in which the interviewee is considered a passive possessor of knowledge, while the interviewer objectively protects the facts from influence or contamination. Questions are rarely formulated and no particular technique is involved. The approach has been criticized because the question format is usually closed-ended and the manner of questioning is abrupt. Historically it has not encouraged interviewee participation or the free exchange of information, therefore its use is considered to be limited. For these reasons, the traditional approach does not enjoy a good reputation as an effective method of interviewing. Also referred to as the standard interview, its purpose is to limit the information from eye-witnesses to that considered specifically necessary for the investigation being conducted (Kebbell, 1996).

The traditional approach to interviewing has been criticized for its excessive simplicity, abruptness, and lack of direction. Other models such as cognitive interviewing and the behavioral approaches, which will be discussed later in the book, have come under fire for extreme complexity, cumbersome techniques, and questions that must be asked in specific and difficult to remember order. The structured interviewing approach uses the best of traditional questioning methods while applying principles used zin cognitive interviewing. This approach provides direction in the questioning to facilitate cooperation. A new approach, which is included in this chapter, is the inferential interview method. Think of inferential interviewing as structural with a twist! The technique improves on prior methods by including simple methods to detect deceit in the interview. The final section expands on the idea of deceit detection with an in-depth section on statement analysis.

Identifying the Sources

Solving crime depends on the ability of the interviewer to acquire accurate information regarding the details of the event. Information typically comes from multiple sources that must be approached to determine their willingness to provide information. The statements must be evaluated for their reliability and applicability to the case. A traditional approach to interviewing provides an adequate way in which to make these preliminary assessments.

In the early stages of an investigation it is important to find out which individuals may have information about the case versus those who do not. Sometimes a person will want to give information about a case or claim to be a witness when he or she is not connected with the situation at all. Referred to as the *side-tracker,* this is a person who is falsely claiming involvement as a witness or suspect to a crime. The side-tracker may be a person with emotional or mental disturbance, one who seeks publicity, or who simply has a grudge against the person about whom they want to provide information. They may be the perpetrator who is purposefully attempting to mislead the investigator. If the motive for the giving of information is not clear, attempt to find out about any relationship the person may have had with the primary individual involved in the investigation. Check all information against the known facts to determine if any of the information is useful before discarding it. The problem with the involvement of a side-tracker is that they can take valuable time away from the focus of an investigation.

Identify your sources! Is he the complainant, victim, or a side-tracker? Is he purposefully attempting to mislead the investigator?

The person who reports a crime or accuses another person of an offense is called the *complainant.* The complainant may be the victim, someone who saw the crime occur, or one who has information about the crime being investigated. Sometimes the complainant is the perpetrator who is attempting to divert police attention away from his or her own actions. If preliminary questions reveal that the complainant may be the suspect, then the approach changes from an interview to an interrogation as necessary.

If the source of the information is the victim, keep in mind that stress or shock may influence the individual's memory of an incident (Artwohl, 2002). Multiple interviews may be needed to obtain an accurate victim statement. The victim may be overly cooperative or highly emotional at the time of an initial interview. It is probably not necessary to do an in-depth interview under these conditions. Obtain enough information to provide emergency or medical attention and to identify a suspect if an assault was committed.

Ask questions to determine if the complainant is a witness. What did this person see or hear about the incident? When interviewing, always separate the individuals and interview them one at time and outside of hearing by any other persons. Encourage the person not to discuss the situation with any other witness. A dilemma exists for someone who does not want to tell something that might be hurtful to another! Not wanting to lie the alternative may be to avoid telling the truth or by not answering the question directly (DePaulo et al., 2003).

Guidelines for the Traditional Interviewing Approach

Asking the person questions that follow the "Five W's and How" guidelines will make the best use of the immediate cooperation being offered. The six guidelines to traditional interviewing involve the questions which answer who, what, when, where, why, how—the five W's and How. A primary purpose of the traditional approach is to gather only the information that is absolutely necessary for the investigation. This approach is used most often in field situations where time for conducting interviews is scarce. It can be followed up with more directed interviewing as time permits in the future. The vast majority of information that is gained through traditional interviewing is helpful for any investigation. The difference between traditional methods of interviewing and other approaches is the manner in which the questions are asked. It is often abrupt and straight to the point. Rather than encouraging narrative responses this interviewing approach tends to limits answers. There is no particular order of questioning and no suggested steps for conducting this traditional approach.

One reason to use the traditional interview approach is for determining the level of cooperation that can be expected from a witness. A potential witness may be called on the phone to determine if a full interview might be helpful to the investigation. An additional benefit of the traditional interviewing approach is to obtain emergency response information and general details of the event at the scene of the crime.

People should be approached in a manner that is most likely going to encourage their cooperation. Understand the reasons why a person may or may not want to provide information. Avoid antagonizing the person being interviewed as they are less likely to provide information if they sense conflict or anger. There is no required order for the guidelines to be used during the interview. Instead, think of the five W's and How as a checklist to make sure that as much information has been gathered as possible.

What?

Questions should not be phrased in a way that leads the person being interviewed to give a particular answer, nor should they be accusatory. Individuals seeking to please the interviewer may inadvertently provide information that is false rather than giving no information at all. Instruct the person that while you are depending on their cooperation, you understand that they will not have all of the answers.

In obtaining complete information about an incident the interviewer should search for what happened before the incident, what happened during the incident, and what happened after the incident. An initial determination of *What* is made for the following circumstances:

- ◆ What offense was committed?
- ◆ What happened?
- ◆ What weapon was used?
- ◆ What was said?
- ◆ What did the eyewitness hear or see?
- ◆ What happened after the event was over?

Is the situation a complaint of abuse, a fight, a theft, or of stolen or damaged property? The initial response of the interviewer will vary greatly based on the general knowledge of what is alleged to have occurred. Is the situation even a violation of the law? Here the interviewer determines the *actus reus,* a term which means the "guilty act" (Schmalleger, 2004). Based on the description of the event by the victim or witnesses, determine if a crime has been committed and the nature of that offense.

Who?

Find out the names and descriptions of all people involved. If this is a primary response, ask the dispatcher for the name of the complainant when en route to the scene. Determine when possible if the complainant or suspect will likely still be at the scene at the time of arrival and request both be instructed to wait there. If the call originated from a neighbor or witness obtain names, addresses, and telephone number through dispatch or within the case file. If an anonymous reporter is involved in reporting, attempt to identify that individual through caller ID or through witnesses. Relevant questions to be asked include:

- Who is the victim?
- Who is the perpetrator?
- Who are the witnesses?

Are there likely to be a group of individuals to be reckoned with, or a situation occurring between two persons? This makes a difference on who might be interviewed relative to the case and how the officer will approach persons at the scene. If the dispatcher has the names of persons at the scene ask for a records check to determine if any of them has been involved in prior offenses; has an outstanding warrant against them; or is the subject of a current restraining order. In particular when the response is to a disturbance, determine if either party has a current firearms license. Find out if there are any children in the home.

Who are the people in relation to each other? Is there a relationship between the victim and the perpetrator? Are they friends or acquaintances? Could they be related through someone? The existence of any relationship opens the possibility of motives to give inaccurate information because of trying to protect someone or having a grudge against someone. Ask people being interviewed about their prior law enforcement contact. Have they been arrested before? Have they been a victim or witness in a previously reported crime? Are they related to a law enforcement person? These questions relative to the relationship of the individual can help in establishing rapport and for assessing the credibility of the individual.

When?

Find out if the incident is still ongoing. Is the complaint about recently discovered missing property or is this an old complaint? The response will be different from an offense involving a recently discovered theft of property and an allegation of violence. Has the complainant made similar allegations about this person in the past? Is this a situation of reoccurring abuse? Is there an order of protection or restraining order that is in effect? Has this type of offense ever occurred against the victim in the past? Possible questions include:

- When did this incident occur?
- When was the event reported?
- When did injuries occur?

Where?

Did the offense occur at the place where the witness or victim is currently? This information may help to determine if the offender is likely to in the vicinity of the crime or not. Of equal importance is whether evidence of the crime may be at a different location than the victim, which would require the preservation of the scene. Consider exploring:

- Where was the location of the incident?
- Where did the event begin and where did it end?
- Where were the witnesses located in relation to the offense?
- Where is the best place to conduct the interview?

In addition to knowing the place where the event happened, questions should be asked to determine why it happened at that particular place. In a purse-snatching example the event may have taken place on a street with a burnt-out light. This may indicate that the perpetrator was familiar with the area rather than it having been a random attack. If the event was in a home, whose home is it? Was the person an invited guest or an intruder? Were there indications of forced entry?

When doing the initial assessment for victim cooperation using the traditional approach it is useful to take into account the place where the interview itself should be held. If this stage occurs in the field, care should be taken to keep the interviewee outside of sight and earshot of other individuals.

Been There . . . Done That! 4–1

A mother left her two children alone in the apartment so that she could get some dope. She locked the children in their bedroom when she left because she did not think she would be gone long. The two young boys started to play with matches and their bed caught on fire. They could not get out of the room . . . they died there. Their death was a tragic accident—their mother did not mean them any harm. Was she responsible? She lacked the <u>mens</u> <u>rea</u> because she did not intend that her actions would cause the deaths of her children. She had a duty to care for these children, but a few years earlier the state had repealed its law on criminal neglect. The mother could not be charged with having committed any crime. In part due to this case, a new law was passed that defined acts of neglect that would be considered illegal. If this same scenario happened again, the mother would be charged with a crime, but the law is not retroactive.

Why?

Motivation for an event may not be readily observable and could be related to the value structure or relationship of the person to the situation. Attempting to determine why something occurs may involve some value judgments on the part of the interviewer. Be careful to properly phrase information that is a judgment rather than a fact in any report that contains it.

◆ Why did this occur?

Interviewing should establish the *mens rea* of the case. *Mens rea* refers to the state of mind of the perpetrator, not the victim. *Mens rea* is the guilty mind requirement or the knowledge of a wrongful purpose (Garner, 2004). This condition is not the same as intent; it is present when a person should have known better, even if they did not intend the consequences.

Been There . . . Done That! 4–2

On a warm summer day the body of a missing 15-year-old girl was located in the river. Her hands were tied behind her back with a man's sock. The autopsy confirmed that she had died of drowning, so she was likely bound and thrown into the river while she was still alive. Why did this occur? It was puzzling since she was still dressed, including her underwear. Early on in the investigation the motive of sexual assault was dismissed because of her being fully clothed. I noted that she was wearing a sanitary pad at the time of her death.

Two suspects were later identified and interrogated. They were two young men who were both under age 20. When asked how they knew the victim they responded that she was a friend. She got into their car willingly because she knew them. Together the three of them went to a secluded spot on the river where kids often go for underage drinking. It still did not make sense. Why would they kill their friend?

During the questioning I asked if they had sex with her knowing that they did not. Immediately one suspect drew his lips tight as if in anger! They wanted to have sex with her but she had said " NO." She had before; they didn't understand why she would not do it then. They fought with her to remove her clothing, she struggled and yelled. In anger one man had taken off his socks and tied her hands. Partially pulling down her underwear it was noted that she was having her period. One of the young men had been arrested for rape in a neighboring state, but had received a suspended sentence. He became frightened that she would tell someone. He convinced his friend that they had to keep her from telling anyone. They threw her (still struggling and screaming) into the river to cover up the attempted rape. While the tragedy still did not make sense to me, the "why" had been answered.

Determining that the individual did not intend the consequences does not mean that he or she is not legally responsible for what happened. According to Schmalleger, there are four levels of *mens rea* (Schmalleger, 2004):

1. Purposefulness—this is when the act is intentional and done for a reason or goal. An example would be when a person kills another for monetary gain, a life insurance, or inheritance.

2. Knowing—if a person engages in activity that they should know would have dire consequences, then responsibility for that act exists. Walking into a crowded room swinging a baseball bat would be likely to hurt someone. Even if the person did not intend to hurt anyone, it is a likely consequence of one's actions.

3. Reckless behavior—when a person engages in activity that is reckless, which increases the risk of harm. Driving at high speeds or under the influence of alcohol are examples.

4. Neglect—this situation may occur though the failure to do something. When a legal duty to care for a child or an elder is established, the failure to provide the care would result in criminal culpability if harm results. Criminal neglect is an extreme failure, for example when a child dies because the parent did not provide food.

How?

The how of a crime is concerned with the event and everything leading up to it. How did the perpetrator get access to the victim, to the money stolen, or to the area to cause damage? Once access was gained, what was the manner in which they committed the act? What were the instruments or tools that were used in the commission of the act? What evidence would there be to support information that is being provided in the interview?

- ◆ How did it happen?
- ◆ How was the victim approached?
- ◆ How did the perpetrator gain access?
- ◆ How often has a similar event occurred?

Of particular importance is the sequence of events, when things happened during the incident. Knowing the exact sequence of events can render the event plausible or not. Now that each component of the traditional interview method has been outlined, look at Figure 4–1 and see how many of the questions you can answer!

What Is Structural Interviewing?

The structured interviewing approach is one that builds on the traditional interview by adding these following components: rapport building; narrative description; and an ample interviewee response opportunity. Many of the positive aspects of the cognitive approach to interviewing are also incorporated into structured interviewing, such as active listening, use of open questions, and appropriate nonverbal behavior (Memon & Higham, in press). The organization of the structured interview is meant to maximize recall and minimize eyewitness contamination (Colwell, Hiscock, & Memon, 2002).

FIGURE 4–1. Look at the picture as if it were a real situation that you are investigating. Can you answer the Who? What? When? Where? Why? How?

Courtesy of Corbis Images.

Steps for Structured Interviewing

Structured interviewing is a method that is planned out and carefully followed to maximize the amount of useful information that is gathered. Following these suggested steps may result in an accuracy rate of about 62% according to a recent study (Colwell et al., 2002).

Step 1: Build Rapport

Establish rapport. Research confirms that rapport may be more important than any particular technique for increasing truthful information (Memon, Wark, Holley, Bull, & Koehnken, 1997). Attempt to build rapport so that the person being interviewed is at ease and is willing to give information. Remember from earlier chapters that the purpose of rapport is to establish a two-way communication between the interviewer and the interviewee. It is a relationship of trust.

Step 2: Encourage Participation

Encourage the individual to participate actively and to report information rather than just respond to the questions that are being asked. Do not volunteer information about the case or the suspect when conducting an interview. Ask open-ended questions frequently and do not interrupt the person who is making a statement. Record the statements accurately and completely. If practicable, take notes during the interview. As soon as possible after the interview, the full statement should be written down using the witness's own words.

To obtain information on an incident ask open-ended questions followed by closed-ended questions to clarify the first answer (Technical
Working Group for Eyewitness Evidence, 1999). Ask non-leading and
open questions that allow for a free narrative account. The interviewer
specifically requests the free narrative. Ask the subject to describe, in as
much detail as possible, everything that is remembered about the event.
In order to avoid contaminating the statement, interviewers avoid introducing any new information or details about the event. Avoid interrupting
the account or asking for clarification of the details at this stage. For
example:

1. "Can you tell me about the car?" This open-ended question
   gives the person an unlimited range of answers without leading
   them to what you might be expecting to hear.

2. "Can you tell anything about the color, make, or model of the
   car?" This is an open-ended question that is not limited to any
   particular aspect of the car. It does not imply that the person
   should remember any particular aspect of the car. It is not leading the witness or suggestive because it does not suggest any
   particular color, make, or model of vehicle.

Specific probing questions are next used to elaborate on the details
that were provided by the interviewee during the free narrative account.
Open-ended questions are preferred. The interviewer may incorporate
the 5 W's and How in this step.

Step 3: Review the Statement

In the final step of the structured interview the subject is asked to recount
the entire scene or event again for the purpose of bringing new recollections into the account. When completed, allow the witness to read this
statement and make corrections to it. Do not write a statement as if it
were the words of the witness unless it actually is. For example, a four
year old would not use the word "intercourse"! Be careful not to substi-
tute your words for someone else's without specifying that the statement
is a paraphrase of the witness statement.

Inferential Interviewing

A promising new approach to interviewing is called the *inferential interview*. The inferential interview is a method to detect deception through
analyzing statement characteristics and a question-by-question analysis.
In a study by Colwell et al. (2002) the inferential interview classification
accuracy was an astounding 82%. This comparison study found similar

To detect deceit according the principles of the Inferential Interview listen for statement coherence, response rate, type-token ratio, and verbal hedging.

accuracy between the structured interview at 62% and the cognitive interview at 68%. The scrutiny of words, phrases, and sentence structure provide clues for further investigation and contain a wealth of information for the interviewer (Rabon, 1994). From this perspective, sentence construction is influenced by the individual's learned communication skills in addition to whether the person is trying to convince, deceive, or be truthful. Statements may be examined for what is missing and what is apparent. A key component is that the interviewer be open to what the words may reveal.

Colwell et al. (2002) suggest that four dependent measures can be used by the interviewer to discover dishonesty in a statement. Deception is associated with less coherence, shorter responses, more verbal hedges and an increase in the type-token ratio.

These are the important factors to consider when using the inferential interviewing method to determine if the statement is deceptive:

1. Statement coherence

2. Response length

3. Type-token ratio

4. Verbal hedges

1. Statement Coherence

A statement should make sense by not violating the rules of nature or contradicting itself. This step is an examination for dishonesty that includes the statement as a whole. Does the statement make sense when it is complete? Are there questions that are unanswered that must be asked to determine if it is complete? Did the statement contradict itself? Does the statement contradict the laws of nature?

2. Response Length

Deception that is highly motivated has been associated with a shorter response length, a slower rate of speech, and more speech errors. These behaviors collectively known as verbal leakage are the unconscious verbal responses that indicate deception. Follow-up questions that are used to probe suspected deception have been helpful in uncovering purposeful deceit by nonskilled lie-tellers (Talwar & Lee, 2002).

Been There . . . Done That! 4–3

Sketchy details of a kidnapping and an attempt to commit murder were the reasons why I was called out in the middle of the night. While en route to the scene I thought about the absurdity of this alleged crime. A woman reporting that while hitchhiking in her rural hometown she had been picked up and given a ride by a man that she knew. She said that she was strangled to unconsciousness by him and later woke up in the trunk of his car. Further, I was told, when the car stopped and the trunk was opened they were parked on the side of a bridge with a long drop to the river below. She reported to the police that he was going to throw her in the river but that she had pleaded with him and he took her home instead!

The report sounded like a lie yet I knew it was important to find out more information. When I interviewed the victim I was looking for more signs of dishonesty. What convinced me that she was telling the truth was that she recounted waking up in the car and described in detail that he had stopped at a gas station —she heard the gas going into the tank and smelled it. She described how frightening it had been in the small dark place without any way to get out. In detail she described the roads as being bumpy or smooth so that she had an idea where they were at the point he had opened the trunk. Taken together the entire statement was coherent. It made sense that she could describe sequentially the experience and feelings while locked in the trunk.

The next day I called for the forensic specialists to look inside the trunk for evidence of her being there. They found one long blonde hair belonging to her . . . it verified that she was telling the truth.

3. Type-token Ratio

The common measures used for a type-token ratio is different words (types) to the total number of words (tokens). For example, if a text is 1,000 words long, it is said to have 1,000 tokens. There may be only 400 different words in the text because many of them are repeated. The ratio between types and tokens in this example would be 40%. The ratio is unique words divided by total words in a statement.

4. Verbal Hedging

Verbal hedging are techniques used to buy additional time for answering the questions or as a way to avoid commitment to the facts. The number of verbal hedges in the interview is counted to gauge the extent to which these have been used.

1. Methods to avoid answering and to buy time include:

    ◆ The unnecessary use of connectors—Uh's . . . Um's . . . and's . . . or's . . . and;

◆ When the subject repeats all or part of the interviewer's questions before answering—"tell you what happened from the beginning?"

2. Ways to avoid committing to the statement include:

◆ A claimed lack of memory and
◆ Extraneous information

Statement Analysis

Based on the idea that statements of experience will contain language characteristics that are absent from statements that are the products of imagination, *statement analysis* is the word-by-word examination of the grammar within a statement (Klopf & Tooke, 2003). Statement analysis provides a more complex method to detect deception as compared to the principles of the inferential approach. It is used as a method to access the credibility and reliability of a statement concerning a crime that has been alleged to occur. It can be used along with any form of interviewing method as an assessment of the information that has been recorded in a statement. Adams suggested that the technique for statement analysis is two-fold: first determine what is a typical truthful statement, this is referred to as the norm; secondly, look for any deviation from this norm, since truthful statements are different in both content and quality from fabricated ones (Adams, 1996). Both written and oral statements can be evaluated using this approach. While the vast majority of statements are believed to be truthful, both structure and content will vary between those that are deceptive and those who are not (Memon, Gabbert, & Hope, 2004).

Conducting Statement Analysis

The four basic components of statement analysis are: parts of speech; extraneous information; lack of conviction; and statement balance.

Step 1: Parts of Speech

Examine the individual parts of speech that are used in the statement, particularly pronouns, nouns, and verbs, and to establish the norm for each. If a change from the norm becomes apparent, the investigator looks to determine the reason for that difference. Word choices are therefore purposeful, even when they are selected subconsciously. Noun, verb, and adjective choices represent a limited example for applying the principles of statement analysis (Adams, 2004). The following phrase used by Robert, a sexually dangerous pedophile, is illustrative: "My story has never changed; I never hurt that boy, I love him." From years of experience, it is not unusual for an offender to refer to their statement as a *story*. When this occurs without prompting, it is noteworthy because the term refers to something that is made up and not real. As Adams (2004) concludes, using this noun to describe what happened may indicate a false statement. The verb *hurt* in this example minimizes the crime of anal rape, which was perpetrated against the young boy. By minimizing the offense the offender is also playing down his role in causing any harm to the child. Using the verb *love* suggests a positive experience rather than the heinous crime that actually occurred. Here the perpetrator uses an adjective *that boy* rather than the name. Distancing himself, this offender objectifies the victim.

Understanding grammatical terms are the first step towards statement analysis. According to the dictionary these following definitions apply (*Merriam-Webster's Collegiate Dictionary*, 2004):

- ◆ *Pronoun*. Words that are used as substitutes for nouns (p. 995).
- ◆ *Noun*. Words that serve as the subject of a verb and refer to an entity, quality, state, action, or concept (p. 849).
- ◆ *Verb*. The part of speech that expresses existence, action, or occurrence in most languages (p. 1389).
- ◆ *Adjective*. A word that modifies a noun to denote a quality of the thing named, indicate it quantity, or extent, or to specify the thing as distinct from something else (p. 16).

Pronouns. Common pronouns are I, me, you, he she, we, they, and it. Truthful people provide statements using the pronoun "I," which is first person singular. Deviating from the use of first person singular during an interview is a signal of possible deception. An overuse of the pronoun "we" indicates a lack of commitment to the statement and unwillingness to take responsibility for something.

Example of truthfulness: I woke up at 7:00 A.M., got dressed and went to school. I met some friends and we went into class. At noontime we all left and drove around.

Example of a lack of commitment: We all met at school and went to class. We left when the bell rang for lunch and drove around.

When the statement concerns more than one person and "we" is the best description, then the lack of "we" is cause for concern, particularly if the subject is talking about a spouse. This signifies a distancing between the man and wife, a lack of togetherness, which is expected between spouses.

Example of the norm: My wife and I went to a local restaurant. We met up with some friends there and had dinner. After dinner we went right home.

Example of a deviation: My wife and I went to a local restaurant. My wife and I then met up with some friends and had dinner. After dinner my wife and I went right home.

In allegations of rape and abduction the interviewer should be concerned when the victim uses "we" to refer to her and the perpetrator. This pronoun suggests togetherness, a deviation from the norm in these reports. The interviewer should ask if the victim knew the perpetrator previously if she refers to her attacker in this way. If there is no relationship then there is reason to believe that the statement was false.

Example of the norm: I got into the car and he pointed a gun at me and told me to drive. He was hiding in the front seat under a blanket. I drove north on Rte. 91 until he told me to take exit 12.

Example of a deviation: I got into the car and he pointed a gun at me and told me to drive. He was hiding in the front seat under a blanket. We drove north on Rte. 91, and then we took exit 12.

Been There . . . Done That! 4–4

It was 2 AM that the phone rang for the report of a kidnapping and rape that had just been reported. Arriving at the scene it appeared strange that the victim had been driven so far off of the highway when the first report I received said she had been abducted from another state. How did the perpetrator know to come off the highway at this particular exit to travel 15 minutes for the location which was secluded? In my interview of the victim she was very calm and matter-of-fact about her abduction, claiming that there was a man hiding under a horse blanket in the passenger front seat who had risen up to abduct her. This did not seem possible given the size of the area or the close proximity to the driver. There were also verbal clues that indicated her situation was questionable. She referred to the kidnapper in a person "we" statement over and over. When pressed for specifics about the assault she used equivocating terms with a lack of

detail. There were attempts to absolve her of responsibility when she stated that she could not have possibly known he was hiding under the blanket. Her statement was difficult to understand because she started at the middle of the incident, went to the beginning and then to the end. It made little sense and I found myself asking her repeatedly to explain things to me—they lacked any chronological order.

The investigation continued after the initial interview with the victim. Even the identification was so unclear that it was meaningless. Finally I called down to the police department where she lived and found that the victim was well known to them. She had made a similar kidnapping complaint a year earlier to that department and to a third police department before that. There was no evidence of a kidnapping, it was a false report. The victim was making a plea for help. Appropriate referrals were made.

Possessive pronouns such as my, our, your, his, her, and their, suggest a relationship between a person or object and the interviewee. Changing the relationship is a deviation from the norm and suggests a distancing from that person or object.

> **Example of the norm:** My grandchild and I were walking in the woods. She needed to go to the bathroom, so I helped her take down her underwear. I did not touch her other than to help her go to the bathroom.

> **Example of a deviation.** My grandchild and I were walking in the woods. She needed to go to the bathroom, so the child was helped with taking down the underwear. The child was never touched in a bad way.

Nouns. Because nouns represent persons, places, and things a change in noun usage may represent a change in the way that the suspect perceives a situation. Interviewers should look for a change in the noun that is being used in the statement. Something has changed in the reality of the suspect when a noun change occurs after frequent usage. It is almost impossible for a perpetrator to admit harming a family member, according to Adams (1996).

> **Example of the norm:** I loved my mother. I did not mean to hurt my mother, but I stabbed her.

> **Example of a deviation:** I loved my mother. I did not mean to hurt her, the devil was stabbed.

Verbs. When someone uses memory to recall past events it is normal to use the first person, singular past tense. It becomes significant if an individual being interviewed varies the verb tense during the statement because the event occurred in the past. Any change in the tense of the verb should provide a signal to the interviewer that deception may exist.

> **Example of the norm:** I saw the shooting. I was so scared that I ran as fast as I could.

> **Example of a deviation:** I saw the shooting. I am so scared that I run away as fast as I can.

Here the sentence starts in the past tense and moves to the present tense, which indicates a lack of commitment to being the witness; it is suggestive of greater involvement than the interviewee has admitted. Change of tense from the past to the present tense may signal deception. Using the past tense when referring to missing persons is also considered a deviation of the norm.

The statement that contains verbs such as "tried," or "started," represents a weakened assertion of the facts. It is not the same as having done something.

Example of the norm: I ran.

Example of a deviation: I tried to run.

Adjectives. Additional information is provided by the use of adjectives. Using the adjectives of "that" and "those" to reference a person or object suggests distancing. Referring to a person through spatial adjectives is a deviation of the norm, particularly when a relationship should exist.

Example of the norm: I did not hurt David.

Example of a deviation: I did not hurt that child.

Step 2: Extraneous Information

Extraneous information refers to irrelevant or unnecessary statements (*Merriam-Webster's Collegiate Dictionary,* 2004). Examine the statement for extraneous information. Extraneous information refers to the situations when the interviewee provides information that does not answer the question and information presented out of order. A truthful person with nothing to hide when asked, "What happened?," will provide the events in chronological order. Subjects avoid revealing information by asking questions in response to interviewers. The extra information is given to avoid talking directly about the event rather than deny the allegation or lie about it outright. Extraneous phrasing that is associated with deception is "I believe," "I think," "kind of," or "to the best of my knowledge." While the subject may actually provide truthful extraneous information, it could be used as an alternative to specific details about the incident. Guilty or involved persons will use this tactic to justify their actions.

Step 3: Lack of Conviction

The *lack of conviction* refers to words that are used to label or change the meaning of something, these are equivocating terms. Examples of equivocating terms are seen in these phrases: sort of, kind of, I guess, little bit, and hopefully. When an individual claims not to remember parts of the narrative this is known as repression (Rabon, 1994). The interviewer should always look closer at the statement where a person consistently says, "I don't recall," or "I don't remember." Other qualifying terms such as "I think," or "I believe" are used to minimize the statement conviction. A victim who uses terms that minimize the event such as "kind of surprised," or "sort of hurt" suggest a deviation from the expected norm. False claims are rarely made as convincingly as truthful ones because liars are unwilling or unable to fully embrace them (DePaulo et al., 2003).

Step 4:
Balance of the
Statement

A truthful statement will contain three parts: prior to the incident, the incident itself, and the events after the incident. The statement should be examined for balance; if any part is missing it is most likely false. More likely the statement is true when it contains equal amounts of information in all three. The person who attempts to justify their actions will give information that does not answer the questions or will include more than is necessary to explain what happened. An extremely large "before" section compared to the "after" section is an indication of a lack of emotion and may be a false or incomplete accounting of what happened.

Missing time within the statement changes the balance and suggests something has been left out. The interviewer should attempt to determine what was not included and whether the information was not important or perceived as not being important to the subject.

Field Statement Analysis

Application of the statement analysis technique is time consuming and can be tedious if the statement is complex. It is further limited by a lack of understanding and training in the entire approach. Preliminary research has suggested a way to use the statement analysis approach quickly in a field situation. Klopf and Tooke (2003) developed a quick method to evaluate statements called the statement analysis field examination technique (SAFE-T). Agent Klopf and Lt. Tooke tested two components of statement analysis in their study to develop an accuracy measure of statements taken in the field: extraneous information and lack of conviction. These terms were defined earlier in the chapter.

Truthful individuals will state events chronologically and concisely when asked what has occurred. To measure extraneous information count the statements' total number of lines, identifying which contain unnecessary information. Determine the percentage of extraneous information as part of the whole statement. If there are 100 lines in the statement and 10 lines contain irrelevant information the amount of extraneous information is 10%. Klopf and Tooke (2003) suggest that fewer than 25% of the statement should consist of extraneous information to be considered accurate.

Lack of conviction is illustrated by the use of equivocating terms—the interviewee is failing to commit to the statement and modifying his or her description of something. When these words are used to quantify or limit the situation described it represents the attempt to avoid personal accountability. In order to detect deception the numbers of terms that indicate lack of conviction are counted. When the count is between six incidents or more of lack of conviction, there is a concern about the truthfulness of the statement (Klopf & Tooke, 2003). The higher the number of terms indicating a lack of conviction is, the higher the possibility that the statement is not true.

Conclusions

This chapter covered the primary methods of interviewing that are used by law enforcement officers today. Each approach has its pros and cons. Traditional interviewing is best used in situations where the intent is to limit the amount of information that is being gathered. As suggested earlier, this approach can be used to make a preliminary assessment of the value of the witness, identifying the individual for future more in-depth interviewing. It is comprehensive, but often is used in a haphazard way that diminishes its importance as a technique.

The structured interview offers a humanistic approach to obtaining information. This approach is more comprehensive and focused than the traditional method. The added value of using a structured interview is that there are no difficult steps to memorize, it is fairly easy to use, and it enjoys a decent response rate. The reason why the structured interview is so widely used is its lack of complexity.

New to the arsenal of interviewing techniques is the inferential interview method. Inferential interviewing is an improvement on the structured interview because it contains the same steps and adds additional ways to detect deceit.

The statement analysis approach contains many useful tools to assist the interviewer in looking for clues to deception and indications that further investigation may be needed. The method is complex and may be difficult to use. An improvement on statement analysis is the modified approach of the field statement analysis.

Chapter Four Questions for Review

Short Answer Questions

1. What does traditional interviewing hope to attain?

2. Why is it important to determine the role the complainant has played in the commission of a crime?

3. Is it important to know why a crime has occurred at a particular location? Explain.

4. Why is learning the proper sequence of events so important to an interviewer?

5. Is it important for the person being interviewed to know the position of the interviewer? If so, why? If not, why not?

6. In a structured interview, should the person being interviewed be encouraged to be an active part of the discussion? If so, why? If not, why not?

7. During an inferential interview what inferences may be drawn from the sentence structure of the answers received?

8. What types of interviews can benefit from statement analysis?

Fill-in Questions

1. The structured interviewing approach uses the best of _____ methods while applying principles used in _____ .

2. In the early stages of an investigation it is important to find out which individuals _____ about the case versus those who _____ .

3. If preliminary questions reveal that the complainant may be the suspect, than the approach changes from an _____ to an _____ as necessary.

4. Questions should not be phrased in a way that _____ the person being interviewed to give a particular answer, nor should they be _____ .

5. Interviewing should establish the _____ of the case.

6. Use _____ and _____ when helpful to make sure that you and the person being interviewed have a mutual understanding of the event.

7. A promising new approach to interviewing is evidenced by the _____ , a method to detect deception through statement characteristics and question-by-question analysis.

8. Based on the idea that _____ will contain language characteristics that are absent from statements that are the _____ , statement analysis is the word-by-word examination of the grammar within a statement.

9. A truthful person with nothing to hide when asked, "What happened," will provide the events in

_____ .

10. When an individual claims not to remember parts of the narrative this is known as

_____ .

Exercises

1. Pair off with a classmate for about 10 to 15 minutes. Interview your partner about the last TV show he or she watched. Use the traditional interviewing approach, only the five W's and How. Verbally or in writing, report what you learned about the program.

2. Pair off with a classmate for about 10 to 15 minutes. Using the structural interviewing approach, interview your partner about the last TV show he or she watched. Verbally or in writing, report what you learned about the program.

Reference List

Adams, S. (1996). Statement analysis: What do suspects' words really reveal? *FBI Law Enforcement Bulletin*, 65(10), 12–20.

Adams, S. (2004). Statement analysis: Beyond the words. *FBI Enforcement Bulletin*, 73(4), 22-23.

Artwohl, A. (2002). Perceptual and memory distortion during officer-involved shootings. *FBI Law Enforcement Bulletin,* 18–24.

Colwell, K., Hiscock, C. K., & Memon, A. (2002). Interviewing techniques and the assessment of statement credibility. *Applied Cognitive Psychology,* 16(3), 287–300.

DePaulo, B., Lindsay, J., Malone, B., Muhlenbruck, L., Charlton, K., & Cooper, H. (2003). Cues to Deception. *Psychological Bulletin,* 0033-2909, 129(1), 74–118.

Garner, B. (2004). *Black's Law Dictionary* (8th ed.). St. Paul, MN: West Publishing Co.

Hand, H. (2003). The mentor's tale: A reflexive account of semi-structured interviews. *Nurse Researcher,* 10(3), 15–28.

Kebbell, M. R. (1996). Enhancing the practicality of the cognitive interview in forensic situations. *Psycoloquy,* 7(16), art. 3.

Klopf, G., & Tooke, A. (2003). Statement analysis field examination technique. *FBI Law Enforcement Bulletin,* 72(4), 6–15.

Memon, A., & Higham, P. A. (in press). A review of the cognitive interview. *Psychology, Crime and the Law.*

Memon, A., Gabbert, F., & Hope, L. (2004). The ageing eyewitness. J. R. Adler (editor), *Forensic Psychology: Concepts, debates and practice* (pp. 96–112). Devon, UK: Willan Publishing.

Memon, A., Wark, L., Holley, A., Bull, R., & Koehnken, G. (1997). Eyewitness performance in cognitive and structured interviews. *Memory,* 5(5), 639–657.

Merriam-Webster's Collegiate Dictionary. (2004). (11th ed.). Springfield, MA: Merriam-Webster, Inc.

Rabon, D. (1994). *Investigative discourse analysis.* Durham, NC: Carolina Academic Press.

Schmalleger, F. (2004). *Criminal Justice.* Upper Saddle River, NJ: Prentice Hall.

Talwar, V., & Lee, K. (2002). Development of lying to conceal a transgression: Children's control of expressive behaviour during verbal deception. *International Journal of Behavioral Development,* 26(5), 436–444.

Technical Working Group for Eyewitness Evidence. (1999). (Report No. NCJ 178240). Washington, DC: US Department of Justice.

Forensic Hypnosis and Cognitive Interviewing

CHAPTER

5

KEY TERMS

Age regression	Cognitive interviewing
Confabulation	Forensic hypnosis
Hypermnesia	Memory hardening
Mnemonics	Scripts

CHAPTER OBJECTIVES

After completing this chapter, you should be able to:

- ◆ Define forensic hypnosis
- ◆ Discuss the advantages and disadvantages of forensic hypnosis
- ◆ Explain the difference between cognitive interviewing and hypnosis
- ◆ Encourage interviewee participation
- ◆ Describe practical techniques to facilitate memory retrieval
- ◆ Articulate the sequence of the cognitive interview
- ◆ Use the four mnemonic principles
- ◆ Explain the limitations of cognitive interviewing
- ◆ Incorporate cognitive techniques into most interviewing approaches

Introduction

There are two forms of memory retrieval included in this chapter: forensic hypnosis and cognitive interviewing. These approaches to interviewing share the same goal, which is to increase the information that the interviewee can remember. They share the use of memory jogging techniques to obtain information. They are different in the methods they use to jog the memory. The forensic interviewing approach seeks to bring out memory through a process of heightened awareness brought about by the interviewer. The cognitive interviewing approach jogs the memory by a process that is completely controlled by the person being interviewed. Both approaches require an interviewee that is willing to participate. Neither of these approaches is recommended as a tool to use with interrogating a perpetrator. Forensic hypnosis is a controversial approach whose popularity has recently resurfaced. The National Institute of Justice recommends cognitive interviewing for criminal justice use.

Forensic hypnosis refers to an investigative memory retrieval technique used to enhance recall in legally relevant situations. Hypnosis itself is a state of increased receptivity to suggestion characterized by an altered state of consciousness. Its use in court testimony has been traced back over 150 years (Webert, 2003).

The *cognitive interviewing method* is also a memory jogging and retrieval tool. It is developed and used for a family of related practices to evaluate survey questions and questionnaires and to conduct interviews. The approaches to cognitive interviewing are as diverse as the individuals who apply them. During the last decade, many institutions from around the world have come to rely on cognitive methods. Federal statistical agencies that are using this approach include researchers from the U.S. Census Bureau who commonly evaluate the quality of survey questionnaires (Honey & Mumford, 1982) and the U.S. Bureau of Justice Statistics. Cognitive methods are being used to facilitate learning for members of the British Air Force (Royal Air Force, 2001), for dealing with depression (Makoi, 2002), and for police interviewing (Fisher & Geiselman, 1992).

What Is Hypnosis?

Hypnosis is a process during which a person allows oneself to become more suggestible; results differ according to individual responses (American Psychotherapy & Medical Hypnosis Association, 2000). Individuals do not lose control but some describe the experience as a heightened awareness, according to the American Psychotherapy & Medical Hypnosis Association (APMHA). Persons under hypnosis are aware of what is going on; those in the state of hypnosis do not become zombies. There are three common uses of hypnosis for a criminal investigation (Newman & Thompson, 2001):

1. To enhance an accused defendant's memory about events occurring around the time of the crime

2. To help an eyewitness of a crime in providing details about the behavior or physical appearance of the perpetrator

3. To assist in generating leads for investigators through recall of a salient detail

Advocates of hypnosis in criminal investigations cite numerous cases when police investigators have successfully solved crimes using hypnosis as a tool (McConkey & Sheehan, 1995; Niehaus, 1999; Niehaus, 1999). The goal of forensic hypnosis is memory enhancement and retrieval for use in a specific civil or criminal case. Strong arguments have been made that forensic hypnosis sessions should be conducted by police officers skilled in relevant interviewing techniques with legally sophisticated skills. Others suggest that clinicians are the most appropriate forensic hypnotics. The debate has drawn attention away from the more important issue of investigative hypnosis being practiced by untrained lay hypnotists (McConkey & Sheehan, 1995).

Forensic Hypnosis Interviewing Methods

The public's perception of hypnosis is quite favorable. Recent research shows that a large percentage of people believe overwhelmingly in the positive use of forensic hypnosis (Webert, 2003). In contrast, the legal and medical community has long taken positions against the accuracy of facts recalled under hypnosis in hotly contested debates regarding its reliability. During the 1970's and 1980's severe attacks were made against the use of forensic hypnosis (Reiser, 1984). In 1985 the American Medical Association recommended the use of hypnosis be limited to the investigative processes and its results not be used as evidence in court because the increased memory is not limited to only accurate recollections (Moenssens, Starrs, Henderson, and Inbau, 1995). Still, hundreds of cases

A child had been abducted and there were no leads to locating the child or identifying the kidnapper. In desperation a hypnotist was called to conduct interviews on the family members. There was no useful information that came from the interviews, but it did cause a lot of discussion among the detectives. In the state of Massachusetts, information obtained after a person has been hypnotized is not acceptable as evidence in court. Sometimes it is worth taking the chance that evidence will not be admissible in court if the process might save a life. The decision is one that should be debated. A number of states do allow hypnotically refreshed memory. What is the status of hypnotic evidence in your state?

presented in court do include testimony enhanced through hypnosis. The primary objection to hypnosis is that eyewitnesses may become more susceptible to leading and misleading questions (Fisher & Geiselman, 1992).

Guidelines for the Use of Forensic Hypnosis

According to McConkey & Sheehan (1995), the successful application of forensic hypnosis methods depends on these following items:

1. The use of forensic hypnosis should be consistent with the government legislation in your state and country relative to hypnosis.

2. Its use must be consistent with clinical and legal safeguards designed to ensure the well-being of the subject involved.

3. A clear statement of the rationale for using hypnosis must be made prior to the session.

4. Hypnosis should be used for major crime investigations and only after all standard procedures have been exhausted in the investigation.

Caution must be exercised in cases involving a juvenile to be hypnotized and with any witness whose ability to give informed consent is questionable. A person who has successfully completed appropriate specific training in its methods may conduct the session. If the hypnotist is not a member of a police department, then adequate credentials on the application of legal forensic procedures is necessary. Hall recommends these guidelines for the hypno-investigator (Hall, 1999):

1. The hypno-investigator should not be involved in the direct investigation of the case.

2. Before the hypnosis, a written record should be made that includes a description of the subject matter and the information that was provided.

3. The session should be both video and audio taped.

4. There should be no "line-up" or mug shot viewing prior to the session.

5. Explain hypnosis to the subject before the session.

The forensic hypnotic approach begins with preparation. There are four phases: the Induction Phase, the Narrative Phase, the Closure Phase, and the Recall Phase. The preparation and phases of the forensic hypnotic session are described next.

Preparing for the Hypnotic Session

Evidence established prior to the session must be documented to differentiate between pre- and post-hypnotic information. The hypnotist should arrange for a quiet room free of distractions. Only the hypnotist and subject are allowed in the room, unless the hypnotist determines that it is necessary to include others. There should be a two-way mirror for session viewing by persons involved with the investigation such as legal representation and police investigators. Ideally, there would be a form of communication from the viewers to the hypnotist, such as a small ear receiver. All conversations between the hypnotist and the subject should be videotaped both prior, during, and after the session. The documentation includes the place, date, and time of the session. Prior to beginning, the hypnotist makes an independent assessment of the subject's suitability for hypnosis and willingness to proceed.

Induction Phase

During the induction phase, the hypnotist attempts to relax the witness and tests his or her responsivity to suggestion. Instruct the witness using an unrushed and calm voice to sit in a comfortable chair without crossing legs or arms. Sitting with a straight back, they should place their hands in their lap so that they can be comfortable during the entire session.

Induction consists of a general relaxation technique; many formats of induction are available to the hypnotist. An approach suggested by Niehaus (1999) begins with an instruction that the subject take three deep breaths and let each one out slowly, closing their eyes at the third breath. Slowly the hypnotist instructs the subject to relax through releasing tension, breathing deeply, and slipping further and further into relaxation. Describing each part of the body to be relaxed encourages the

Courtesy of Corbis Images.

The first phase of hypnosis is the induction phase. Eye-fixation is a common approach.

subject to drift further into a relaxed state of hypnosis. The hypnotist may suggest pleasant surroundings such as a beach or vacation be envisioned to encourage relaxation. Induction into hypnosis can be induced through these approaches adapted from the Ohio Academy of Hypnosis Basic Forensic Hypnosis manual (Niehaus, 1999):

◆ **Eye-fixation method** — requires that the subject fixate on some point or object overhead

◆ **Chiasson's technique** — helping the subject put his hands directly in front of his face, the fingers pressed together. Instruct the subject to see his fingers spread apart as they come closer to his face. When the face is being touched he then will go deeply into restful, peaceful hypnosis.

Narrative Phase

A major technique used for memory recall in forensic hypnosis is *age regression* (Newman & Thompson, 2001). Age regression is the used during the narrative phase. It is the most common technique used in hypnosis. Here the hypnotist suggests that the subject will return to an earlier age. To regress the subject, the imagery of a calendar going backwards, watching television, or walking toward the scene of the crime, are among the ways to get the subject to the time of the crime. In step one of the narrative phase he or she is asked to tell the events as they see them, once the subject has reached the crime scene. The approach should be not to lead the subject in any way. The hypnotist can only ask the person to describe their senses. In other words, what the subject sees, hears, smells, or feels, regarding the event. "What do you see?"; or "what is happening now?" are suggestive phrases that are non-leading.

The calendar procedure is a popular age regression technique. According to Howell the subject is instructed to imagine a calendar on the wall (Howell, 2003). The person is then instructed to look at the calendar and see that it is _____ (month) _____(date) _____(year) which is a _____ (day of the week). The hypnotist takes the subject backwards by each day until reaching the date prior to the event. The subject is asked to state the sequence of events as they are occurring.

During step two of the narrative phase the hypnotist asks specific but non-leading questions. It is important that the subject be told that, "I don't know" is an acceptable answer. For example, the subject may be instructed to view the back of the vehicle (used in the crime) and slowly describe everything that is seen. The hypnotist gives the subject the opportunity to make comments on anything he or she wishes prior to closure.

Closure Phase

Hypermnesia is another major technique used in forensic hypnosis (Newman & Thompson, 2001). Through direct suggestion, this technique enhances the memory of the individual after the hypnotic session. The suggestion may be as simple as instructing the subject to remember what was discussed during the hypnosis once he or she awakens. Non-relevant suggestions made by the hypnotist to the subject are cancelled at this time. An appropriate de-induction procedure to end the hypnosis session is then used during the closure phase. A simple count of 1 to 5 or similar technique may be used to close the session.

Recall Phase

The final phase, recall, actually occurs after the hypnotic session has ended and the subject is deinducted. During this phase, the subject is asked to recall all that he or she has remembered about the crime since the memory enhancement. Any questions can be asked of the subject regarding the incident. The subject may also want to make comments or ask questions about the process.

Challenges to Hypnotic Memory Retrieval

As with any approach to interviewing, there are challenges to the use of the forensic hypnotic technique. Situations of abuse, particularly child abuse, should be approached with extra caution. There are indications that events are altered, deleted, and created by events that occur during and after the time of encoding, during the period of storage, and during any attempts at retrieval (McConkey & Sheehan, 1995). In other words, the memory of abuse may be influenced by abuse that occurs after the initial event or at any time including the hypnotic session.

Forensic hypnosis is not recommended for use on a defendant or person suspected of being involved in the crime under investigation. People can and do lie while under hypnosis. Confabulation can occur. The results of a hypnotic session with a suspect are of questionable value.

Few states allow hypnotically refreshed recall as evidence in court. Among these are Texas and Nevada. Hypnotically refreshed recall has been admissible in Texas in both criminal and civil cases since 1988 (Howell, 2003). Texas mandates minimum training standards, testing, and certification of police officers who use investigative hypnosis. In 1997 the Nevada legislature declared that hypnotically refreshed testimony was admissible in both civil and criminal cases (Nevada Revised Statutes, 1997). Nevada specifically named police officers trained in forensic hypnosis as among the persons whose interview may qualify as admissible in court. It is suggested that all information be independently verified when possible and its use limited to witness and victim statements.

The Federal Bureau of Investigation revised its guidelines on the use of hypnosis in 1979, mandating that certain safeguards be in place for hypnotic sessions (Newman & Thompson, 2001). Among these requirements was the recording of hypnotic sessions. Concern has also been raised regarding police biases along with the noted increase of police officers using hypnosis as a part of the criminal investigation (Newman & Thompson, 2001).

Confabulation

Critics claim that *confabulation* is very common while under hypnosis (Newman & Thompson, 2001). Confabulation is a filling in of the memory gaps to make the event more comprehensible. It may result from the subject's desire to please the hypnotist through the creation of complete and coherent memories.

> A confabulation is a *fantasy* that has unconsciously replaced *fact* in memory. A confabulation may be based partly on fact or be a complete construction of the imagination. It is used to describe the memories of people claiming to have been abducted by aliens, as well as false memories induced by therapists or interviewers, memories that often involve bizarre notions of satanic ritualistic sexual abuse of children (Adams, 2004).

In response, advocates suggest that forensic hypnosis does tend to increase recall with witness who are motivated and cooperative and that the accuracy of information in these cases may be as high as 90% (Reiser, 1984).

Faking

Hypnosis can be faked and people are capable of lying in hypnosis. While it is extremely difficult to determine if an individual is faking during the hypnotic session, McConkey and Sheehan (1995) state that it does occur. They suggest that no single indicator exists to be sure that the subject is faking, but an accumulation of factors make the possibility probable. Here are some possible indicators of deceit:

1. Frequent occurrences of logical thinking that are unsolicited and unsuggested

2. Reflection on what he or she is saying to the hypnotist

3. Zealous overplaying the role of the hypnotized subject

4. Indications of behavior consistent with expectations communicated outside of hypnosis

5. Behavior atypical of an individual under hypnosis

Memory Hardening & Suggestibility

Opponents to the use of forensic hypnosis believe that hypnotism is *memory hardening*. The phenomenon gives the subject increased confidence regarding the facts remembered during hypnosis, regardless of whether the facts are true or false (Webert, 2003).

Post-hypnotic suggestion can become permanent if it is repeated many times or over several sessions (Niehaus, 1999). Additionally the effect of hypnosis varies with individuals; some individuals may be hypersensitive to these techniques. Critics argue that a person undergoing hypnosis experiences an increased susceptibility to suggestion and a loss of critical judgment regarding cues planted by the hypnotist (Webert, 2003).

Courtesy of Corbis Images.

The admissibility of hypnotically induced evidence is determined by each state.

Hypnosis Evidence in Court

Rock v. *Arkansas* (1987) is the most significant case concerning the admission of forensic hypnosis evidence. The Supreme Court in *Rock* ruled that the lower courts could not ban the use of evidence retrieved under hypnosis as a *per se* inadmissibility by the Supreme Court in *Illinois* v. *Gates* (*Illinois* v. *Gates,* 1983). The majority of states however, do not allow post hypnotic memories as evidence in court (Webert, 2003).

Scientific evidence must meet certain tests in order to be admitted into evidence. According to the *Frye* test, the scientific method must have gained general acceptance in the medical and psychological communities as a reliable method in order to be acceptable (*Frye* v. *United States.,* 1923). The *Frye* rule was first articulated in this criminal case, which attempted to introduce evidence from a polygraph test. Forensic hypnosis is used in both medical and legal settings, but is not generally accepted as reliable. Those states that determine scientific reliability based on use of the *Frye* rule generally exclude the use of hypnotic memories. A more recent test for the reliability of scientific evidence is articulated in *Daubert* (*Daubert* v. *Merrell Dow Pharmaceuticals.*, 1993). The four-part *Daubert* test, which has become the federal standard concerning the admissibility of scientific evidence, has replaced *Frye* in some states. It asks:

1. Whether the type of evidence can and has been tested by scientific methods

2. Whether the underlying theory or techniques has been subjected to peer review and published in the professional literature

3. How reliable the results are in terms of potential error rate

4. General acceptance can have a bearing on the inquiry (the old *Frye* test)

Some courts may allow the testimony of information gathered prior to the witnesses being subjected to hypnosis, providing that there is evidence documenting the evidence as being provided prior to the hypnosis and others ban its use in criminal proceedings altogether.

Edward Geiselman and Ronald P. Fisher, professors at UCLA and Florida International University, utilized cognitive methods to develop a technique to overcome the challenges that limit the use of hypnosis in criminal investigations (Geiselman & Fisher, 1985). Fisher and Geiselman worked closely with the Los Angeles Police Department and Metro-Date Police Department to develop the method that would address the specific needs of police interviewing. Their success was evidenced when a *Frye* hearing in a California Court in 1995 concluded that the cognitive interviewing method was a reliable investigative tool (Geiselman & Fisher, 1985).

What Is Cognitive Interviewing?

Often called CI, cognitive interviewing is an approach for increasing the amount of information recalled by a witness, without increasing the level of confabulation. Deceptively simple, it might not seem to be particularly useful or different. However, the four methods for jogging memory used along with several specific techniques becomes a very powerful and effective means of eliciting a complete and accurate picture of the events recalled. The most important thing about cognitive interviewing is that when it is done properly, it works.

Although cognitive interviewing has been compared to hypnosis, its original authors maintain that there are major differences between the two (Geiselman & Fisher, 1985). For example, there is no hypnotic induction in cognitive interviewing. Evidence indicates that while it is a successful memory retrieval tool, it does not heighten the interviewees' confidence in the memories or increase the error rate (Geiselman, Fisher, Cohen, Holland, & Surtes, 1986). There is no evidence to suggest that cognitive interviewing techniques increase the misleading question effect and it may even reduce the effect. Although cognitive interviewing involves memory jogging and retrieval techniques, there is no induction phase and the interviewee is a full participant in this process.

Studies testing the usefulness of cognitive interviewing have taken place in Germany, Britain, and the United States (Geiselman & Fisher, 1985). Results have indicated that it is an effective approach. With relatively little training, the results from a cognitive interview may increase the gain in information by almost 50 percent compared to interviews without its use (Fisher, Geiselman, and Amador, 1989). In trials where individuals were re-interviewed after a standard interview, they reported new facts with the cognitive approach.

Both specific and general memory jogging guidance techniques are combined to form the cognitive interview technique. Since a memory is composed of a collection of several elements, the more elements a memory retrieval aid has in common with the memory of the event, the more effective the aid is. The general idea is that memory is accessible through several access routes, so information that is not accessible though one retrieval cue may be reached though another. For an interview to be successful, the details of the crime are recalled and are communicated to the interviewer.

Been There . . . Done That! 5–2

There are a number of approaches to cognitive interviewing; one is a seven step enhanced method. Another has been published recently by the National Institute of Justice (NIJ) in its manual on Eyewitness Evidence (U. S. Department of Justice, 1999). The NIJ incorporated many of the principles found in the cognitive approach interviewing in an updated traditional approach. For more information on the national recommendations for police interviewing go to their web site, http://www.ncjrs.org/pdffiles1/nij/178240.pdf The shorter version is provided in this chapter purposefully. Familiarity with the concepts along with the willingness to practice the mnemonics will prepare the student for its use. The concepts can be incorporated into a more elaborate interviewing approach or incorporated into the more traditional approach. The concepts are flexible.

The cognitive interview technique has been adapted for use with child interviews. The version specific to interviewing children can be found in this book in Chapter 7. The technique has been shown to be very effective when interviewing children (Geiselman, Bornstein, & Saywitz, 1992).

Cognitive Interviewing Techniques

The approach stresses using a secluded, quiet place free of distractions for the interview as well as urging subjects to speak slowly. Cognitive interviewing encourages the witness to do the talking while the interviewer listens. It attempts to avoid some of the mistakes commonly associated with police interviewing such as interrupting the narratives and rushing the account. Witnesses must feel comfortable in taking the time to think and reflect about what happened. They should feel free to say anything, knowing that there is sufficient time to speak and that the interviewer will not make judgments on the statements. Specific questions are for clarification. The interviewer holds these back until the narrative is fully stated. It is common knowledge that cases are solved when someone talks about what happened! Cognitive interviewing is designed to get the interviewee talking. A major challenge is not to interrupt.

Mnemonics

Mnemonics are methods for remembering information that is otherwise difficult to recall. The three basic stages of memory are encoding, storage, and retrieval (Wrightby & Merrill, 2002). Encoding is a process that the brain goes through when something happens. The information received is filtered and stored. Mnemonics are merely ways to find the information. Think of the brain as a filing cabinet. There are many drawers; within the drawers are file hangers. Typically, the files are labeled by category or alphabetically, but that depends on who is doing the filing! If you cannot find a file then it is necessary to think about how you categorized the information. Was the order by the case number, incident type, perpetrator, or victim? Was the date or the location used as a method to file the information? This is a similar process used for mnemonics.

Recall through mnemonics requires the use of imagination, association, and location. Use of imagination does not suggest fantasy but imagery. The description of an event will be more realistic and complete if an individual verbalizes how he or she felt or reacted at the time of a crime. The association aspect of cognitive interviewing allows the individual to remember one thought in order to move to another (asking for example, if there was a familiar smell, shape, or feeling during the incident). The third principle evident in the attempt to promote recall has to do with the location of the incident. The interviewee pictures the place where the incident occurred in order to describe in detail everything about the place.

Mnemonics are not complicated; they are simply ways to jog the memory in order to find the information that is not easily accessible. The foundation of the cognitive interview is the use of these four mnemonics that are the memory jogging techniques (Geiselman & Fisher, 1985):

- ◆ Mentally reconstruct the context of the event
- ◆ Report every detail, regardless of apparent importance
- ◆ Recall the events in a variety of orders, moving back and forward in time
- ◆ Change perspectives and recall from a different points of view

These four principles are the tools to use within the interview process. Explained to the witness before the interview begins, they allow the witness to approach memory recall and retrieval from several different

Been There . . . Done That! 5–3

On a back country road in the middle of the afternoon a female jogger sprinted effortlessly. It was warm and sunny that summer day. The woman being interviewed said that her mind was blank as she enjoyed her run, until a truck stopped in front of her and a man came towards her. Grabbing her, the man pushed her into the tall corn stalks along the side of the road. She struggled while he lay on top of her and fought until she got free. Once free she ran in the other direction like she was in a marathon and went into the first house to call the police.

During the interview it was apparent that details were missing that would enhance the case. By use of imagery I asked her to tell me every detail, no matter how small. She changed the order of the attack and reconstructed the context of the event. She was able to describe the smell of the field and the sound of a car going by. He did not rape her; he struggled to get her pants down. His own pants were unzipped and part way down his hips when she escaped. From this information I knew there was at least one other witness who had seen the truck parked on the side of the road. A check with the local police department confirmed that someone had called them with information on that suspicious truck. We now had a plate number and were able to locate the driver. The driver was located and interrogated. His clothing was taken and evidence of his being in a corn field were evident. His pants and underclothes were taken and sent to the lab. Pre-ejaculatory fluid in his shorts confirmed his sexual intentions. He was convicted of an assault and attempted rape.

avenues. The first two methods attempt to increase the overlap of elements between the stored memory and retrieval cues. The goal is to encourage witnesses to construct a new description of the event. The last two methods encourage using many retrieval paths.

Reconstruction Technique

For reconstruction, the investigator assists the witness in recreating the incident scene. Instructing the interviewee to think about the circumstances that surrounded the incident, the investigator suggests the interviewee think about the room where the incident occurred, the location of furniture, vehicles, weather, lighting, any nearby people, objects, or smells. The individual interviewed is to think about how he or she felt at the time and their reaction to the incident. The purpose of this line of inquiry is to return the witness deeply to the scene of the crime. Visualizing a situation strongly through imagery helps an individual to remember. Reconstruction is accomplished by asking witnesses to relive mentally the events prior to, during, and after the crime.

Instruct the witness that reconstruction includes talking about the time of day, day, month, and year of the event. In other words, reconstruct the scene according to when it happened. What was the weather?; how did he or she know? Was it light or dark? This line of thought will open up thoughts particularly when multiple events or assaults had occurred in an effort to separate them into single occurrences that are blurred over time. Reconstruction also includes talking about the location of the incident in relation to other houses, furniture, equipment, or any other tangible item that can be described.

Reporting Everything Technique

For the reporting phase, the investigator explains that some people hold back information because they are not quite sure that the information is important. Instruct the witness not to edit anything, even things that may not seem important. Providing this permission to recount everything may cause the witness to remember something otherwise forgotten. Throughout the interview remind the interviewee that you would like them to talk about everything they remember. Continue to encourage their participation.

Changing the Order of Events

The process includes instruction to recall the events in a different order. Typically, a witness is asked to begin at the beginning, which may cause them to fill in gaps so that the story sounds logical. Sticking to an expected order may present an account that may not be completely accurate. The instruction for this technique may include that the beginning point be the thing that impressed (scared, frightened, made them aware that something was going on) them. Ask the witness to try starting from the point that they remember most vividly and either go backwards or forwards from that point.

Changing the Perspective

In the fourth phase of this process, instruct the witness to recall the incident from different perspectives or adopt the perspective of others who were present. Depending on the circumstances of the event, the investigator may also instruct the witness to place himself or herself in the role of someone else in the incident and think about what he or she must have seen.

Additional Memory Jogging Techniques

1. **Appearance.** What type of clothing was the witness or perpetrator wearing at the time of the event? Was there anything unusual about the physical appearance of the individual involved? What was it that seemed unusual? Did the perpetrator remind the witness of anyone, and why? The characteristics that are familiar to an individual may cue him or her to think of someone else. The behavior, speech, or physical appearance may be one of many characteristics that lead the witness to remember the individual in more detail than previously thought. As a description of physical appearance evolves, the investigator should take note of mention of details that go beyond a typical description. Examples include a hat, haircut, condition of the hair or skin, jewelry, tattoos. Keep in mind that individuals have preferences in underclothing that may not change, for example the kind of underwear or t-shirt worn.

2. **Conversation.** In what place did conversation occur, if any? What was said and by whom? Was something happening that prompted the statements? Were there particular words that seemed to be significant? Was there a way that the person spoke which was peculiar?

3. **Names.** If a name was spoken, does the witness remember it? Instruct the interviewee to think about the number of syllables or letters of that name.

4. **Senses.** Was there a smell that is associated with the event? What did the person, the place, or surroundings smell like?

5. **Speech.** Did anyone involved have a speech impediment or speak with an accent? Was the conversation loud or soft, high-pitched or deliberate?

Steps of the Cognitive Interview Method

The interviewer is expected to have developed the skills for establishing rapport, listening actively, and avoiding interrupting as basic skills for effective cognitive interviewing. Additional competence is required for encouraging intense concentration and the use of imagery. Asking open-ended and compatible questions assist in obtaining detailed descriptions and recreating the original context of the event.

The order of the cognitive interview is important; each step must take place one after the other in order to be effective.

Step 1: Meet and Greet

In this first step, the interviewer explains to the interviewee that there will be seven steps of the interview process. This first step is when they will learn about cognitive interviewing and what to expect during the interview. Tell the person that their full cooperation is expected and that they should not leave out any information or details, regardless of whether they appear important or not. Most of the interview will consist of the interviewee doing the talking! Instructions will come on how to jog their memory along with techniques proven to improve the interview process.

The interviewer asks questions in a standard approach but instructs the interviewee to think aloud, express his or her opinion, and to say if they have any difficulty in answering questions. In other words, the investigator is giving the control of the interview to the person who is being interviewed. Police officers and other interviewers are used to asking the questions. In this approach, they are the listeners who encourage the witness to do the talking.

- ◆ Control anxiety and develop rapport with the interviewee. This may be done by helping the subject to feel more comfortable through the development of rapport. Refer to Chapters One and Three to refresh your memory on rapport and its development. Nervousness and anxiety are sometimes evident through laughing, yawning, sweating, shaking, or crying. Be concerned about his or her comfort and ask about it. Avoid comments that may be judgmental or are confrontational.
- ◆ Encouraging active participation, outline what you expect from the interviewee during the interview. Explain that you are not going to ask all the questions but depend on him or her to explain what has happened.

◆ The witness is asked to reveal every detail regardless of whether they think the information is important or not. **Note: This is one of the mnemonic memory jogging techniques.**

◆ Give the interviewee permission to say that they do not know the answer when a question is asked.

Step 2: Narrative Phases

This step involves three parts: a free recall, a guided recall of the event, and clarification. First, the interviewee is asked to supply a narrative report of the incident in their own words. Active listening requires that the interviewer avoid interrupting or asking for details during this phases. Paying particular attention to the narration, the interviewer notes the perspective of the statement. For example, where does the subject alter the level of description, alter his voice to mimic the assailant's speech, or deflect his gaze away from the interviewer?

Next comes the part where the interviewer assists the interviewee in recall. Talking about the need for concentration, instructions may include questions such as "how did you feel?"; "what did you hear?"; and "tell me what happened." The investigator asks for the witness to think about what happened through their senses; what did the interviewee see, hear, smell, feel, or touch? The interviewee is reminded to talk about all they remember, even if it seems unimportant. Reconstruction techniques are employed in this directed segment of the interview. Initiate a context reinstatement to help the interviewee go back to the place or context that the event occurred. This is done by asking open-ended questions designed to stimulate stored memories. The interviewer should not attempt to fill in gaps or interrupt even if questions arise or something needs clarification.

At this third point in the narrative-gathering process, the interviewer may have a list of questions concerning missing or unclear information. Taking care not to verbally pounce on the interviewee, remind him or her to share all information by reporting everything. Now is the time for extensive note taking and asking of questions. Avoid closed-ended questions that will limit the response of the interviewee.

Step 3: Extensive Recall through Mnemonics

The interviewee should be encouraged to retrieve more information through memory enhancing techniques. The interviewer would explain that the strategies to obtain more information are not being used because the statement was faulty, but that these techniques have been shown to increase their memory retrieval of the event. Two primary techniques

Courtesy of Corbis Images.

Recall with mnemonics is an important part of cognitive interviewing

that provide more information include "recall from a different order," and "changing the perspective."

Talk to the interviewee about concentration and ask that he or she thinking about the sound, environment, the rooms, furniture, weather, lighting, or people. Ask what they were feeling or hearing at the time of the event. This is the reconstruction technique.

Recalling events from a different order, also called "switching the temporal order," is another mnemonic to use during this stage. The instructions are that the interviewee recalls the incident backwards. Prompting takes place by asking, "What is the last thing you remember?; What before that?; What happened before that?"

Changing perspectives is also a helpful technique to use during this stage of the interview. Being clear to the interviewee that he or she must only report facts that were actually witnessed and not to fabricate or guess, the purpose is to see the event from the eyes of another. Additional memory jogging techniques that were described earlier in the chapter may prove helpful at this time.

Step 4: Summary and Closure

This may be the last chance for getting information from this individual! Ask if there is anyone that he or she would recommend you speak with or anything else you should know. Briefly summarize the information that the interviewee has provided.

Closure occurs by reestablishing the personal connection with the interviewee. Always end on a positive note with appreciation for the time and effort put into the interview. Update the contact information and encourage the interviewee to call with any new information.

Challenges to Memory Retrieval

Everyday memory encoding problems such as lighting, distance to the event, and distractions will negatively affect the way that recall occurs. Individual emotions and the process of scripting cause interference on memory retrieval. Memories do change over time and the new memories may or may not reflect the reality more accurately.

Contamination

One of the most common sources of eyewitness error occurs when the witnesses' memories become contaminated by information that they have acquired since they witnessed the event. Sometimes referred to as misinformation, the source of contamination is typically someone involved in the case who shares his or her bias early on in the investigation.

Leading, misleading, and forced questions can confuse your witness and produce contaminated information. For example, "Did you hear her scream?" implies that someone did scream. The interviewee is now led to believe that someone screamed, misled if that did not occur, and forced to state that they did not miss something. The answer will probably be "Yes, I heard her scream"—even if that did not occur. An investigator may not know if the question he or she is asking IS misleading, therefore open-ended questioning will avoid this problem. In the same situation the witness may be asked, "Did you hear anything?" Or "What did you hear?" Avoid mentioning any new information that has not been previously given.

Been There . . . Done That! 5–4

Memory can be changed by contamination, high emotion, and scripting. Recall of an event is different than playing back a movie with all of the details of what happened. Memory is more delicate and can be influenced by what a person should have done and guilt for having done something. I once interviewed a woman whose child was in the hospital with apparent shaking syndrome. The baby was not expected to live due to massive injuries to the brain. Stella told me that the baby woke up crying in the middle of the night and woke up her live-in boyfriend. The boyfriend was very angry and yelled at her to do something to stop the crying of the baby. There were two rooms in this apartment, the bedroom where two children slept with their mother and boyfriend and the kitchen. Stella got up from bed and carried the baby into the kitchen. On the way she tripped over a toy that was left on the floor and dropped the baby. It was a horrible accident. At my request Stella drew a picture of that kitchen and indicated where she had tripped and where the baby had landed after the fall.

I served a search warrant on the apartment to collect the toy and document that accident. What I found was surprising. There were no toys at all in the apartment, not one — nothing to trip over. Looking at the drawing that Stella had provided, the place that the baby landed was not where the trip occurred; the baby was to the left of where Stella "tripped." To the right was a stove with a small dent. If the baby was thrown against that stove to the right he would have landed to the left and forward where Stella indicated he lay. Was this faulty memory or a lie? You decide.

Emotion

Memory of an event is challenged by the emotions of the individual recounting the event. The witnesses' guilt about what happened or their participation in the event will likely affect their perception. Stress or fear will also influence the memory encoding process. It has been suggested that individuals process information differently at high and low emotional arousal states (Artwohl, 2002). During the high emotional state, the individual may switch from rational thinking to experimental thinking. The memory is more likely during life-threatening or highly emotional situations to become fragmented, to include past events, become intuitive instead of analytic, and become oriented toward immediate action instead of reflection. This situation may be described as being seized by emotions. Tunnel vision, diminished hearing of loud sounds, temporary paralysis (short-term freezing), and distracting thoughts are among the problems experienced by individuals who experience traumatic events. Cognitive interviewing techniques are helpful in facilitating accurate memory retrieval and dissociated experiences of a high stress experience (Artwohl, 2002).

Scripting

Since memory may have gaps due to encoding problems, the brain fills in with scripted memories. *Scripts* are the memory of how things are supposed to happen (Wrightby & Merrill, 2002). For example, a driver who hits and kills a young child may recall having slowed down the vehicle prior to the impact. That is what is supposed to happen, right? Onlookers who do not have the same perspective may give an account that the driver struck the child at full speed. The use of scripting is not an indication that the individual is lying but that he or she may be filling a memory gap. To avoid interviewee scripting encourage narrative responses without prompting or interrupting. Allow the individual to reflect and respond after having been involved in stressful situations.

Conclusions

Forensic hypnosis remains a controversial evidence-gathering technique. Numerous court cases have provided guidance on its use and standards for admissibility as evidence in court. Hypnotically refreshed evidence should be used as tool in the investigation and not as the sole source of information. Corroboration is necessary to support the information gathered through hypnosis. The professionalism of forensic hypnosis has been increased through uniform training standards, testing, and certification. Despite the controversy, hypnosis seems to be making a small comeback in recent years as a positive and reliable information-gathering tool!

Cognitive interviewing is the most respected form of interviewing available. Proper use of the memory jogging techniques along with the overall atmosphere of cooperation has been shown to improve interviewing results. The use of cognitive interviewing does increase information recalled by the witness without increasing confabulation. It has successfully survived court challenge! Cognitive techniques can easily be incorporated into any interviewing method that the investigator chooses to use; this flexibility increases its potential use. It will also work well with interviewing children.

Chapter Five Questions for Review

Short Answer Questions

1. What are some of the arguments against the use of hypnosis during court testimony?

2. What are three common uses of hypnosis for a criminal investigation?

3. What does the successful application of forensic hypnosis methods depend on, according to McConkey & Sheehan?

4. What is the calendar procedure age regression technique?

5. Why is hypnosis not recommended for use on a defendant or person suspected of being involved in the crime under investigation?

6. What is the federal standard, known as the *Daubert* test, concerning the admissibility of scientific evidence, which has replaced *Frye* in some states, based upon?

7. How do Mnemonics jog the memory in order to find information that is not easily accessible?

8. What is the Reconstruction Technique?

9. What is the correct order of the cognitive interview and why is it important?

10. What is scripting?

Fill-in Questions

1. _____ refers to an investigative memory retrieval technique used to enhance recall in _____ situations.

2. Persons under hypnosis are _____ ; those in the state of hypnosis do not become zombies.

3. The goal of forensic hypnosis is _____ and retrieval for use in a specific civil or criminal case.

4. During the induction phase, the hypnotist _____ the witness and tests his or her responsivity to _____ .

5. The two major techniques used for memory recall in forensic hypnosis are _____ and _____ .

6. The final phase, recall, actually occurs _____ and the subject is deinducted.

7. Critics argue that a person undergoing hypnosis experiences a _____ to suggestion and a loss of _____ regarding cues planted by the hypnotist.

8. The _____ refers to the consideration of all relevant information in determining reliability, a test advocated by the Supreme Court in *Illinois* v. *Gates*.

9. _____ encourages the witness to do the talking while the interviewer listens.

10. One of the most common sources of eyewitness error occurs when the witness's memories become _____ by information that they have acquired _____ .

Exercises

1. Think about something that has happened to you in the past. This incident will be the basis for the practice interview; it can be a positive or negative experience. The interview will be concerned with obtaining information about that experience. Form interview teams of two students each. Students will practice the cognitive interview steps in these exercises.

   1. Practice Step One of the Cognitive Method. Meet & Greet = 5 minute exercise

   2. Practice Step Two of the Cognitive Method. Narrative Phases = 20 minute exercise

   3. Practice Step Three of the Cognitive Method. Extensive Recall through Mnemonics = 25 minute exercise

   4. Practice Step Four of the Cognitive Method. Summary and Closure = 10 minute exercise

2. **Enhancing Recall through Mnemonics**
   Pair off the students for this brief 15-minute exercise. Identify one as the interviewer and one as the interviewee. Instruct the interviewer to ask the interviewee "What was the last program you watched on TV?" The interviewer should next use step three of the cognitive interview method — extensive recall through mnemonics. Asking for recall from a different order and changing the perspective, the interviewer should attempt to obtain more information about the particular TV program.

Reference List

Adams, S. (2004). Statement analysis: Beyond the words. *FBI Enforcement Bulletin, 73*(4), 22–23.

American Psychotherapy & Medical Hypnosis Association. (2000). Definition of the process of hypnosis and trance states. Retrieved 2005, from http://apmha.com/page8.htm

Artwohl, A. (2002). Perceptual and memory distortion during officer-involved shootings. *FBI Law Enforcement Bulletin,* 18–24.

Daubert v. *Merrell Dow Pharmaceuticals.,* 113 S.Ct 2786 (1993).

Fisher, R. P., Geiselman, R. E., & Amador, M. (1989). *Memory-enhancing techniques for investigative interviewing: The cognitive interview.* Springfield, IL: Charles C. Thomas.

Fisher, R. P., & Geiselman, R. E. (1992). *Memory-enhancing techniques for investigative interviewing: The cognitive interview.* Springfield, Il: Charles C. Thomas.

Frye v. *United States.,* 23 Fed. 1013. (1923).

Geiselman, R. E., Fisher, R. P., Cohen, G., Holland, H., & Surtes, L. (1986). Eyewitness responses to leading and misleading questions under the cognitive interview. *Journal of Police Science and Administration,* 14, 31–39.

Geiselman, R. E., Bornstein, G., & Saywitz, K. (1992). *New approach to interviewing children: A test of its effectiveness.* (Report No. NCJ 135011). Washington, DC: National Institute of Justice.

Geiselman, R. E., & Fisher, R. P. (1985). *Interviewing victims and witnesses of crime.* (Report No. NCJ 99061). Washington, DC: National Institute of Justice.

Hall, E. G. (1999). Watch carefully now: Solving crime in the 21st Century. *Police,* 23(6), 42–45.

Honey, P., & Mumford, A. (1982). *The learning styles questionnaire.* Maidenhead, ENG: Peter Honey Publications.

Howell, J. (2003). *Preventing and reducing juvenile delinquency: A comprehensive framework.* Sage Publications, Inc.

Illinois v. *Gates,* 462 U.S. 213 (1983).

Makoi, K. (2002). What are emotions? Retrieved 2003, from http://www.kimakoi.com/emotions.htm

McConkey, K. M., & Sheehan, P. W. (1995). *Hypnosis, memory, and behavior in criminal investigation.* New York, NY: The Guilford Press.

Moenssens, A., Starrs, J. E., Henderson, C. E., & Inbau, F. E. (1995). *Scientific evidence in civil and criminal cases.* 4th ed.,). Westbury, NY: The Foundation Press, Inc.

Nevada Revised Statutes. (1997). Testimony of witness who previously underwent hypnosis to recall subject matter of testimony. Vol. Title 4 *Witness and Evidence,* Chapter 48 Section 039.

Newman, A. W., & Thompson, J. W. Jr. (2001). The rise and fall of forensic hypnosis in criminal investigation. *Journal of the American Academy of Psychiatry & the Law,* 29(1), 75–84.

Niehaus, J. (1999). *Investigative forensic hypnosis.* Boca Raton, FL: CRC Press.

Reiser, M. (1984). Police use of investigative hypnosis: Scientism, ethics, and power games. *American Journal of Forensic Psychology,* 2(3), 115–143.

Royal Air Force. (2001). Learning forces. Retrieved January 10, 2005, from http://www.learning-forces.org.uk/2-10/learnbetter.htm

Webert, D. R. (2003). Are the courts in a trance? Approaches to the admissibility of hypnotically enhanced witness testimony in light of empirical evidence. *The American Criminal Law Review,* 40(3), 1301–1327.

Wrightby, K., & Merrill, K. (2002). The wilderness incident investigative interview: Mitigating memory challenges utilizing the enhanced cognitive interview (ECI) technique. Retrieved January 12, 2005, from http://www.outdoored.com/articles/Articl.asp?ArticleID=141

Behavioral Interviewing and Interrogation

Auditory thinkers	Behavioral interviewing
Emblems	Facial coding system
Hedging	Mirroring
Modeling	Neuro-linguistic programming
Shifting	Qualifiers

CHAPTER OBJECTIVES

After completing this chapter you should be able to:

♦ Define the term *neuro-linguistic programming*
♦ Explain what is meant by the term *facial coding system*
♦ Describe the visual person and their methods of verbal communicating
♦ Provide the verbal characteristics of an auditory thinker
♦ Explain kinesthetic verbal processes
♦ State how eye movements are reflective of learning processes
♦ Describe the eye movements that characterize visual reasoning
♦ Explain eye movement when the auditory learner is recalling or constructing information
♦ List clues of possible deception

Introduction

Behavioral interviewing and interrogation is based on theories of communication and learning which influence unintended communications that can be observed by the astute interviewer. The techniques described

in this chapter can be used for behavioral interviewing or interrogation. The common thread to all of the techniques is the belief that human communication is affected by learning which in turn affects the behavioral indicators that can be observed and interpreted. The behavior indicators such as nonverbal posturing, sensatory verbal communication and eye movement will be among those phenomena that are presented. The techniques involve the recognition of unintended communications also called neurocommunications, when they may present themselves and possible interpretations that may be made by the interviewer. Rather than a method, behavioral interviewing is an increased awareness through the application of numerous techniques that may have relevance in any form of interviewing. There is no step-by-step method to use for behavioral interviewing. These are tools that should be used along with any other form of interviewing and are not a stand-alone method.

Knowledge of the learning processes and its application to behavioral responses provides a means for persons conducting interviews and interrogations. Acknowledging that individuals will vary in their responses due to differential encoding, this chapter will provide a broader understanding of human interactions.

Knowledge is only potential power. True personal power is the ability to take action and implement your knowledge (Hogan, 2002).

Brain development begins in vitro; incomplete at the time of birth, it continues to mature. Experiences during childhood affect intellectual function and some aspects of normal language skills. Due to the influence of experience on the processes of learning, no two people will think exactly alike. Some forms of communication appear to develop independently of experience. These involve the complex nervous system, the brain, and the senses (Bloom, Nelson, & Lazerson, 2001). Sensation, the unconscious reception of information by our sense organs, begins shortly after birth and matures over time (O'Leary, 2002). This occurs through touching, hearing, tasting, seeing, and smelling. By the age of one most aspects of visual development are complete. Approximately 99% of the stimuli to the brain are received unconsciously with about 80% of this taken in by the eyes (ATF, 1997). The importance of appealing to the unconscious/subconscious mind cannot be underestimated and is a central tenet of behavioral interviewing. Since we learn though our senses, then it makes sense that we might be persuaded through them also. The remainder of the chapter will refer specifically to these techniques for interviewing and interrogation.

What Is Behavioral Interviewing?

Behavioral interviewing is the application of communication theory and patterns of behavior to guide the interview process. It involves taking cues from the interviewee, whether these involve subconscious behavior responses or verbal patterns. The introduction to kinesics and neuro-linguistic programming provides the background and history for these approaches. Not only is it important to listen to what is said during an interview, but also how it is said. Emotional outbursts and inflections of the voice may give a clue to sensitive areas of the interview. Sudden silence, uncertainty or confusion, or the shifting of conversation to an unrelated subject may indicate that information is being withheld (Massachusetts Municipal Police Institute, 1981). Nervous bodily reaction or facial characteristics may also signal that a sensitive area has been reached. By noting these things, an interviewer will know what portions of the statement may require further probing or clarification. It is estimated that nonverbal communication often conveys a larger share of social information, approximately 65% or more; while verbal communication plays a less salient role, 35% or less (ATF, 1997).

Kinesics

A "kine" is the smallest observable unit of body movement and *kinesics* refers to the scientific study of gestures and other body movements (Wainwright, 2003). As introduced in Chapter One, kinesics is a form of nonverbal communication known as body language (Sandoval & Adams, 2001). Anthropologist Ray Birdswhistell coined the term *kinesics* during the late 1940s. According to this pioneer, up to 65% of a message's meaning is communicated through nonverbal cues (Birdwhistell, 1970). Since its inception the term has been widely used in discussions on nonverbal communications for behavioral interviewing. The premise is that behavioral communication is determined by individual learning styles. The three categories of learners are visual, auditory, and physical (also known as kinesthetic). From the *Learning Styles Questionnaire* developed by Honey and Munford (1982) we know that approximately 30% of people are visual learners; 30% are auditory learners; and 40% are physical learners (Royal Air Force, 2001).

Ekman and Friesen (1969) classify kinesics into five categories: emblems, illustrators, affect displays, regulators and adaptors. Of these categories, emblems are most frequently referred to within the context of interviewing and interrogation. *Emblems* are nonverbal gestures that have a verbal counterpart. By themselves emblems have little meaning, but are widely understood within the culture (Ekman, 2001). Examples of these deliberate and often unconscious slips of body movements include:

- Giving a person the "finger" means "fuck you."
- Shrugging indicates "I don't know" or "What difference does it make?"
- Head nod means "Yes."
- Head shake means "No."

Clues that the emblem may be a leakage of information that the individual did not intend includes the incomplete gesture, such as only one shoulder raised; or when the emblem is presented out of a normal position, such as two hands are slightly tilted outward on a table. Look for a slight nod of "yes" while saying "no." While every liar does not evidence emblematic slips, when they occur, they are very reliable as to the true sign of a message that the person does not want to reveal (Ekman, 2001).

Neuro-linguistic Programming

The term *neuro-linguistic programming* (NLP) refers to the interconnectedness between primary forms of human communication: thinking, speaking (verbally and nonverbally) and patterns of behavior. Developed during the 1970s by John Grinder and Richard Bandler it involves the psychology of how individuals think, communicate, and decipher information. Grinder and Bandler define NLP as *the study of subjective experience* (Dilts, Bandler, & Bandler, 1980).

"Neuro" refers to the brain and neural network that feeds into the brain. Neurons or nerve cells are the working units used by the nervous system to send, receive, and store signals that add up to information. It includes the idea that behavior originates from the five senses; seeing, hearing, smelling, tasting, touching, and feeling. Incorporated into the theory are the psychological reactions to ideas and events. The way that we communicate both verbally and nonverbally, is referred to as "linguistics," which follows the paths provided in the brain. The "programming" part of the description refers to the unique way that human beings manipulate the signals and convert them into useful information. The brain directs the programming process based on prior experience into thinking patterns and behaviors that become part of our life experiences and emotions.

Cultural and Personal Considerations

Nonverbal communication is generally considered to be culture constrained. Dahl reminds us that while facial recognition appears to be universal, the way that feelings and emotions are expressed through facial expression is dictated by culture. Interpretations are therefore most accurate within a similar cultural background. Demographic changes and growth of ethnic minority populations in the United States suggests that behavioral indicators must be used with caution. By 2050, Asians are expected to make up 8.2 percent of the population, African Americans will compose 13% and Hispanics will be at 24% (Leigh, 1998).

Nonverbal communications are also affected by gender. Interpretation and use of facial expressions can be different. Men appear to use different nonverbal communication styles when speaking to other men than when they are speaking to women (Dahl, nd). Women may smile more frequently than men. Age differences may also impact communication styles.

Because of variances due to personal characteristics, ethnicity, gender and age (to name a few), a critical aspect of behavioral interviewing is the establishment of a baseline through conversational speech in order to determine the normal communication modes of the individual. It is important to analyze the responses during conversational speech prior to beginning the interview itself.

Emotions and Observable Behaviors

Because of the different neural networks involved in emotion and conscious reasoning responses, emotions seem to short cut the circuits for reasoning. Once believed to be psychologically based, scientific discoveries have shown that emotions are physiologically based. Emotions seem to occur spontaneously and can't be called forth on command, nor can they be terminated simply by choice (Ekman & Davidson, 1994). Facial expressions however, may fake emotion or attempt to cover it. Whereas the expression of an emotion can be suppressed, the feeling cannot. Studies suggest that some emotions elicit observable responses. If noted, these emotional behavior states can be observed and evaluated in the context of the situation. Those of potential value to the interviewer include:

- ◆ Facial expression
- ◆ Body Posture

Facial Expression

Extensive research conducted by Ekman and associates suggest that emotions include facial activity which may be visible or not, and that certain

Courtesy of Corbis Images.

Real emotions are difficult to control. Some individuals may attempt to cover up their emotions through fake facial expressions.

facial expressions of emotion are universal (Ekman, 1999). Facial configurations may relate to specific emotions felt by the individual being interviewed according to Ekman. Facial expressions may include movements to emphasize speech, so note movements that are not typical of the individual. Form a baseline through conversational speech. A lie catcher should never rely on one clue to deceit; there must be many. It is only liars who know they are lying when they lie who are likely to be caught. The liar who succeeds in deceiving him or herself, believing the lie to be true, is not likely to exhibit signs of deceit. Facial clues should be confirmed by clues from voice, words, or body.

People may attempt to conceal emotion with facial expressions. The smile is the most common cover or mask, noted when there is not a full expression across the face. A smile that indicates pleasure may be concealed by pressing the lips together and pushing the chin muscles up. Some expressions are more reliable than others, examples include (Ekman & Rosenberg, 1977):

◆ Sadness, sorrow, or grief is indicated when the lip corners go down; this expression is reliable and difficult to fake.

◆ Sadness, grief, distress are indicated by center forehead muscles wrinkling. The inner corners of the eyebrow typically are pulled upward. These facial movements should not be present due to a false sense of distress or sadness.

◆ Fear, worry, apprehension, or terror are noted when the eyebrows are raised and pulled together. This eyebrow configuration is also common when someone is concentrating.

◆ One of the best clues for anger is seen by a narrowing of the lips; they are not sucked in or pressed, just thinner and less visible.

◆ A crooked expression, particularly more visible on the left side of the face is one that is faked and not felt.

◆ Expressions of long duration are likely to be false.

◆ A contempt smile involves a tightening of the muscle in the lip corners, producing a muscle bulge in and around the corners, often a dimple, and a slight angling up of the lip corners.

◆ A miserable smile, indicating negative emotion, involves the lower lip pushed by the chin muscle, and the corners tightened or down without any evidence of the muscle around the eyes tightening.

◆ The false smile will not be accompanied by the involvement of the muscles around the eyes.

♦ The smiling face with the lower eyelids straight across, covering part of the iris of the eye and the wrinkles below the eye seem to disappear can indicate an underlying wariness, guardedness, or even anger that is not being expressed.

Some dangers exist for the interviewer who relies solely on expressive characteristics to determine innocence or guilt. These are tools which should be used in conjunction with other interviewing techniques for the optimum results. Failure to recognize that an innocent person may feel guilty about something else or afraid of being disbelieved and may leak emotion is one hazard to be aware of. Most guilty people will not avert their gaze since they know that everyone expects experts to be able to detect deception in this way. Psychopaths and natural liars have an extraordinary ability to inhibit facial signs of their true feelings.

Here are some other indicators of emotional information indicative of the face and eyes which complete a picture of deceit.

♦ When the gaze is averted: downward may signal sadness; down or away may indicate shame or guilt; the person may look away due to disgust.

♦ Blinking increases when people are emotionally aroused; this can be due to excitement, anger, or fear.

♦ When hearing something they disagree with, the person's eyelids tend to close longer than a normal blink

♦ Pupils dilate when people are emotionally aroused which may be because of excitement, anger, or fear.

♦ Face blushing could leak embarrassment or shame.

♦ The face turning red indicates anger.

Facial Coding. Ekman has introduced an aspect of neuro-communication through the coding of facial behavior (Ekman, 1993). The *facial coding system* (FACS) is a comprehensive anatomically based method of measuring all visually discernible facial movement. There are five universal expressions controlled by the autonomic nervous system. They are: anger, fear, disgust, sadness, and enjoyment (Ekman & Rosenberg, 1977). The 44 muscles of the face contract in a particular way in response to unconscious stimuli to the brain, according to this theory. Embarrassment is a recent addition to the five original universal expressions. Embarrassment has been identified as: gaze down, smile, head turn or face touch, and then lip press (Ekman, 1993).

Facial coding research has initiated practical application for interviewing and interrogation. A group of persons working under Terrence Sejnowski have already discovered ways to distinguish between false facial expressions and genuine emotional ones (Howard Hughes Medical Institute, 2001). Using the facial coding system developed by Ekman (1993) the team designed a computer program to recognize facial movements and measure the variables such as the degree of skin wrinkling at various points on the face. The CIA is funding research on a similar software program that could result in the future of improved lie detection (Howard Hughes Medical Institute, 2001). Using face recognition software the researchers have claimed a 91% accuracy rate on the recognition and coding of facial expressions. Computer software programs are currently used by law enforcement for face recognition in London, England (The Human Face, 2001). Cameras strategically located throughout the city of London scan thousands of faces and match them against those in the law enforcement database for terrorist identification. The accuracy of recognition is not only improved through computer software use, but it also takes the pressure off of investigators to overcome barriers to uncovering deceit.

Been There . . . Done That! 6–1

Susan was a very religious woman whose brother was a Catholic priest. She knew and respected many of the local priests and was very involved with the ministry. Frequently she volunteered at the church and got to know Father Tom. She reported that he had come to her home while her husband was at work and had forced her to have sex against her will.

I later interviewed Father Tom who denied that he had raped his parishioner. He had difficulty looking at me while he answered my questions; during most of the interview his head was down and his eyes averted. He was fidgety and appeared very nervous. Verbally, he was hedging frequently. Continuing the investigation I learned that Father Tom was promoted within the week and transferred to Rome. Was he guilty? Rome is one of the few places in the world where rendition of a suspect is impossible.

Body Posture

Behavior indicators are well-known body positions that make a statement about the individual or send signals about the way they think of themselves. Authority stances are among the most common. When you see someone that stands with hands on hips and feet spread apart it indicates defiance or aggression. It is also seen when someone is making a power play. Take on the same stance and you are telling the individual you represent that same power. Then modify your stance, for example, if confronted with someone who has their arms crossed, uncross your arms to see if they will follow your behavioral lead. If they do, you have achieved control over the situation! Truthful people tend to lean forward, indicating they are listening. Through posture, deceitful people tend to move away. Kinesic posturing have been long been taught by interviewing experts. The following examples are common suppositions (Naramore, 1988):

Generally Truthful Body Postures

- Open and relaxed posture
- Frontally aligned
- Upright in the chair
- Smooth changes in body positions

Generally Deceptive Body Postures

- Rigid posture
- Head and body slump
- Rapid abrupt changes of posture
- Slouching a chair
- Head and body slump (toilet position)

Personal Gestures Indicative of Stress

- Rubbing of hands
- Picking one's nose or earlobes
- Hair twirling
- Licking of lips or difficulty swallowing
- Nail biting
- Profuse sweating

Studies have shown when an individual is introduced to a group, their status influences their perceived size (Cialdini, 1993). A person introduced as a professor is estimated as being taller than when he is introduced as a student. Without being pretentious let the individual know what you represent by introducing yourself as a police officer or other official if you are not wearing a uniform. Be confident, but not cocky. Any attempts to mask or downplay your authority serve to reinforce to the person that "This important person is just like me." The majority of individuals have a deep seated sense of duty to authority (Cialdini, 1993). Further establish your status through your clothing. If you wear a uniform, take care that it fits properly and that it is clean and pressed prior to an interview. For those in civilian clothes, wear professional looking attire that is well suited to your work. Looking sloppy does little to promote confidence or respect.

Actors are taught that there are two body postures: rising/approaching and sinking/withdrawing. Rising energy is reflected in a lift of the body, ebbing energy in a drooping body. Upward movement is associated with life: a growing plant, a young child, a person of vigor. Downward movement is related to death, the sick, the weary, and the discouraged. This fundamental rising/sinking action is usually motivated by our inner feelings and emotions. Excellent posture suggests power, such as the stance taken by a military individual. Exhibiting respect and attention, they will stand with heels together and toes pointed out at a slight angle. Male aggression is communicated when the individual stands with feet wide apart. Typically, people who walk rapidly and swing their arms freely tend to be goal oriented. When people habitually walk with hands in pockets, they tend to be critical and secretive. When people feel depressed, they shuffle along with their hands in their pockets and seldom look where they are going, making it difficult for them to be goal oriented. Stooped or bowed shoulders usually mean something negative. One could be afraid, submissive, guilty or self-conscious. Raised shoulders denote fear or tension. Squared shoulders suggest strength or responsibility.

A major strategy in the NLP method is *modeling,* which refers to learning to reflect individual behavior (Ekman & Friesen, 1969). Also referred to as "pacing," or "matching," it is a form of imitation that indicates to the subject (subconsciously) that you are alike. Used during an interview, modeling suggests harmony and agreement between the interviewee and the subject. When two people adopt similar sitting positions the nonverbal statement is "We are alike." Numerous possibilities exist on what might be matched with a subject in either posture or gesture. Notice if the individual presents with stiff-fingered palms and an extended rigid thumb. This is a control gesture warning people to remain at a distance. It also signals, "I will not give up my position." The interviewer would want to match this gesture to relay the same emotional position.

Modeling is an approach that is also used to establish rapport. Matching posture and gesture must be done in a subtle way that does not appear to mimic the person or it will have the opposite effect. When the person changes body position, wait an appropriate period of time and change yours to match. Don't assume that you must be exactly like the individual to use the method described as modeling. Establish yourself as the authority through your status, clothing, and other symbols to achieve a meaningful figure worth modeling to maximize your influence on the subject.

Eye Movement

Gaining knowledge into the dominant sensatory mode of the subject through their use of language is insightful, yet sometimes the terms people use are neutral. How do we know the best way to respond? The eyes provide another window of opportunity to access the information needed to make an appropriate response. Rapport and control can also be established through the unconscious or subconscious movement of the eyes. To determine the person's preferred representational system look for patterns of movements or clusters within the same modality. For more information on eye movements and NLP a concise description of the theory is available online in an article by Robert Dilts (Dilts, 1998).

Everyone processes in all three modes and develops a preference or dominant pattern of response. Prior to identifying the eye pattern in response to questioning, a baseline must be established to find out the dominant response for that particular individual. Watching the direction of the subject's eyes in response to visual, auditory, or kinesthetic terms during a rapport-building phase where nonthreatening, nonobtrusive, and nonoffensive information is being asked establishes the "norm" for that individual. Eye movements should only be seen as deviations from that norm and should occur in clusters for greater reliability (ATF, 1997). Generally, when the eyes are defocused or staring straight ahead it indicates recalled or remembered images. Hogan (2002) suggests that knowledge and application of eye accessing cues is a powerful way to enhance all communication processes. Some people's eye movements will appear reversed from the patterns discussed below. This may occur when someone is left handed; look for consistency when evaluating the individual.

The Visual Right Handed Person

People communicate that they are in the visual channel by looking up or lifting up their head. When asked a question containing visually constructed images the eyes tend to go up and to *his/her* right if the image is new; if the question brings out a recollection his eyes go up and to *his/her* left (Hogan, 2002). Other possible indicators of a visually communicating individual include their gesturing up with their hand or pointing up or out; standing erect with their shoulders more or less straight across; their voice is usually higher and faster; and they have less color in their face as they use visual process words.

If during the investigation of arson, for example, the owner/suspect is asked, "When did you last visit your property at Warren Wright Road?" you would expect that the owner would have been at the property at some time. The reason for asking would be determine if the last visit could

Visual—Right Handed Person

Visual—Right Handed Person

be related to the time of the fire. Upon answering, the suspect that is visually oriented will typically look upward to the left and then the eyes look straight ahead. The answer might be, "Well let's see, I got there about 7:30 P.M." The movement to that section of the brain allows the mind to recover visually stored data. Both the eye movements and the verbal response indicate visual orientation to something that has actually occurred. On the other hand, if the owner looks up and to his/her right one might question why the information was being visually constructed.

If a subject who was attacked is asked what their assailant looked like, and the response is "I did not see it that well; I think he had a mustache" while the eyes shift up and to the right, the information is being constructed versus remembered. The quandary for the interviewer is then to determine why the person would have to construct that piece of information that had already happened—is it not true? Taken by itself little importance could be attached to this perceived inappropriate eye accessing response. Other factors should be taken into consideration to help determine if this information is fabricated. First, has a definite pattern of visual thinking been adequately established through both verbal communication and eye movements?

The Auditory Right Handed Person

People communicate that they are in the auditory channel by cocking their head as if they were on the telephone. The responses to questions that are constructed for the auditory person tend to elicit eye movements that are level to the right, or left, of the face. Therefore when the subject is confused or unaware the eyes level to *his/her* right; if a recollected is sparked, the eyes tend to level towards *his/her* left (Hogan, 2002). You

Auditory—Right Handed Person

Auditory—Right Handed Person

might note the individual pointing to their ear; gesturing to their side; drumming their fingers or toes; moving their eyes from side to side or down to their left and holding their shoulders back.

The Kinesthetic Right Handed Person

When people access their kinesthetic system, they'll look down to the right or usually have more skin color. They generally have a lower, slower voice tone; gesture down by their middle or stomach; point to their heart or put their hand over their heart; and they breathe low and deep in the abdomen. The person kinesthetically orientated will look down to his/her right when sensing past feelings, smells, or tastes or imaging future ones (Hogan, 2002).

Kinesthetic—Right Handed Person

Rabon suggests that additional eye patterns associated with feelings occur when the person looks straight down, closes their eyes, or is seen blinking rapidly (Rabon, 1992). The downward gaze is often associated with the "giving up" of a suspect. It signals a change in the behavior of the suspect from being unwilling to now willing; this is the time to press for the investigator to press for information. Rapid blinking and the closing of eyes signify that the person is feeling mode.

Sensatory Verbal Communication

The learning methods in this NLP model involve visual, auditory, and kinesthetic (tactile) properties. Voice characteristics can provide important clues to the truthfulness of the person speaking. Changes in the speech are notable during the interview.

Generally, people will speak in the same sensatory manner to which they learn. To aid in the building of rapport, the interviewer will mirror the same sensory language used by the subject. *Mirroring* occurs when the interviewer uses the same sensatory language as the interviewee to establish common ground on which the subject feels comfortable. It is a legitimate way to "speak the same language" as the subject in order to improve rapport. Another use of the information regarding sensatory communication is for the purpose of shifting. *Shifting* is when the interviewer uses the same sensatory language to ask the subject questions and to move that person into the area under investigation through comfortable and familiar language. This occurs when the interviewer has determined the preferred sense of communication and uses the terms provided by the subject to move to the preferred topic for discussion. Involving the senses in descriptions by victims and witnesses tends to increase the credibility in many cases, particularly for sexual assault complaints, for children, and when interviewing developmentally delayed adults.

To attempt shifting the interview from one sense of relating to another new terms are incorporated into the investigator's questions. For example, the victim might state, "It was awful, I can still feel his hands on me." A response calculated to shift the conversation to the visual mode would be, "When you felt his hands on you, what did you see? Did he wear any rings, were there any tattoos on his fingers?" To move the conversation into the auditory type of thought the interviewer might ask, "When you felt his hands on you, what did you hear? Did he say anything while he was touching you?" Another use of sensatory analysis would include exploration of other kinesthetic areas such as smell or taste. An example would be "When he was touching you, what did he smell like?"

The vast majority of the population is believed to be visually impacted by charts, graphs, and pictures. They think in visual terms, when asked a question a picture of thoughts go through their minds. The language of these learners will therefore be visually constructed. Those that communicate through the sense of sight will use phrases such as "Do I have to draw you a *picture?*"; "I don't *see* why I am here"; You are *looking* at the wrong guy!" Interviewers should mimic their acuity with appropriate verbal cues such as "I *see* what you mean, *picture* this, *look* at it this way." Some common gestures noted in visual persons include the hand

and arms moving near their neck level when they are talking. They become quick and animated, with a similar quick, shallow method of breathing. These traits should help in identifying the visual person. *Mirroring* is a method used by the interviewer who reflects the same sensory language used by the subject as a means of achieving rapport. For mirroring, the visual personality it is recommended that your speaking rate match his, using the same types of words (Hogan, 2002).

A small portion of persons; the musicians, singers, and speakers of the world; are considered auditory. Those that rely primarily on the sense of hearing will tend to speak moderately and rhythmically. *Auditory thinkers* hear the thoughts as they are being processed and in turn are impacted by what they hear. To reach these individuals the interviewer's language should use similar auditory expressions: "I *hear* what you're saying"; "*listen* to this"; and "*tell* me what you mean." When asked to explain something the interviewer might notice the person's hands or arms move below the shoulder while pointing to their ear. According to Hogan (2002) the way to persuade an auditory thinker is to moderate your vocal rate and breathe deeply.

A small percentage is the emotional thinkers, depicted with a kinesthetic thought process. Facts and charts are not impressive to these persons; they may be athletes and those with heightened spiritual awareness. Their language will contain "feeling terms" which the interviewer should also use. These include phrases like "I *feel* your pain;" "I know what you are *going through*, how you *feel* . . ." Note if their gaze is frequently down and their breathing is slow and deep during an interview. Slow down and be particularly calm to communicate with this personality!

Been There . . . Done That! 6–2

Historically child allegations of sexual abuse are viewed with skepticism. During an interview with a six year old, she told me that he had put IT in her mouth. I asked, "What did IT taste like?" She shuttered and exclaimed, "Ugh, white stuff came out and it tasted like spinach." The spontaneous description accomplished two things: First, it verified the elements of the crime of rape, oral penetration had occurred; secondly, the manner in which she screwed up her face and described the taste of the ejaculate gave strong evidence that this was not a situation of coaching or witnessing sex. The child was describing an experience based on her senses. When the defense attorney saw the videotaped interview a plea bargain was struck that sent the perpetrator to prison.

Qualifiers, Hedging, and Manipulators

Physiological variations that occur during the course of an interview or interrogation may also give clues to the truth of a statement. One example would be a change in speech pattern and the use of qualifiers or hedgers. The *qualifier* is a word that modifies or limits the general meaning of the phrase (Rabon, 1992). An example of a qualifier occurs when the witness uses the term "it" for referring to the assailant. This could be an attempt to soften the image or it might be that there was not an individual, but an imagination at work.

Hedging is a lack of commitment to the statement. For example, "I think . . ." would be considered a hedger, a failure to commit to the description. When a person becomes less fluent and begins to stutter, it may signal deception. When answers become deceptive the use of fillers, such as "uh," or "ya know," often increases.

According to research, most people associate lying with "shifty eyes" and fidgeting behavior (Ekman, 2001). Referred to as *manipulators* these are poor indicators and are unreliable when attempting to detect deceit. These movements may indicate discomfort or relaxation and vary according to the stakes involved. Liars will consciously control these behaviors because of their known interpretations. Lip biting and lip sucking are other manipulative behaviors easily constructed to feign concern or hide other emotions. Instead, look for physiological changes that people cannot easily control. Changes in skin color, voice tone, and breathing rate are examples. An irregular breathing rate is associated with increased anxiety levels. Stress also causes a dry mouth that may result in repeated clearing of the throat or cracking of the voice. A liar will raise irrelevant issues, such as remarking about a relative that gets him into trouble or that the police are always picking on him.

Detecting Deceit

Ekman said it best, "There is no sign of deceit itself—no gesture, facial expression, or muscle twitch that in and of itself means that a person is lying. There are only clues that the person is poorly prepared and clues of emotions that don't fit the person's line" (Ekman, 2001). Knowing that liars will be held to task for their words, not their behaviors or the display of most emotions, words are more closely monitored by the individual involved in deceit.

When attempting to detect deceit the greatest danger is in disbelieving the truth; it occurs when the lie catcher mistakenly judges a truthful person to be lying. The following considerations are suggested when using the techniques in this chapter.

1. Remember that the absence of a sign of deceit is not evidence of truth.

2. Comparisons must be made between the suspect's usual behavior and that when under suspicion.

3. Consider the possibility that a sign of an emotion is not a clue to deceit but a clue to how a truthful person feels about being suspected of lying.

4. Discount the sign of an emotion as a clue to deceit if the suspect's personality would make the suspect likely to have such a feeing even if the suspect were being truthful.

5. Know that the polygraph only measures the arousal of emotion, not which emotion is felt. Studies indicate that while it is "better than chance," a person feeling strong emotion at being suspected may actually fail the polygraph while being truthful (Ekman, 2001).

The implication on learning about neuro-communication is that the improvement of interviewing skills through behavior awareness increases the detection of deceit. Knowledge on sense behaviors, both verbal and nonverbal, should raise the level of proficiency in accurate statement taking. However, studies have shown that police officers are extremely poor at detecting deceit, no better than the general public in fact. Measuring the ability of law enforcement officers from the C.I.A., D.E.A., F.B.I., and others, attempts were made to determine the extent to which we can identify liars (Ekman, 1996). He found that these trained professionals fared no better at detecting deceit than mere chance, fifty-fifty. He forwarded five explanations to account for this situation: we live in circumstances which encourage lying; our parents teach us not to identify lies; we generally prefer not to catch liars; that we often want to be misled; and that we are too polite to steal information.

The first explanation refers to the increased mobility of our society without an increase in sensitivity to the monsters that roam among us. In today's modern society the social consequences are not disastrous for lying (or worse); one can change jobs, spouses, and a damaged reputation does not follow. Yet we have not been prepared by our evolutionary history to be sensitive to the behavioral clues that suggest someone is lying. Secondly, parents conceal their activities from their children. They have a stake in not educating offspring to detect lies from demeanor in order to protect their own privacy. Therefore, awareness of deceit is not part of the growing up educational process. Thirdly, Ekman suggests that we generally prefer not to catch liars, because a trusting rather than a suspicious stance enriches life (Ekman, 1996). Trusting people makes life easier, regardless of the cost in not detecting someone who may take advantage of you. Ekman (1996) further suggests that those whose lives are at risk if they are not constantly alert to betrayal are more accurate in detecting lies than those who live with peace of mind. The fourth explanation that we often want to be misled exists because we have a stake in not knowing the truth. Using the example of a philanderer husband, Ekman (1996) says that neither husband nor wife wants the infidelity confirmed, particularly if funds to care for their children are not being diverted. Lastly, we are raised to be polite in our personal relationships and interactions. To steal information would be worse than staring at the person while picking his nose (Ekman, 1996). The true messages are often not the ones that we care to hear about on a daily basis, so we learn to tune them out.

Ekman acknowledges that these reasons seem to fall short of explaining why criminal justice professionals do so poorly in identifying liars from their demeanor. An added dimension, he states, lies in the fact that more than 75% of people they talk to lie to the police (Ekman, 1996). With such a high base-rate of lying it is difficult to spot the liar; the emphasis is therefore diverted to getting the evidence to convict the liar. Effectiveness would be increased if the two goals were converged.

A study on the method using facial movement, voice, and speech netted an 80% chance of correct classification of who was lying and who was telling the truth in a high stakes situation (Ekman, 1996).

Conclusions

Communication takes place that is both verbal and nonverbal, influenced by the way that we learn through our senses. Since the majority of our stimuli to the brain are considered to occur on an unconscious level, appeals to persuade through the subconscious may occur. Interviewers can gain insight to the people they question by identifying the primary learning mode and using that information to mirror and model. Shifting is a method of playing back to the individual the mode in which they feel most communicating in.

Behavioral interviewing is not an interviewing model but a rich source of techniques which incorporates nonverbal communications awareness. During an interview or interrogation it will be helpful to the investigator to be acutely aware of the behavioral indicators that may signify deceit.

Chapter Six Questions for Review

Short Answer Questions

1. Define neuro-linguistic programming and neuro-communication through facial coding system. Briefly state their implications for interviewing.

2. What are the three primary learning methods? What is their role in mirroring? How does it differ from modeling?

3. What techniques should you use for each type of sensory learner?

4. What is the significance of facial expressions? What cautions should interviewers take in regard to facial expressions during an interview?

5. What are examples of qualifiers, hedging, emblems, and manipulators?

6. What is the greatest danger when attempting to detect deceit and how can you prevent it?

Fill-in Questions

1. _____ refers to the interconnectedness between primary forms of human communication: thinking, speaking, and patterns of behavior.

2. _____ sensory learning method thinks in verbal terms. When asked a question, pictures of thoughts go through their minds.

3. A small percentage of the population has a _____ thought process. They are emotional thinkers and their language will contain "feeling terms."

4. When this person is recalling an event their eyes will move up and to his/her left

    _____ .

5. This person keeps their eyes level to the right, or left, of the face when responding to questions

    _____ .

6. _____ look down and to the right or usually have more skin color when responding to questions.

7. Facial clues should be confirmed by clues from the
   _____ , _____ , or
   _____ .

8. Narrowing of the lips indicates
   _____ .

9. _____ is indicated when the lip corners go down; this expression is reliable and difficult to fake.

10. It is better to focus on _____ changes instead of _____ ones when detecting deceit.

Exercises

1. The class must break into pairs for an exercise on eye accessing cues. The instructor reads these questions while one person in each pair answers and the other watches their eye movements. Switch roles every other question.

   - **How many windows are in the front of the house where you live permanently (not at school)?** Eyes up and left represent a visual remembering.

   - **Describe your mother.** Eyes up and left represent a visual remembering.

   - **Which one of your friends has the most annoying voice?** To the side and left represents an auditory recall.

   - **What is the name of your favorite song?** To the side and left represents an auditory recall.

   - **What was the color of your first car?** Up and left indicates a visual remembering.

   - **Imagine what your best friend would look like with purple hair.** Up and right is a visual construct.

2. Practice mirroring. Pair up with a member of the class for this exercise for 10 minutes. Sitting across from one another and facing each other, one of the students is asked to describe what he or she did since that they got up that day. During this "interview" the listening partner should match posture and gesture in a subtle way that does not appear to mimic the interviewee.

Reference List

ATF. (1997). *Advanced analytical interviewing program.* Washington, DC: The Bureau of Alcohol, Tobacco, and Firearms.

Birdwhistell, R. (1970). *Kinesics and context: Essays on body motion communication.* Philadelphia, PA: University of Pennsylvania Press.

Bloom, F., Nelson, C. A., & Lazerson, A. (2001). *Brain, mind, and behavior.* U.S.: Worth Publishers.

The Human Face. (2001). [DVD]. British Broadcasting Corporation (Producer), & J. Erskine, & D. Stewart (Directors). Buckinghamshire, England, UK: BBC.

Cialdini, R. B. (1993). *Influence: The psychology of persuasion* (2nd ed.). New York, NY: William Morrow and Company, Inc.

Dahl, S. (nd). Cultural and non-cultural aspects of non verbal communication. Retrieved January, 2006, from http://stephan.dahl.at/nonverbal/culture_and_nonverbal.html

Dilts, R., Bandler, L. C., & Bandler, R. (1980). *Neuro-linguistic programming.* Capitola, CA: META Publications.

Dilts, R. (1998). Eye movements and NLP. Retrieved 2005, from http://www.nlpu.com/Articles/artic14.htm

Ekman, P. (1993). Facial expression and emotion. *American Psychologist, 48*(4), 384–817.

Ekman, P. (1996). Why don't we catch liars? *Social Research, 63*(3), 801–817.

Ekman, P., & Davidson, R. J. (1994). *The nature of emotion: fundamental questions.* New York, NY: Oxford University Press.

Ekman, P., & Friesen, W. (1969). The repertoire of non-verbal behaviour: Categories, origins, usage and codings. *Semiotics,* 1, 49-98.

Ekman, P. (1999). Facial expressions. T. Dalgleish, & M. Power *Handbook of Cognition and Emotion.* New York, NY: John Wiley & Sons Ltd.

Ekman, P. (2001). *Telling lies: Clues to deceit in the marketplace, politics, and marriage.* New York, NY: W. W. Norton & Company.

Ekman, P., & Rosenberg, E. (1977). *What the face reveals.* New York, NY: Oxford Press.

Hogan, K. (2002). *The psychology of persuasion.* Gretna, LA: Pelican Publishing.

Howard Hughes Medical Institute. (2001). Facing the truth. Retrieved 2005, from http://www.hhmi.org/bulletin/may2001/faces/faces2.html

Leigh, J. (1998). *Communicating for cultural competence.* Prospect Heights, Il: Waveland Press.

Massachusetts Municipal Police Institute. (1981). *Police and procedure: Interviewing witnesses.* Unpublished.

Naramore, D. (1988). *Psychology of interviewing.* NESPAC: Homicide School unpublished.

O'Leary, K. D. (2002). Conjoint therapy for partners who engage in physically aggressive behavior: Rationale and research. R. Geffner, & A. Rosenbaum (editors), *Domestic violence offenders: Current interventions, research, and implications for policies and standards* (pp. 145–164). Binghamton, NY: Haworth Press, Inc.

Rabon, D. (1992). *Interviewing and interrogation*. Durham, NC: Carolina Academic Press.

Royal Air Force. (2001). Learning forces. Retrieved January 10, 2005, from http://www.learning-forces.org.uk/2-10/learnbetter.htm

Sandoval, V., & Adams, S. (2001). Subtle skills for building rapport using neuro-linguistic programming in the interview room. *FBI Law Enforcement Bulletin*, 1–5.

Wainwright, G. (2003). *Teach yourself: Body language*. Chicago, IL: McGraw-Hill Companies.

Interviewing Special Populations

The next three chapters of *Smart Talk* provide unique experiences for students to become familiar with interviewing and interrogation approaches that differ for special populations. Criminal justice professionals frequently are involved in circumstances which require interviews and interrogations with children, elders, and persons who have a disability. This section will prepare the learner for some of the unusual circumstances that might be encountered in situations with these populations.

Chapter Seven covers interviewing children. The different models of child interviewing are provided along with the child-adapted version of cognitive interviewing and forensic interviewing. These can be practiced for increased understanding and proficiency. Of importance when interviewing children are the developmental considerations according to the child's age. Knowledge of the developmental stages can assist the interviewer in avoiding the limitations inherent with child interviews.

As the elder population explodes in America the criminal justice community must grow to meet the needs of that population. A greater understanding of the complexities of interviewing older persons is addressed in Chapter Eight. The types of crimes and approaches to interviews are among the topics discussed. Although physical limitations due to aging can be expected, these can be anticipated by the interviewer. In most cases the limitations can successfully be overcome.

Interviewing persons with disabilities is the topic of Chapter Nine. The legal requirements of the Americans with Disabilities Act as it pertains to criminal justice personnel are an important part of this chapter; reasonable accommodations must be made for persons having a disability.

The courts are increasingly holding criminal justice professionals accountable for their actions when confronted with persons that have a disability. This responsibility translates into the need for increased awareness
on the part of the police, court personnel, and corrections. Persons with
mental retardation, mental illness, and personality disorders are overly
represented in the jails and prisons in the United States.

Interviewing Children

CHAPTER OBJECTIVES

After completing this chapter you should be able to:

◆ Compare and contrast the forensic and cognitive approaches to interviewing
◆ Explain what is meant by the term *secondary abuse*
◆ Describe the methods for risk assessment
◆ Provide information on the tools for interviewing children
◆ Explain problems associated with child interviewing
◆ State how the accuracy of the child statements may affect the process
◆ Describe the multidisciplinary approach
◆ Explain the CM preparation method
◆ List the child stages of development and their characteristics

Introduction

Interviewing children can provide unique challenges and opportunities for crime investigators. It is helpful to understand child mental development from the subjective experiences of a child, for a variety of reasons.

Communicating with children through interviews is highly dependent on their developmental level. As criminal justice professionals we are concerned with the violence perpetrated by children and against children, and in the effects of their being witnesses to domestic violence. Child eyewitness testimony is potentially important in the decision making for a range of criminal and civil matters (Hayes & Delamonthe, 1997). In addition to the theoretical reasons for exploring methods of effective interviewing is the practical and pressing concern of forensically documenting the abuses against children (Saywitz, Goodman, & Lyon, 2002).

Both the identification and recognition of child abuse and the impact of violence are also of consequence to the investigator. Insight into the reactions of the victim may provide a more detailed and accurate portrayal of the situation that is harmful to the child. The investigator has a unique opportunity to document the full extent of injury, both physical and psychological, if those signs and symptoms present themselves. The likelihood of successful prosecution is enhanced with increased documentation and evidence of harm.

The role of criminal justice investigators differs and may be in conflict with investigators from social service agencies. Criminal investigators have the duty to determine *what* happened rather than an emotional belief that *something* happened (Lanning, 2002). The determination of whether a crime has been committed and the development of admissible evidence are central to the criminal justice perspective. To be effective, interviewers and investigators must be in control of their feelings about abuse and have the ability to react dispassionately.

During the investigation of suspected child abuse the most likely source of information will come from the victim. Second-hand disclosure regarding the abuse of a child should never be considered reliable without corroboration. It is necessary to verify as much of the information as possible. Reliability issues compounded with the suggestibility of children and limited memory development heightens the search for methods to improve child testimony as an urgent investigation.

Been There . . . Done That! 7–1

A multidisciplinary task force was established in my county to jointly investigate major crimes committed against children. We came from many different professions: I was the police officer; there was a medical doctor, prosecuting attorney, social worker, clinician, and victim-witness advocate. After the interview the team recommended I arrest the perpetrator. Even though I also believed that the child had been sexually abused there was a lack of sufficient probable cause. It was a heated discussion, without compromise. Now what—leave the child unprotected from further abuse? No, the suggestion was made that we offer the suspect a pre-trial diversion. In exchange for him admitting guilt and going to counseling as well as staying away from the victim we would not prosecute. He agreed! It was a win-win for everyone. Never compromise your reputation by effecting an arrest that lacks probable cause—it will come back to haunt you!

Child Developmental Stages

The ability of the child witness or victim to accurately report experiences is limited by the child's developmental stage. Since children do not mature at the same rate, one should be careful about overgeneralization. Poverty, culture, exposure to violence, and a variety of other variables affect cognitive development. The investigator can go into the interview with a rough idea of what might be expected from the interviewee. This knowledge is most helpful before the interview begins. Use it to determine where to conduct the questioning, who should be present, and for structuring the questions to be asked.

The Limitations on Reporting by Age

The child is expected to be pre-verbal during *infancy* and direct questioning is unlikely to be productive. Documenting connected terms or crying that indicate an injury or express pain are worthwhile for the investigator to include in the report of suspected child abuse. During *early childhood* their ability to verbalize is increased particularly through play. The best approach for eliciting information from a child under the age of six is within a play therapy framework. *Middle childhood* brings an improvement in the ability to answer questions and to describe events. Exact dates are still a problem, but seasons associated with clothing and events occurring around holidays help to establish the timing on assaults.

Infancy: The first 2 years
Their language consists of utterances, crying, and gestures. A high anxiety level is reached when immediate needs are not met; hunger and relief of pain are examples. The earliest documentation regarding the infant

victim is the recognition of pain or discomfort. In addition to the medical report of injury, the investigator should take note of the verbal expressions that indicate pain while the child is being examined by a physician in addition to the reports given by the caretaker. Slowly their vocabulary is established through single and then connected words. By the time the child is 24 months of age he/she is likely to be using expressive terms such as "me want," "man bad," "hit you." Behavioral indicators of abuse are more likely the "language" during infancy.

The investigator should obtain interviews with all caretakers, regardless of their status as a suspect. A parent who says that the infant does not cry excessively or appear in pain may later become a suspect if the child is found to have extensive internal injury, for example. Early documentation of suspected infant abuse is extremely important. Physical examination by a medical professional is required to provide evidence of a crime; a team approach is most beneficial in cases involving an infant victim.

Early Childhood: Ages 2 to 6

These years are collectively referred to as the pre-school stage. During early childhood there is an expectation that the child will verbally communicate particularly thorough play. This child will have an active imagination that is grounded in reality; fantasies are about things similar to which they have experienced, but not necessarily what has happened to them. There is a need to clarify if they heard, saw, or felt something in order to determine the origin of their experiences regarding the topic of the interview. They have an inability to concentrate on any one thing for more than a few minutes, their attention span increases as the child grows older. Interviewers need to assess the attention span and structure the interview to accommodate the need of the child. For example, a child can be encouraged to color between questions.

An intense single experience or a repeatedly rehearsed situation may be retained in their long-term memory. Time and space are concepts that the young child has difficulties expressing. The extent of recall is dependent on the level of their social interactions. By age five most children can recall and recount things that have occurred in the past (Morison et al., 2000). Extended questioning should not be expected; this does not mean that the interview will be short. The opposite is true; the structure needs to involve natural breaks provided purposely. The interview will require significant time with a great deal of concentration on the part of the interviewer. Only in rare instances should this child be interviewed longer than one half hour.

As the young child matures he or she will push their physical limits by running, leaping, and climbing. Unsupervised or neglected children are susceptible to self-injury caused by falling.

Middle Childhood: Ages 7 to 12

During their middle years a child's mental processes develop at a faster rate than in the earlier stages. Their language is well developed along with an improved understanding of time and space concepts. These children can be more specific with explaining when and where they have had the experiences that you want to document. Having a strong need for trust, a victimized child at this age may require additional attention and support to compensate for the violation that occurred towards them.

Play remains their primary expression supplemented with emotion language. This age group should be capable of explaining what they felt as a result of their experiences. During an interview follow-up questions such as, "What did that feel like?"; "What did it taste like?"; and "How did that make you feel?" are quite appropriate in response to their descriptions. Their cognitive development becomes more sophisticated; including increased reasoning capacity, and the ability of distinguishing fiction from reality. "How do you know?"; and, "What is he/she like?" can stimulate expressive responses. Their perception of others may be categories as "good," or "bad," and they will be able to tell why.

Field Assessment

In cases where the police officer is responding to the complaint of child abuse or neglect in the field, an assessment is made to determine if criminal action should be sought. This assessment includes an interview of the child in the field. The majority of calls will not be acted on independently by the police officer; he or she may act as the first responder who then makes a report to the social services. In making the assessment in the field, the child should be interviewed at the scene. The name, address, and age of the child are documented in addition to the demeanor of the child. The names and addresses of the caretaker and family situation are documented.

After explaining the reason for the visit to the caretaker, police officers should ask to see the child. If the child is old enough to understand, explain why the police are there and what they will be doing. Depending on the allegations and/or the child's age, the investigator will need to visually examine the child for signs of obvious trauma. Investigators should document any injuries noted and, if possible, photograph areas of injury or of questionable physical findings.

The child should be interviewed outside the presence of the caregiver. If the child has sustained life-threatening or severe injuries, the first priority is securing emergency medical attention for the child. The

Department of Health and Human Services (Pence & Wilson, 1992) suggests that the following information should be determined from the interview:

- establishing the child's developmental level;
- the child's explanation of any injuries;
- who the child perceives as his/her caretakers;
- how the child is disciplined;
- how other children in the home are disciplined;
- how often have the victim and/or siblings been injured in the past;
- what type of weapon or implement was used, and where it is now;
- if they bled after the assault, where their clothing is now, or any other item that might have been stained;
- who else saw the incident; and
- whom the child told of the incident.

Initial Considerations for Child Interviews

As this chapter progresses, differences will emerge regarding interview techniques with children. That is because the purpose and scope of the interview with a child may change at any point during the interview process. A child that is being questioned primarily for having been victimized may also have begun perpetrating. The child may have been victimized by more than one person and through different forms of abuse. Children that have been victimized may also have witnessed other victimizations; they may have information from the perpetrator of others that have been abused. These variables will in turn affect the choice of the person to conduct the questioning.

Step 1: Risk Assessment

Before beginning any investigation that involves interviewing a child a determination must be made on whether that child is safe. Assessing the present and future risk of harm to a child is more than just an indication about the investigator's level of caring, it is a legal requirement called *risk assessment*. All fifty states and the District of Columbia have legislation that requires certain professionals to report when a child is at risk due to suspected child abuse and neglect. The standard of proof necessary to make this assessment is a mere suspicion alone. Some questions that are helpful in making a risk assessment include:

1. Is there *any* reason to believe that this child has been abused, neglected, or witnessed abuse towards a parent or sibling in his or her home?

2. Has the child received a suspicious injury or threat of injury?

3. Has another child in the home been abused or neglected?

4. Are there weapons or ammunition that is accessible to this child? Note: some states make it illegal to have unsecured weapons or ammunition in the home.

5. Does the primary caretaker abuse alcohol or drugs?

6. Is the child depressed or suffering from lack of medical attention?

If the answer to any of the questions above is "yes," then a report of suspected abuse must be filed with the appropriate receiving agency for that state. Child Protection Services, Department of Social Services, and police departments are examples of agencies that are designated by law as obligated to receive these reports.

If the child divulges during an interview that abuse has occurred by a caretaker, the interviewer must determine if he or she is likely to be punished for having made the report about a family member or intimate of a parent. This would be a high risk situation that requires immediate intervention. A local child protection agency should be called regarding this case before the child is released to the caretaker. Police officers in every state have temporary or emergency removal powers for the purposes of protecting children. Removal of the victim to a safe living environment is an option that should be exercised only if a non-offending parent or guardian is unwilling or unable to protect the child from the suspect.

Step 2: Models for Evaluating Abuse

After conducting the risk assessment and determining that appropriate measures have been taken to assure the safety of the child, the approach to be used for interviewing the child should be determined. Step 2 requires that the model be consistent with the goals of the investigation. The approach to child interviewing may vary widely based on this decision.

The American Professional Society on the Abuse of Children (APSAC) categorizes the approaches to child sexual abuse evaluation into three different models. While these are specifically suggested for evaluating sexual abuse, they provide a way to conceptualize the way that abuse is determined by external agencies. This framework is helpful for the criminal justice professional in understanding the complexities of child maltreatment allegations from the perspective of clinicians. The recommended approaches consist of the child interview model; the parent-child inter-action model; and the comprehensive evaluation model (Faller, 1996).

The *child interview model* relies most significantly on the interview with the child to determine if abuse has occurred. The inherent assumption in this model is that children are usually reliable when they give accounts of their sexual abuse and that they rarely make false allegations (Faller, 1996).

The *parent-child interaction model* is theoretically based on expected behaviors between an offending and nonoffending parent and their children. Mere conversation is the method to determine if the relationship between the parent and child is appropriate. This is a controversial method even among clinicians and should not be used as the basis for criminal complaints.

The third model is the comprehensive evaluation or *multidisciplinary team approach*. Teams may consist of physicians, social workers, psychologists, lawyers, and police officers. Medical exams of the victim and psychological testing may be conducted and considered by the team for the abuse evaluation. Interviews with the victim are an important aspect of this approach. Due to the time and expense of the multidisciplinary approach, it may not be appropriate in all allegations of maltreatment. However, it is commonly accepted that abuse against children is a complex problem which requires the coordination of efforts through a multidisciplinary approach to ensure that the needs of the victim is met as well as the criminal justice requirements (Walton, 2003).

The multidisciplinary approach to investigating child abuse requires a substantial knowledge of child development. Current trends are leaning towards the use of non-police persons to conduct these interviews. FBI Agent Lanning suggests that police officers should become familiar with child development and the interviewing processes from other disciplines in order to remain an active participant in investigative interviewing of children (Lanning, 2002). Lanning (2002) cautions that police officers should not blindly accept the opinions of clinicians and always maintain control over the interview, even if it is conducted by a social worker or other child advocate.

Step 3: Preliminary Considerations

Step 3 consists of a checklist that will assist the interviewer in determining the type of interview that will be needed. There are four components to the *preliminary considerations checklist:* determine the reason for questioning, determine the purpose of questioning, identify the population, and identify the interviewer.

1. *Determine the Reason* for questioning

   ◆ Has the child been victimized?   = Lengthy Interview

   ◆ Has the child been witness to a crime?   = Short Interview

   ◆ Is the child suspected of having committed a crime?   = Interrogation

2. *Determine the Purpose* of the questioning

   ◆ Abuse Determination — what is the best model to meet your needs?

   ◆ Risk Assessment — is this child at risk for future victimization?

   ◆ Obtaining Evidence — will the child be able to give verbal or written evidence?

3. *Identify the Population*

   ◆ Age — what are the expectations and limitations of this child?

   ◆ Gender — what are the expectations and limitations of this boy or girl?

   ◆ Special Needs — are accommodations necessary to conduct the questioning?

   ◆ Cultural background and ethnicity — can outcomes be predicted or avoided?

   ◆ Current or recent traumatizing events — what do you know about this person?

4. *Identify the Interviewer*

   ◆ Age — can he/she interact with the target?

   ◆ Gender — would this make a difference on target response?

   ◆ Ethnicity — will the interviewer have credibility with the target?

   ◆ Interviewing or Interrogation specialization

   ◆ Experience of the Interviewer — what is the skill level with the target population?

   ◆ Approach — what attitude is required according to the purpose of questioning?

   ◆ Confidence — is he/she comfortable with the target?

Step 4:
Remain Neutral

Approaching each interview without bias is essential. The purpose of the interview is to determine the truth; this is done based on facts and evidence. The kind of evidence that is sought includes the interview with the child, corroborating physical evidence, and testimonial evidence such as statements taken from persons with knowledge about the case.

To obtain testimony for legal evidence the investigator cannot rely on second-hand information garnered from another agency. Even statements that were taken by another police agency should not be accepted per se without the present investigator having had an active role in the interview process. This is extremely important in order to protect the victim as well as the rights of the accused. Just like any other criminal investigation certain criteria must be satisfied for the matter to be considered a criminal offense. Resist the temptation to run out and make an arrest without reviewing the statement to determine if probable cause has been adequately established through the following information *for every allegation.* Here are some questions that the interviewer must know in order to proceed with the criminal process.

1. What, if any, crime has occurred?

All elements of the crime must be satisfied. For example, if the allegation is the rape of a child, penetration must have occurred. What is the evidence of penetration? Penetration may be perpetrated by any object into any orifice. Determine the genitalia that were penetrated and the object that was used. It may be a body part or a physical object inserted into the child. Depending on the age of the victim, force may also be an element of the crime. The issue of force may be satisfied by any level of force; depending on the relationship this might be a "command." Identify what level of force was used, if any. For a young child this is not an issue.

2. Who is the person that committed the crime?

It may be difficult for a young child to adequately identify the perpetrator! A person cannot be accused of a crime without having been positively identified. If the child only knows the first name of the individual (and this is not unusual) it is necessary to follow up with a question on where he or she knows "John," or where the abuse occurred. With a younger child the information might be obtained from the guardian. For example, if "John" was responsible, how does the child know him? Where did it happen—if the offense occurred in "John's house" find out if that is the grandfather, or uncle, or babysitter. It is not appropriate to suggest that a child has been abused, but once the statement is made that abuse did occur, direct questions for the purposes of clarifying what has already been stated is permissible. Keep asking questions until satisfied that the perpetrator identity is firmly established.

3. Where did the crime occur?

Expect that the description of the place will be age appropriate. "In the woods"; "In the house"; "At school" are examples of what you might hear. Build on what the child says if clarification is needed. If the place of victimization occurred at a day care, find out the times and dates that the child had been enrolled and attended day care. If the abuse occurred at the house of a relative, find out if the person cared regularly for the child or on a sporadic basis.

4. When did the crime occur?

Many young victims will not be able to state the exact date that they were victimized. Their concept of time is different than adults, and they may have been victimized over a long period of time. In order to clarify the times of victimization ask questions to help the child in narrowing down within a time frame period. For example: "What were you wearing?" The answer may indicate the season. Determine the last time that the perpetrator had access to the child being interviewed. Children over the age of six are more likely to be able to accurately define the time period in relation to an important event in their life such as a holiday or birthday. Ask, "Was it before your birthday or after?" If you know that the perpetrator had frequent access to the child ask if "it" happened the last time they were together.

5. Against whom was the crime perpetrated?

Clarify with the child if he or she was the victim versus that they might have seen something happen to someone else. If there is any question in the mind of the interviewer, be direct; ask, "Did this happen to you?"

6. How was the crime perpetrated?

This part of the questioning can be most difficult for the interviewer. He or she must be comfortable asking for specific clarification on how the crime was perpetrated. It can be helpful for the interviewer to feign misunderstanding; ask the child to help understand what happened. Here are a few examples (depending on the crime being investigated): "You told me that a stick was there, what happened with the stick? Can you show me on the doll (or picture) where the stick was put? Did it touch you outside or did it go inside? What did that feel like?" When asking questions for clarification interviewer neutrality is important. Do not act surprised, angry, happy, or thankful. It is appropriate to thank the child for clearing up the misunderstanding.

What Is the Forensic Approach to Child Interviewing?

The forensic approach to child interviewing is used when primary victimization is suspected. Based on the multidisciplinary model it involves multiple individuals with different expertise working together to gather information and collect evidence. The approach is legalistic with an effort towards maintaining integrity of the case to meet possible future court challenges. All interviews and collection of evidence must be conducted by individuals who are trained and familiar with the legal standards of the state where the offense is alleged to have occurred. The interviewer may be a police officer, a child psychologist, or a certified forensic interviewer; or by any member of the team who is qualified to conduct the questioning of the victim based on the preliminary considerations. Collaboration with mandated reporting agencies means that members of the forensic team are consulted and have full participation in the process.

When asked if she would draw a picture of the person who "touched her in a place she didn't like" a four-year-old girl drew this picture. It was used as evidence of her sexual assault.

A recent trend is towards the use of a certified forensic interviewer who can establish a nonbiased position as neither an advocate for the child nor an employee of the court. This method is meant to reduce the number of interviews that may ultimately contaminate the child's testimony through repetitive questioning. It involves a standardized procedure that documents the affect or nonverbal report of the child as well as the verbal account. Often this is accomplished though videotaping of the victim during the interview. There is no legal requirement that children be informed that they are being interviewed. The decision on giving this information to the child is a matter of organization policy. The permission of a parent or guardian should be obtained prior to the videotaping of a child.

Forensic interviewing is a traditional structured format for a child interview that is designed to minimize future challenges through strict adherence to legal principles. The interview requires planning and precision. A detailed history of abuse or suspected current abuse is obtained prior to the interview. An interview room is specifically designed for the comfort of the designated age group to be interviewed. Direct questioning is necessary to elicit details of an assault, but care is taken not to be suggestive in the form of questioning.

Forensic Interviewing Techniques

Interviewing children takes time and can be a difficult process. The purpose of the interview will determine how complex it will be. Young children are easily distracted and often reluctant to disclose abuse. When they feel attached to the abuser they may fear the consequences, including what you the interviewer might do to them as a result. To avoid this problem the interviewer should not show approval or disapproval at anything the child says. The emotions of the interviewer must be held in check. Signs of disgust, disbelief, or even approval are not appropriate since they may influence the child.

Phase I: Caretaker Instructions

Prior to meeting with the child instructions should be provided to the caretaker. The caretaker should be advised not to answer any questions about the interview from the child. No attempt should be made by the caretaker to gain further information from the child about the event. Warn the caretaker not to discuss case specifics since others may also be involved that have not yet been identified. Explain to the caretaker that a bathroom break needs to be provided for the child just prior to the interview.

If it does not compromise the investigation, attempt to put the caretaker at ease by telling him or her about the process at this stage. Include the fact that you will need to talk to the child alone.

Immediately prior to the interview have the guardian sign a prepared form of release to conduct and document the interview. This is important since the process may result in information that implicates the caretaker himself or those that the caretaker wants to protect. When an interrogation of a juvenile is the focus, additional legal requirements must be met. See Chapter Thirteen for issues concerning juvenile interrogation.

Phase II: Evaluation Phase

Using the common preliminary considerations checklist, conduct an evaluation of the upcoming interview. From this exercise the interviewer will know the approximate length and approach that will be needed. Lengthy interviews with a young child should be no more than one-half hour!

Determine the appropriate place to conduct the interview. For all interviews the room should be quiet and free of distractions. There should not be any electronic devices in the room that will make noise: any phone, cell phone, beeper, pager, clock, or radio. For a child interview, no chairs are necessary if there are comfortable places to sit on the floor. This puts the interviewer at a more even level with the child and is less threatening. Audio or video recording devices should not be visible to the child since he or she may "ham it up" for a camera. For an interrogation there should be a table for writing and a visible recording device if one is to be used.

Preparation for the interview includes the reading of any statements that may have brought the child to the attention of the police. Any information regarding past or present allegations of abuse should be researched. A background check of the alleged perpetrator should be made prior to the interview with the victim.

Phase III: Prepare the Child

Interviewers are often frustrated by inaccurate and unreliable statements taken from young children. This is in part due to developmental limitations on children's ability to communicate when they don't understand the questions. The interviewer is not made aware of the situation because children will merely provide an answer that is false rather than communicate that they don't understand. Current research on this issue suggests a method to greatly diminish the error rate. The *Comprehension Monitoring (CM) preparation method* is a practice session for assisting the child in identifying information that he or she does not understand and improving their ability to tell the interviewer when they don't understand. Using the CM preparation method, someone other than the interviewer should prepare the child for the interview. The approach may cut erroneous reports in half by improving the communication between the interviewer and the child (Saywitz, Snyder, & Nathanson, 1999).

Children being prepared for the interview should (a) practice identifying instances of non-comprehension, (b) practice responding with verbalizations that indicate their lack of understanding (using explicit feedback, modeling, and praise), and (c) increase their awareness of the negative consequences of responding to questions not fully understood (e.g., misordering in a restaurant and receiving the wrong food, missing out on a favorite activity). After the preparation phase the child should be given adequate time for some food, beverage, and of course, a bathroom break.

> ### Been There . . . Done That! 7–2
>
> Building rapport is a critical component any interview. When first meeting the child to be interviewed it is important to get down to their level and say hello. Introduce yourself properly and treat the child with respect. They do know the difference at any age! Although I have conducted interviews with children in civilian clothes I would typically introduce myself as a police officer whose job it was to talk to children about things that might be important to them.

Phase IV: Establish Rapport

The interviewer should meet and greet the child in a relaxed and comfortable manner. Rather than asking for his or her name, say, "Hi, you must be Bill," and state your first name. Tell the child that you have been expecting them, and then ask the guardian if it is alright for "Bill" to take a walk with you. This simple act reassures the child that you are someone to whom he or she is able (given permission) to go with and to talk to. Make this introduction appropriate to the age of the child to be interviewed. If this is a young child, kneel down to the same level at the beginning of the meeting. The interview should be conducted without the presence of the guardian unless absolutely necessary.

Take whatever time necessary to ensure that the child is relaxed and does not feel threatened. The interview room should afford flexibility for the child to move around, but not large enough to "escape." Crayons and paper should be available to occupy the child and allow him or her to talk unguarded. Talk about the child's likes such as colors, activities, games, videos—get to know them. Let the child know a bit about you. This is the time to access the developmental level of the child and their ability to communicate. For very young children it might be sufficient to say that you are someone who talks to kids about things on their minds. Older children may want to know more about your role, a police officer, social worker, etc. This is the stage where you determine the sexual terminology of the child if the interview concerns sexual abuse. Use appropriate tools to aid in this vocabulary development. You may want to ask questions to determine their sophistication, "Can you write?"; "Do you know your alphabet?"; "Do you read?" With an interrogation, the child must be told if you are a police officer.

Phase V: Conduct the Interview

At this point the interviewer is ready to find out what happened. Establish that the child knows the difference between the truth and a lie and that the child is willing to tell you if he does not understand questions. Example: "Do you know what a lie is?" Ask for an example. "Do you know what telling the truth is?" Ask, for an example, "If I said your name was Bill, is that a lie or the truth?" "If I say that this crayon is red, is that the truth or a lie?" Give license by saying that you will ask when you don't understand something also.

Don't use cop talk. Use language that is appropriate to the age and developmental level. Words like incident, occur, penetration, prior, ejaculation, and perpetrator can be confusing to a child. Look for signs that the child does not understand you. Avoid using language that sounds accusatory, such as "Why?" Don't say, "Why did you do that?"; "Why did you go to that house?"; "Why did he touch you?" Never threaten or try to force a reluctant child to talk. If gentle coaxing is insufficient to overcome their unwillingness, stop the interview.

Do not lead the child by offering a possible place for the event or name for the perpetrator. Start the conversation by asking what happened, or "I need you to tell me what happened to you." Ask simple and direct questions for clarification. Be as open-ended as possible to solicit narratives. Don't ask questions that can be answered with "yes" or "no". Determine whether threats were made if the child divulged. Close the interview by thanking the child for his or her cooperation. Do not try to exact promises about testifying.

What Is the
Cognitive Approach to Interviewing Children?

The *cognitive interviewing method* is a memory jogging and retrieval tool which was developed in the hope of improving the completeness and accuracy of eyewitness accounts. Originally designed for adults, it has been modified for use with interviewing children. Studies have determined that the cognitive interview increased the amount of correct information elicited from eyewitnesses without increasing the proportion of incorrect information (Geiselman, Bornstein, & Saywitz, 1992). However, it does not prevent the child from reporting false information after having been subjected to a misleading suggestion.

Cognitive Interviewing Techniques

The cognitive approach is thought to be useful when interviewing younger children because they tend to give less complete information, although their cognitive ability is not that different from older children (Hayes &

Delamonthe, 1997). The method is deceptively simple, but requires practice in order to become proficient! It stresses the use of a secluded quiet place, free of distractions along with urging subjects to speak slowly. It is useful for questioning both victims and witnesses. Most of this approach incorporates traditional interviewing techniques, but includes the improved method of recalling information through memory jogging techniques rather than direct questioning. This method is only used with a willing participant.

Caretaker Instructions Phase

Prepare the guardian, parent, or caretaker in the same way that is expected for any forensic interview. Request that the person not ask the victim-child about the abuse. Put them at ease by answering any questions that would not jeopardize the investigation. Obtain the necessary release forms from the guardian, parent, or caretaker to conduct the interview with the child.

Practice Interview

A practice cognitive interview is optional, but recommended (Geiselman et al., 1992). If a practice interview is used, the interviewer should be different from the person who conducts the practice session. Giving the child experience with being interviewed serves to clarify the methods that will be used in the actual interview and encourages the child to use recall techniques. Introduce the child to a scenario that will be used to practice for the actual interview though a short video or the introduction of a person that has short conversation with the child and leaves the room. Tell the child that they will now practice for the interview that will happen another time with . . . the "detective," or "Mary," or the "social worker." Research has indicated that children who were given a practice cognitive interview on an unrelated event prior to the actual cognitive interview gave the most complete reports about the event (Geiselman et al., 1992).

Establish Rapport: Cognitive Interview Step 1

The new interviewer must establish rapport and prepare the child prior to questioning. Instruct the child that this is the interview he or she has been waiting for to talk about what has happened to them. Rapport development here is the same as with the forensic interviewing approach. Consideration must be given to assuring that the child is relaxed and comfortable prior to the interview. Positive and open-ended questions promote expanded conversation, such as asking the child about his or her favorite TV show.

Interviewers prepare the child for upcoming questions with the following instructions (Geiselman et al., 1992):

1. There may be some questions that you do not know the answers to. That's okay. Nobody can remember everything. If you don't know the answer to a question, then tell me "I don't know," but do not guess or make anything up. It is very important to tell me only what you really remember. Only what really happened.

2. If you do not want to answer some of the questions, you don't have to. That's ok. Tell me, "I don't want to answer that question."

3. If you do not know what something I ask you means, tell me, "I don't know what you mean." Tell me to say it in new words.

4. I may ask you some questions more than one time. Sometimes I forget that I already asked you that question. You don't have to change your answer. Just tell me what you remember the best you can.

Been There . . . Done That! 7–3

Leading questions are so dangerous in interviewing because they may provide misinformation to the person being interviewed. It can happen very subtly that a victim or witness is given misinformation without specifically stating the answer; they come to believe a response is expected. If they don't know the answer, one is made up. Once a victim or witness has misinformation there is a chance that they will repeat it with increased emphasis. One day I took a 6-year-old boy though the station as a way to establish rapport. He went over to my desk and was allowed to sit in my chair. We lingered a few moments making easy conversation. We then started walking though the office back to the room where the interview was to occur. This child knew exactly why he was

there and started talking about being abused before we made it past all of the desks in the office.

My mistake was in not insulating him from distractions that would cause misinformation. Walking past the rows of detectives sitting at their own desks, he caught a glimpse of the shiny gold badge worn by the Sergeant. At that exact time I asked, "What did he (the man who sexually abused him) look like?" Without hesitation the child pointed to the Sergeant with the shiny gold badge and loudly exclaimed "he looked like HIM!" As I ran the child out of the room I heard something like, "get that _____ _____ kid out of here!" I would not recommend starting an interview while walking . . .

Reconstruction and Report Everything: Cognitive Interview Step 2

In step 2 the first two mnemonic techniques are used. The child is asked to **reconstruct the circumstances** surrounding the incident. The child is coaxed to give a narrative account of what happened. The interviewer should listen intently and not interrupt. Notes should be taken sparingly; it would best if the interview were being video or audio taped. Someone listening to the interview, but outside of the view of the child, would take more complete notes.

Instructing the child to reconstruct the circumstances of the incident, include these sample directions. Example: "Picture the time when [the scenario], as if it was happening right now. Tell me what it was like. Tell me out loud. Where there any smells? Was it dark? Was it light? Was there anyone else there? Who? What things were there? How were you feeling?" This description includes not only the appearance of the scene, the people present or nearby, but also the child's thoughts and feelings at the time of the scenario.

The next part is to ask the child to start at the beginning and say from the beginning to the middle, to the end, everything they remember, even little parts that they don't think are very important. Ask the child to **report everything** that happened. Do not interrupt while the child is talking. Prompt by asking what happened only when needed. Clarify at this point by asking open-ended questions whenever possible. Do not ask more than one question at a time. Speak in a relaxed tone. When clarifying details that the child has provided a positive questioning approach is recommended.

Praise the child's effort, not the content of the responses. For example, the interviewer should say, "I understand what you are saying," or, "you are doing a great job in explaining to me." Do not say, "Thanks for telling me what Uncle Joe did to you."

Changing the Order and Perspective: Cognitive Interview Step 3

The third step in the child version of cognitive interviewing consists of using the second two memory-jogging techniques to enhance the narrative account. Any or all of these techniques may used in the interview depending on the information that is being sought.

- ◆ **Change the order.** The child is asked to recall what happened in backward order, from the end to the beginning. Prepare the child for that technique before asking. After each response ask the child, "What happened right before that?"
- ◆ **Change the perspective.** The child is asked to recount the incident from a new perspective. This is done by instructing the child to say what they would have seen through the eyes of an inanimate object, such as a stuffed animal that was present. Avoid asking the child to recount from the perspective of the perpetrator.

Additional memory jogging techniques may be useful when looking to clarify specific information that has been provided by the child. Examples include:

- ◆ **Alphabet search.** In order to help the child to remember names or places, ask the child to go through the alphabet to help recall the information.
- ◆ **Speech characteristics.** Probe for speech traits if the offender was not identified. Ask if the voice reminded the child of anyone or was unusual in any way.
- ◆ **Conversation.** Ask how the child felt about what was said. Were there any unusual phrases or words used by the perpetrator?

Research suggests that using only two of the original cognitive procedures will have a positive impact on the quality of the interview with a child (Hayes & Delamonthe, 1997). In the most recent version of the cognitive method the two methods incorporated into the child interview were **reconstruct the circumstances** and **report everything**. The overall approach of thinking out loud and giving a narrative account add to the completeness of the child report.

The Child as a Reporter

The only people that should be present in the interview room are the child being interviewed and the one designated to conduct the interview. The presence of significant others to the child WILL affect the interview process (Morison, Moir, & Kwansa, 2000). The interviewer cannot know beforehand if that influence will be positive or negative. Supporting parents or friends may act to encourage the child to divulge and a disapproving parent (or one the child perceives to be disapproving) will have the opposite effect.

The nature of the relationship between the child and the interviewer is one of the most important components of a successful interview. A child that feels respected and secure will communicate more openly and honestly than those who feel threatened by the process.

Been There . . . Done That! 7–4

Early in a career of interviewing children I learned from trial and error what items should be kept out of the interview room! One particular child grew increasingly anxious as he began to divulge being sexually molested. As he was pressed with follow-up questions about specifics he became avoidant. Everything that could be picked up became a focus for him. Gently I would take the toys away and ask for him to explain things to me. Exasperated, he picked up a bottle of glue and poured it into my hair! That was quickly followed by a toy hurled in my direction. We did talk some more, but afterwards, everything sharp and sticky was removed from the room! Don't expect children to enjoy the process any more than you would if you were asked to talk about your own negative experiences. Your goal is to make a potentially uncomfortable situation as comfortable as possible though your attitude and kind nature. The articles in the child interviewing room should be selected carefully. Do not include toys or otherwise distracting items, and leave out the glue!

Accuracy

A child's account of events may be incomplete. This does not mean that they aren't telling the truth. They tend to block out events, and the interview may produce information regarding a prior incident intermingled with a present event. The interviewer should know before beginning any history that might exist of prior victimization so that clarifications might be made during the interview. If leading questions are asked the responses may be distorted. Inaccurate responses also occur if the child does not fully understand the question, but will rarely acknowledge that comprehension was an issue. Interviewers will increase the probability of accurate responses through the use of age-appropriate language and confirming throughout the interview that the child understands.

Children may have difficulty disclosing events that they find embarrassing or humiliating (Morison et al., 2000). Then again, adults have similar problems! This means that the interviewer should be sensitive to the child's self-esteem. Compliance during the process can be increased if the child is a willing participant to the interview. Taking the time to engage cooperation through the rapport building stage is extremely important. Neutralizing the setting for the interview may help in decreasing shyness.

Memory and Fantasy

Research suggests that when children are interviewed it is difficult to determine with certainty whether the child is recounting something suggested, coached, or actually witnessed by the child on the basis of the child's memory alone (Lindberg, Chapman, Samsock, Thomas, & Lindberg, 2003). The best results for a pristine memory recall might be obtained from interviewers learning to keep quiet and allow the child take over in the first open free recall attempt. Although adult memory is not always accurate we do not question adult recollections to the same extent as we question the memory of children. Always investigate for corroborating evidence in cases of child abuse. To minimize fantasy during a child interview avoid using terms such as *pretend* or *imagine*.

The Child as a Victim

There are numerous considerations when interviewing a child who is suspected of being a victim of abuse. The interview may uncover both direct and indirect forms of abuse. An injury or a pattern of injuries that is nonaccidental characterizes direct child abuse. It is damage to a child for which there is no explanation that is reasonable or fitting to the injuries that the child has sustained. Such abuse may take these forms: emotional and psychological maltreatment; physical injury abuse; and sexual abuse. Another form of direct maltreatment is considered passive; the action or inaction of a legally recognized caretaker who fails to fulfill his or her responsibility to a dependent child. These neglectful categories of abuse are becoming more familiar to criminal justice and social service agencies as they struggle to enforce an increasing number of child protection statutes. Examples of passive maltreatment are neglect, which may be physical or emotional; educational neglect; inadequate care in such areas as food, clothing, and shelter; lack of supervision; denial or the lack of medical care; nonsupport of minor child; and parental kidnapping.

Two categories of *secondary abuse* are covered here: witnessing domestic violence and witnessing the homicide of a parent. Secondary abuse occurs as the consequence of residing in a violent home. Violence toward an intimate partner causes a variety of psychological problems for the children and places them at greater risk for delinquency and adult criminality. Research has suggested that those children subjected to violence through child victimization and the witnessing of abuse in the home have higher rates of violence as adults (Heyman & Slep, 2002). In homes where a parent is battered there is approximately a 50/50 chance that children in the home are also being abused. Although we cannot predict which children will become victims of abuse, those that reside in violent homes are at greater risk. When responding to calls of domestic abuse an officer should interview all children residing in the home. This type of interview is generally short. Questions should not be asked within sight of either parent. An initial question is, "Are you ok?" Watching for the response, the officer/interviewer will determine if they need to sit down and talk in depth about the situation.

The victims can be found throughout society with no regard to age or gender. This does not mean that all children are victimized, but that boys and girls of all ages are represented as victims. A child is defined as a person under the age of 18, except in those states that specify a younger age. Always interview the children in a home when responding to domestic violence.

Been There . . . Done That! 7–5

The interviewer needs to speak the language of the child. Allowing children to get comfortable with the anatomical dolls and to supply me with vocabulary to use during the interview, I would point to the eye, to the nose, to the chest, etc. on the doll. Each time I would ask, "What is this called?" Sometimes it is hard to keep from laughing; no positive or negative response should be given! Be prepared for anything! Wingy, dingy, fred, flop, friend, mine, po, pet, ping are among the many responses I have heard!

Tools for Interviewing Children

The use of drawing is very helpful when interviewing any child under the age of twelve, and some cases older children. Paper and crayons are important tools to have available in all interview rooms. Use crayons to build rapport. Ask the child what their favorite color is; allow them to use one crayon that they have chosen. This simple act gives some control to the child, acknowledges something of value to him or her, and it establishes if they know colors. The rest of the crayons may be then put aside so that they do not become a distraction. Do not have glue, scissors, or toys available in the interview room that will provide an opportunity to avoid distressing topics. Drawings may be used to express better what has happened to them.

In recent research ninety 4- to 13-year-old victims of sexual abuse were interviewed by police officers who showed the children a human figure drawing and asked questions (Aldridge et al., 2004). The drawing and associated questions brought an average of 86 new forensically relevant details of the event and was particularly helpful with 4- to 7-year-olds. The authors of the study recommend that a gender neutral drawing be used and that it should be introduced in the later part of the interview to expand recall. When using the pictures instruct the child to mark a picture using their crayon. Instructions should be clear and simple. For example: Put an **X** on the picture where you were kissed and circle the place on you where you were touched.

Anatomically correct dolls are a helpful tool for a variety of reasons. First, they help to establish the child's vocabulary so that the interviewer can use language that is understood by both of you. The dolls can also be used by the child to demonstrate what had occurred against them. Caution should be exercised in using dolls with extremely young children whose reasoning is not developed to the point of realizing that an object can also serve as a representation of an object (Morison et al., 2000).

Bolstering Credibility through Evidence

Credibility refers to the believability of the witness or victim. It is a major factor that must be established during an interview. To help determine if a person is credible the interviewer considers if the person can comprehend what is being said. How is her or his observation of things around them? Can they see well enough to describe events as they observed them? Does the nonverbal behavior indicate possible deception? For states that do not have a pre-determined age required to testify, credibility would

---

Been There . . . Done That! 7–6

Nine-year-old Tim reported that mommy's boyfriend made him stand in front of Mickey Mouse while he shot him. Tim stated that he thought he was dead when the bullets went so close to his head. When Virgil put the gun down Tim ran into the bedroom and jumped onto the bed. Virgil came after him and tried to break his head open with the end of the gun, but it hit the wall instead. A search warrant was obtained for Virgil's one-bedroom house. The wall next to the bed evidenced a hole that was consistent with the butt of a rifle. Small ammunitions and a handgun were retrieved in addition to a rifle. As the search continued, a poster of Mickey Mouse was located between the mattresses. There were small holes that perfectly matched the ones found on the hall door. One hole was measured as being one inch higher than the height of Tim. The door was seized along with the other evidence. At trial mom testified that Tim was a liar and had fabricated the assault. Nothing spoke louder than the poster of Mickey Mouse and the door riddled with bullet holes. The jury gasped when Tim was instructed by prosecution to stand in front of Mickey Mouse and they saw that bullet holes aligned with his little body. Virgil was convicted!

This is a picture of the door where Tim was made to stand while being shot at. Notice the bullet holes and the place where the Mickey Mouse picture had hung.

Note the bullet holes on Mickey's face! This was the poster that was found in a search of the home where the assault in *Been There... Done That 7–6* occurred. It was hidden under a mattress.

be established as part of the process when determining competency. Gathering physical evidence is a way to enhance the credibility of a child.

There is no substitution for physical evidence to support the child's statement. When interviewing a child, make note of any object that is involved with the crime that might later be seized with a legally obtained search warrant. Clarify during the interview the exact location and description of any possible evidence. Obtaining physical evidence for use in prosecution is helpful when the victim is an adult. For abuse against children this is a critical part of the case! Merely presenting the word of a child against the word of an adult makes prosecutions more difficult. Seek a search warrant if the place of the event is exactly known and the perpetrator has positively been identified.

What would the interviewer search to bolster credibility? Anything! If a child describes being physically assaulted with any object, the investigator should seize that object. If the place is anywhere other than his or her own residence, it might be photographed inside to compare with the child's description of the area. When the victim divulges sexual molestation the subject of the search includes any area where tissues, towels, magazines, lubricants, or photos are kept by the perpetrator.

If the victim child is severely injured or has died the place of death must be searched to determine, if possible, if the explanations for the injury are consistent with the environment.

Determining Competency and Reliability

During the investigation of suspected child abuse the most likely source of information will come from the victim. Standing alone, eyewitness testimony is considered the least reliable form of evidence. Reliability issues compounded with the suggestibility of children and limited memory development heightens the search for methods to improve child testimony as an urgent investigation. Studies have confirmed that children do have the ability to communicate reliably when questioned properly (Morison et al., 2000).

Competency is a preliminary question of law that the judge must decide before the witness will be permitted to testify. There is no federal standard for determining competency. The 1974 federal rules of evidence abolished the competency rule for trial in federal courts. Over one third of states followed the federal example when it comes to the child witness and do not require a competency inquiry (Abrams & Ramsey S. H., 2000). We assume all adults to be competent; thirteen states presume that a person over the age of ten is competent to testify. Eighteen states require demonstration that the child understands the nature and obligation of the oath to tell the truth. Competency determination hinges in one part whether the child has the capacity to recall events, separate fact from fantasy, and maintain those memories independently without being influenced by others. The second part of the determination is that the child has a sense of moral responsibility defined as understanding the duty to speak the truth (Abrams & Ramsey S. H., 2000).

Conclusions

This chapter begins with a description of the child developmental stages. This section is an important foundation for conducting interviews with children. While children do not develop exactly the same, knowledge of children's development can assist the interviewer in determining who the best individual to conduct the interview is. The chapter also provided some insight into the role of the criminal justice investigator when interviewing children. Throughout are discussions on the problems specific to obtaining reliable and credible statements from children given their suggestibility and immature cognitive development. Specific techniques, cognitive and forensic, were explained in detail with example questions suggested. The cognitive approach has been shown to provide more accurate information, but it is a more lengthy method.

Chapter Seven Questions for Review

Short Answer Questions

1. What are the considerations in the Common Preliminary Checklist?

2. What are the three models for evaluating abuse?

3. In regard to obtaining evidence, what are the questions an interviewer must know in order to proceed with the criminal process?

4. Compare and contrast the Forensic and Cognitive approaches to interviewing on each dimension.

5. What are some of the concerns that an interviewer should be aware of regarding the child as reporter?

6. What are the types of abuse that can occur with a child being interviewed?

7. Briefly discuss the developmental stages of a child.

8. What are the four mnemonics used in the cognitive child interview approach?

Fill-in Questions

1. The three approaches recognized by the American Professional Society on the abuse of children are

_____ ,
_____ , and _____ .

2. A _____ will assess the present and future risk of harm to a child.

3. How many states have legislation that requires certain professionals to report when a child is at risk due to suspected child abuse or neglect?

4. Evidence that is sought through a police investigation of child abuse includes _____ , _____ , and _____ .

5. The _____ is conducted when primary victimization is suspected.

6. The two categories of secondary abuse include _____ and _____ .

7. _____ and _____ are helpful tools when interviewing children.

8. During _____ children communicate with utterances, crying, and gestures.

9. _____ age group usually needs to gain your trust and need more attention and support to compensate for the violation that occurred toward them.

Exercises

Practice your cognitive interviewing techniques. Divide into pairs. One student will be the interviewer and the other will be the interviewee.

1. The interviewer is to find out as much detail as possible about the interviewee's last experience taking an exam. Instruct the interviewee on the **report every detail approach.** Take five minutes for this mnemonic exercise.

2. The interviewers are asked to recall what they learned about their partner's last exam. Take five minutes for this discussion.

3. Continue with the interview. Instruct the interviewee on using the technique to **reconstruct the circumstances** surrounding their exam experience. For example, they should be asked to describe the surroundings, room, furniture, etc. Remember that the interviewer should not interrupt their partner once they begin. Take five minutes for this mnemonic exercise.

4. Share any new information with the class that came out of this approach. Take five minutes for this discussion.

5. Continue with the interview. Ask the interviewee to recall the story in reverse order, and then from the perspective of someone else who was there at the time. Take ten minutes for this mnemonic exercise.

6. Discuss with the class any new information they learned about the exam.

Reference List

Abrams, D. E., & Ramsey S. H. (2000). *Children and the law: Doctrine, policy, and practice.* St. Paul, MN: West Group.

Aldridge, J., Lamb, M., Sternberg, K., Orbach, Y., Esplin, P., & Bowler, L. (2004). Using a human figure drawing to elicit information from alleged victims of child sexual abuse. *Journal of Consulting and Clinical Psychology, 72*(2), 304–316.

Faller, K. C. (1996). *Evaluating children suspected of having been sexually abused.* Thousand Oaks, CA: Sage Publications.

Geiselman, R. E., Bornstein, G., & Saywitz, K. (1992). *New approach to interviewing children: A test of its effectiveness.* (Report No. NCJ 135011). Washington, DC: National Institute of Justice.

Hayes, B. K., & Delamonthe, K. (1997). Cognitive interviewing procedures and suggestibility in children's recall. *Journal of Applied Psychology, 82*(4), 562–577.

Heyman, R. E., & Slep, A. M. S. (2002). Do child abuse and interparental violence lead to adulthood family violence? *Journal of Marriage and Family, 64*(4), 864–871.

Lanning, K. (2002). Criminal investigation of sexual victimization of children. J. Myers, L. Berliner, J. Briere, C. T. Hendrix, C. Jenny, & T. Reid (editors), *The APSAC Handbook on Child Maltreatment* (2nd ed., pp. 329–348). Thousands Oaks, CA: Sage Publication.

Lindberg, M. A., Chapman, M. T., Samsock, D., Thomas, S. W., & Lindberg, A. W. (2003). Comparisons of three different investigative interview techniques. *The Journal of Genetic Psychology, 164*(1), 5–28.

Morison, M., Moir, J., & Kwansa, T. (2000). Interviewing children for the purposes of research in primary care. *Primary Health Care Research and Development, 1,* 113–130.

Pence, D., & Wilson, C. (1992). *The role of law enforcement in the response to child abuse and neglect.* Washington, DC: National Center on Child Abuse and Neglect.

Saywitz, K. J., Goodman, G. S., & Lyon, T. D. (2002). Interviewing children in and out of court. J. E. Myers, L. Berline, J. Briere, H. Terry, C. Jenny, & T. Reid (editors), *The APSAC Handbook on Child Maltreatment* (2nd ed., pp. 349-377). Thousand Oaks, CA: Sage Publications.

Saywitz, K. J., Snyder, L., & Nathanson, R. (1999). Facilitating the communicative competence of the child witness. *Applied Developmental Science, 3*(1), 58–69.

Walton, S. (2003). When violence hits home. *State Legislatures, 29*(6), 31–34.

Interviewing Elders

KEY TERMS

Abandonment	Active neglect
Aging-out	Conversation-observing evaluation
Fiduciary Abuse	Passive neglect
Self-neglect	Source contamination

CHAPTER OBJECTIVES

After completing this chapter you should be able to:

- ◆ Explain the changing demographics of the elder population
- ◆ State the concerns regarding elder perpetrators
- ◆ Define self-neglect
- ◆ Explain the difference between active and passive abuse
- ◆ Compare and contrast the interviewing techniques involving older persons
- ◆ List the categories of crimes targeting the elderly
- ◆ Describe the characteristics of the most common perpetrators against the elderly
- ◆ Explain the concept of a multidisciplinary approach to elder crime
- ◆ List ways of building a case involving an elder victim

Introduction

There is a growing awareness among professionals that older Americans are targets of illegal activities; crimes are committed with little intervention from traditional sources. These targets are identified by age and graying hair; they are perceived as being vulnerable by offenders who may be bullies, impaired or overwhelmed caregivers, and by narcissistic or greedy individuals. The situation has not developed purposefully, but may be the result of undervaluing the nation's elderly for so many years. Responding to the crimes against the elderly, or committed by the elderly, is historically of low priority for the criminal justice community. The offenses are viewed as crimes against individuals instead of the traditional view of crimes against society. Few perpetrators are prosecuted; even less crime is reported.

These cases present many challenges to the criminal justice community; our responses produce less than stellar results. Listening to the complaints of elder citizens is time consuming and often arduous; seldom acknowledged as meaningful police work. Policy makers and researchers are now recognizing the extent of problems that affect elders and are only recently identifying the role of the criminal justice system to combat them. Protecting the victim and holding the offender accountable *is* real police work, regardless of victim characteristics or relationship to the offender. Unless the criminal justice community views the criminal acts of elder abuse as criminal behavior, experts suggest that the violence will continue (Rohn, 1999).

Responses to elder crime are being modified, but what has changed? Demographics are the largest contributing factor to the shifting policy concerning elder crime. No longer is America dominated by the youthful. The number of teenagers in the United States was surpassed by the elderly in 1983. Seniors are the fastest growing segment of the population, which is expected to double by 2030 when 1 in 5 Americans will be age 65 or older (CDC, 2000). Along with this population explosion, comes the shameful problem of crime committed against the elderly. Every year an estimated 2.1 million older Americans are victims of physical, psychological, or other forms of abuse and neglect. These high numbers exist in spite of the majority of older citizens (70%) reporting their health as good or excellent (Bonnie & Wallace, 2002).

Past practices have relied almost exclusively on the interview with the elder victim along with their request for prosecution. This approach puts the senior in the position of being further threatened and physically abused by the perpetrator. Caregiver stress is often cited as a major cause of elder abuse. This "excuse" has been dismissed for the majority of cases involving domestic abuse to elders (Brandl, 2000). Unreliable memory, infirmity, and even the concern of impending death to the victim place an extraordinary reliance on the victim interview. For these reasons, this chapter will be broadened to include a general approach to these crimes in addition to suggestions on interviewing. Legislative changes have amplified the role of the criminal justice community to cases involving crimes against the elderly. Simply put, law enforcement must be concerned about its response to elder abuse because it is the law (OVC, 1993).

Crimes Targeting the Elderly

According to the Bureau of Justice Statistics, elders in the United States are victimized by crime at rates far below that of younger people (Klaus, 2005). Elderly is defined as being aged 65 or older. Only personal larceny, such as purse snatching and pick-pocketing, occurs against the elderly at approximately the same rate as other age groups. While persons aged 65 and older are not victimized by violent crime as often as younger persons, when they are targeted they are as likely to be seriously injured.

Domestic Violence

The majority of violence against elders is domestic abuse. In 1987, the federal government first described elder abuse, neglect, and exploitation under the Amendments to the Older Americans Act (National Committee for the Prevention of Elder Abuse, 2005). Abuse is categorized as domestic abuse and institutional abuse. Within these broad categories, physical, sexual, emotional/psychological abuse may occur, along with neglect, self-neglect, abandonment, and financial exploitation. It is estimated that for every one case of elder abuse, neglect, exploitation, or self-neglect reported to authorities, about five more go unreported (National Center on Elder Abuse, 1998).

Examples of domestic crimes that may be directed at the elderly include:

1. *Self-neglect,* the failure to provide for one's own essential needs is the most frequent form of elder abuse. This is a non-criminal activity that might result in civil intervention by criminal justice and social services on the victim's behalf.

2. *Abandonment* is the desertion of an elderly person by an individual who has assumed responsibility for providing care for an

elder, or by a person with physical custody of an elder (National Committee for the Prevention of Elder Abuse, 2003).

3. *Active neglect* is a deliberate attempt by a caregiver to inflict injury or emotional stress on an older person; examples include intentional withholding of needed medication or food due to the costs involved.

4. *Passive neglect is* the unintentional failure to fulfill a caretaking obligation where no willful desire to inflict physical or emotional distress exists; examples include the denial of adequate food or health services due to ignorance or carelessness on the part of the caretaker.

5. *Physical abuse* results in harm to the victim which can involve a number of activities including hitting, slapping, and physically restraining the victim.

6. *Sexual abuse* is forced sexual contact with an individual due to the lack of consent or who is incapable of exercising consent because of physical or mental impairments.

Questions need to be asked by the investigator that will determine if the condition of the elder is the result of self-neglect or is the consequence of criminal activity due to any of the above categories. Information that may be helpful in making this determination includes the following:

- Interview neighbors and other witnesses to identify those who might have relevant information and how they might be contacted.
- Identify and interview the victim's doctor, conservator, attorney, social worker, and any agencies that provide services to the victim.
- Ask the victim who lives with them or makes visits.
- Look to see if there are any ligature marks on the wrists, legs, or around the neck of the victim that would indicate the use of restraints.
- Check to see if the elder has food in the house: ask if someone prepares meals for him or her and determine who does the shopping.
- If the elder is in a confused state, determine through medical personnel if the individual is being overmedicated, or is suffering from mental impairment.
- If the abuse occurred in a residential setting, interview the staff to determine who has witnessed the abuse.

Fiduciary Abuse

A major category of crime against the elderly is fiduciary abuse. *Fiduciary abuse* is the financial exploitation or economic abuse of elders; it covers a range of criminal conduct concerning misappropriated property belonging to the elder. Two categories of fiduciary abuse are the fraud

Been There . . . Done That! 8–1

In response to a call on stolen property I went to the home of Mr. James
who was 82 years old at the time. The
elder man stated that someone had
stolen his wallet. He told me that
he was in his barn putting blueberries
in boxes when he realized the wallet
was not in his back pocket. Since he
sold blueberries from a street stand,
Mr. James claimed any one of the people who bought berries that morning
could have been a pickpocket. Before
jumping to any conclusions I asked Mr.
James to retrace his steps with me.
As we moved from the farm stand to
the barn I noticed a wallet lying on
the ground. He claimed the wallet was
in fact his. After checking its contents he proclaimed that nothing was
missing. Mr. James was very embarrassed—so I assured him that it was
no problem and we shared a few blueberries. Were Mr. James's fears of a
pickpocket victimization unrealistic?
Had we not found the wallet, what
would have been done next?

committed by strangers and financial exploitation perpetrated by family
members or caregivers. These two categories require different approaches
by law enforcement due to the offender/victim relationship (Johnson,
2003). In some states there is a legal expectation that the elder suffers
harm due to the financial abuse or that the perpetrator gain from the
financial transaction (Johnson, 2003). Indicators of fiduciary abuse
include:

- Uncharacteristic bank activity for the elder.
- Suspicious activity on the elder person's credit card accounts.
- Frequent or unauthorized use of the person's ATM card.
- A will has been drawn up that has not been witnessed.

Although the exact numbers are believed to reflect underreporting,
elders are victimized by consumer fraud at a rate that exceeds the victimization of those under age 50 (U.S. Department of Health and Human
Services, 2000). Telemarketing scams, in addition to health care and
investment schemes are examples of stranger fraud.

Initial Considerations When Questioning the Older Person

The priority of the crisis responder is to render first aid and identify the
victim. Once the scene is safe, the persons at the scene should be separated and interviewed. Videotape the interview whenever possible, the
alternative should be an audio tape. This serves to document the abuse

and the condition of the victim at the time of the offense. The videotape serves to preserve the evidence if a prosecution determination is made that does not include the victim testimony. Photographs of injuries and of living conditions should be taken for documentation.

When investigating complaints of crime committed against an elder the interview process is similar to the approach taken with any other population. An additional initial step helps to determine which interviewing technique would be most suitable.

The Pre-Interview

The initial recommended step is a pre-interview of the elder in order to make an assessment. The *conversation-observing evaluation* is an approach for the assessment of the elder through direct observation for the purpose of identifying the limitations of the interviewee and the nature of the offense. The evaluation should not be biased by the opinion of persons who care for the elder or those who have a relationship with that person. Except for a police officer or social service worker observer, no other persons should be present besides the elder and the interviewer at this stage. While a determination must be made on the extent of victim participation that can be expected, the mental or physical status of the abused does not dictate the failure or success of any investigation. Medical and physical evidence in addition to witness statements and expert testimony should be considered in all cases, and in particular to those that involve vulnerable victims.

- ◆ Begin this phase without preconceived ideas on the ability of the victim to testify or about the nature of the offenses. Health concerns need to be identified, but are not the primary consideration in the investigation of crimes against the elderly.
- ◆ Speak with the elder at the place where he or she is most comfortable. For most elders this will be the place that they live, although the situation may dictate that this pre-interview take place in a hospital room. The approach necessitates that the interviewee be as comfortable as possible.
- ◆ Think of this stage as a "friendly visit." Avoid making statements that are judgmental. Have a cup of coffee and talk . . . at the same time remaining alert to behavioral indicators displayed by the victim. This is not the time to delve into specifics of alleged abuse or neglect. A common error made by police officers in other situations that is to be avoided is the failure to develop the situation.
- ◆ The interviewer should put him or herself at the same level as the interviewee, asking the victim where he or she wants you to sit. Place yourself face front to the person so that you can observe the individual and where the elder can also see your face clearly.

◆ Refrain from taking notes before asking permission to do so.

◆ Introduce yourself and state generally your purpose. For example: "My name is Denise Gosselin. I am a police officer. I have been asked to come and talk with you today. Is that ok?"

◆ Ask the person for their full name, even if you already have that information. Refer to the elder by her or his title — Miss, Mrs., Mr., Dr., etc.

At this point it should be obvious if the interviewee is having difficulty communicating. You are evaluating the ability of this person to answer simple questions. Look for signs that she or he is having difficulty hearing or seeing you. Does the elder lean forward towards you? Are you noticing the tendency to look at your lips when you speak? If you notice problems, ask the person if he or she needs ancillary devices such as a hearing aid.

◆ Encourage the elder to talk about him or herself and comment in ways that promotes discussion. During the conversation these points should be covered, but the questions are not asked in a traditional interview format.

Suggested questions include:

1. "How are you feeling today?" This question helps to determine what physical conditions and limitations, if any, exist. When the conversation turns to illness, ask if the person needs medication for the condition. If so, how often is it needed and do they take the medication regularly? Does she or he take the medication themselves, or does someone give it to them to take? Determine if the interviewee drinks alcoholic beverages on a daily basis, documenting the preferred drink.

2. "How old are you?" Encourage the elder with positive comments regarding age. Use the information to facilitate conversation about the individual's ability to hear, see, and walk. Determine what forms of aid the individual needs, if any. While the physical condition may seem apparent, the investigator should still talk about the strengths and weaknesses faced by the individual.

3. "How long have you lived here?" And, "Is this your house?" These questions help to determine if dependency exists with respect to the living arrangements. Listen for indications that *it used to be my house, but . . . .* Determine if the elder is financially dependent on another person.

4. "Do you live here by yourself?" Ask this even if it seems apparent. Clarify if anyone lives temporarily with the elder such as a family member or friend. Look for signs of discomfort when the

older person is talking about family or friends that spend time with the elder. How isolated is this person? Are there any social supports?

5. "Do you live with your husband (or wife)?" or "How does your spouse treat you?" Be particularly aware of anxiety or discomfort when discussing a spouse or if the individual begins to offer excuses, such as "I am so difficult to take of" or "He doesn't mean to take it out on me." Listen and be patient. Do not attempt to be friendly by adding to or acknowledging the validity of statements regarding behaviors. Attempt to learn as much as possible about the dynamics of the relationship. Remember that both males and females may be abusive to an elder spouse.

6. "Excuse me for prying, but may I ask if you are on a retirement pension or receive social security?" "Are you doing ok financially?" "Have you made any financial arrangements with someone to take care of you?" Attempt to get a sense of the anxiety level associated with the financial situation of the person. Is there a fear that their money will be depleted? What is the source of that fear?

7. "Is there anyone that helps you out with your daily living?" Identify who the individuals are that occupy a caretaking role and the relationship between the elder and the caregiver. "Do you pay this person?" "Do they ask for money or gifts?" Does the older person have reasonable expectations on the extent of care that they receive?

During this stage you have been gathering information on the living conditions of the victim and the relationships that are involved with her or him. You are slowly coming to an assessment of the individual; the ability of the person to relate information, and the overall ability to communicate. If the victim's skills are within the normal to high range with seemingly accurate information being related, then the traditional methods of conducting the actual information might be the best approach. If the individual appears confused or has difficulty remembering events, the cognitive method may be the future interviewing choice. When the questioning appears difficult due to a mental illness (including Alzheimer's disease) an interdisciplinary team approach might offer the best interviewing alternative. In the rare event that the elder is unable to relate any information that could be considered credible, or the elder has died, the investigator must rely on collecting sufficient evidence in the event prosecution needs to take place without the victim's testimony.

If evidence of abuse is discovered and the perpetrator is defined as having a domestic relationship to the victim, such as a spouse, former spouse, child, parent, or live-in person, then proceed according to your department policy for domestic violence. Mandatory and preferred arrest policies do not make an exception when the victim is an older person! Financial abuse, physical or sexual abuse, intimidation, and threats are domestic violence offenses when the perpetrator is in a legally recognized domestic relationship to the victim. There are no exclusions for police action in cases of domestic violence that are based on age or infirmary. The opposite is true in many jurisdictions; where a victim is elder, the crime is enhanced.

Case Creditability

Case creditability may be enhanced through physical evidence in addition to the testimonial evidence from a victim. Some states allow for evidence to be admitted to court testimony when a victim is unavailable due to death or sickness (Zahner, 1999). Your state law should be researched in the anticipation of cases involving absent elderly victims. Evidence obtained from medical personnel, home-health aides, and advocates are particularly relevant to cases involving elder victimization. In a study on institutional abuse conducted by Pillemer and Moore (1989) approximately one third of the resident physical abuse by staff members was witnessed by other staff members (Loue, 2001).

Medical records are an invaluable tool for the investigation of elder abuse cases (Boutin, 1999). Among other things, the medical records contain information on the physical status of the individual, names of the physician, and contact information for family members. Photographs of

---

Been There . . . Done That! 8–2

A female resident of a nursing home in her early 80s was refusing to eat. She had instructed the staff that she was not to be fed intravenously. On investigation it was determined that she was not physically impaired and had no history or indication of mental illness. There was no history of prior abuse. In conversation she stated that her only daughter had abandoned her. The adult daughter had gone on vacation with her husband. I asked the woman if she was aware of the consequences of not eating; she stated, "yes." She then asked, "Why is it taking so long [to die]?" I told her that she was not sick and only needed food. The woman told me that she knew what she was doing and that she did not want to be fed. This extreme form of manipulation called the "hunger strike" is documented through case examples (Duggal & Lawrence, 2001). In this example the elder was angry at her daughter for having gone away on a vacation.

injuries taken at different stages should be taken. Bank records and checkbooks provide evidence for building a case of financial abuse. Videotaped interviews with the victim may be introduced into evidence in some circumstances.

The perpetrator should be arrested if probable cause exists to do so, and the offender should be interrogated. Avoid premature determinations on the probability of prosecution. Assuming that a crime will not be prosecuted due to victim frailty or desire may result in the insufficient collection of evidence which will render the case inadequate for prosecution. In serious cases consult with the district attorney and ask what information would be helpful to aid in the successful prosecution of the case.

Conducting the Interview

The steps to interview the victim are similar to that of other populations. Preparation for the interview and the establishment of rapport with the interviewee are critical steps towards ensuring a cooperative subject.

Step I: Prepare for the Interview

Prepare for the interview by choosing a quiet location that is free of distractions and noise. Get as much information on the suspect as possible, including prior arrests and commitments. Speak with the victim's neighbors and service providers prior to the interview with the victim. The purpose of this extra step is to determine their impression of the medical and cognitive status of the interviewee and of the suspect, if one is known.

Step 2: Establish Rapport

One of the most important ways to establish rapport with an elder is through respect. Avoid treating the elder as if he or she were a child. Explain your role and what the interviewee might expect during the investigation into the allegations.

Step 3: Conduct the Interview

Begin the interview by using non-leading questions. Avoid asking questions that require a yes or no response. Keep questions short and to the point. Use language that is easily understood but not patronizing. Questions should be open-ended to encourage conversation.

If the interviewee is having difficulty remembering when events took place it may help to relate to normal daily activities such as eating or watching television. Allow the victim to relate the crime in his or her own words. Avoid the tendency to make suggestions if the elder seems slow in responding; some elders need extra time to collect their thoughts. Encourage the older person to draw pictures to describe abuse or to write down answers if necessary.

Determine if anyone was present when the offender came. Was anyone witness to the abuse? Ask if the older person if she or he knows the person who did "this." Address the fears that the elder may be reluctant to discuss the incident and to report the incident to the police or social service agency. Avoid the personal tendency to react when a victim gives information regarding any crime committed against them. Remain professional and empathetic to any abuse.

Ask the elder what the suspect will say about the allegations. The interviewer can anticipate some of the possible scenarios (Morris, 1999):

- Has the victim been told by the suspect that it was an accident (and apologized), a normal part of aging, or a figment of the confused elder's mind? (physical abuse case)
- Has the victim been told by the suspect that is what the elder wanted, that it was an accident, that there was no money for medicine (eyeglasses, food, etc), or that the suspect was a stressed care giver? (neglect elder abuse case)
- The defense will center on consent or on an argument that the event never occurred. (sexual abuse)
- Has the victim been told by the suspect that "it was a gift," (and the elder doesn't remember it), or that "it was my inheritance," or "you loaned it to me." (financial/fiduciary abuse)

Look for all of the above possible defenses when discussing the allegations and the victim's perceptions of what the suspect may have relayed to the victim. Such perceptions may be very revealing.

Step 4: End the Interview

Address any objections concerning family members. An elder may be reluctant to give permission for charges to be brought against a loved one, particularly if he or she is dependent on that person. Explain that decisions regarding the criminal charging of any person will be left to the district attorney. Advise the elder that you are mandated to report suspected abuse or neglect to the elder services. They might expect to be contacted by someone who can address their needs.

Step 5: Follow-up

Subsequent to the interview referrals to other agencies should be made, if warranted. Examples of referrals include a report to the state-mandated elder abuse hotline or social services. When injury to the elder was noted, a future interview should be scheduled to document the abuse. Documentation of an injury may necessitate photographing it days after the initial response, when bruises and marks are more prominently visible.

Been There . . . Done That! 8–3

A 90-year-old woman had been sexually abused by her adult son according to a report from the home health aide who visited Mrs. Jane at her home. The aide found that the elder was complaining about being hurt "down there." The victim was believed to have dementia. The aide thought that because the victim could not testify in court that there was no case. Is she right? What are the options?

Empowering the Elder Victim

Laws specifically protecting vulnerable adults have been enacted across the country. Legislation devised specifically for the intervention in cases where elders are unable to protect themselves against fraud, financial abuse, and from personal violence should be used where ever possible. Practices have evolved to investigate cases involving the elderly that center around the empowerment of this population in order to increase the chances of successful prosecution. When interviewing older victims respect and deference should always be a consideration. Advocates suggest providing education and enhancing the level of safety awareness and safety planning to the elder (U.S. Department of Health and Human Services, 2000).

Do not leave the final determination regarding prosecution with the victim. In all cases, victim safety must be the primary consideration, just as it is in all other criminal investigations. Legal provisions and mandated arrest policies that exist for victims of domestic violence must be utilized regardless of the age of the victim or of the perpetrator. If the victim is overly concerned with prosecution the reasons should be explored and if possible discussed with a multidisciplinary team for a final determination. When the objections of the elder victim involve fear of isolation or loss of a caretaker, then the individual's needs for services must be in place prior to a prosecution.

The Elder as a Witness

Sexual predators, drug abusers, and thieves may involve themselves with an elder they view as being vulnerable. Con-men and greedy caretakers target those that are perceived as being needy. While the likelihood of being afflicted with intellectual deterioration known as dementia or senility increases with age, it is not considered part of the normal aging process. The Office for Victims of Crime suggests that it is false to assume that older persons suffer from dementia; it is typically a reversible condition brought on by illness, malnutrition, dehydration, and other physical problems (1993). Only five to seven percent of the population is diagnosed with the well-known Alzheimer's disease (OVC, 1993). An interviewer can expect that the majority of elders are capable of giving accurate and reliable information regarding victimization.

Physical Limitations

A factor to consider when interviewing elders is the extent of substance abuse within this population. Explained as an invisible epidemic, alcohol and prescription drug misuse is thought to affect as many as 17 percent of older adults (Levin & Kruger, 2000). An elder may be overly reliant on drugs or alcohol due to changes that come naturally with aging. Remember that the responsibility for victimization or perpetration does not center on substance abuse, it is only a factor to be identified for appropriate referral and intervention.

Compared to men, elder women who are socially isolated and have hearing impairments are at greater risk of contracting late-onset schizophrenia (Sajatovic, Madhusoodanan, & Buckley, 2000). Characterized by hallucinations and delusions, this mental disease was once thought to only affect individuals with onset prior to age 45 (Sajatovic et al., 2000). The disease may be treated successfully; therefore, medical referral is an absolute necessity if this is suspected.

Normal sensatory changes due to aging include visual and hearing loss. Visual acuity may interfere with distant identifications and descriptions of strangers, but is not significant when the perpetrator is known to the individual. Older persons commonly lose the ability to hear high frequencies and experience hypersensitivity to very loud speech. When questioning seniors, the Office for Victims of Crime suggests that it is easier for an older person to understand a male rather than female since the pitch of men's voices is usually lower than that of women (1993). Persons with hearing loss often compensate by lip reading and viewing facial expressions. The individual may have a hearing aid that is not working properly or is not being worn at the time of the interview. If the interviewee is having difficulties with understanding ask if he or she has communication devices that can assist them.

When interviewing older persons the following should be considered:

- Schedule the interview for mid-morning, a time when the victim is most likely to be at her or his best.
- Refer persons for medical screening when substance abuse is suspected.
- Ask the interviewee if he or she is having difficulty in hearing, but do not assume that is the case.
- Many elders elect not to wear their hearing aid at all times. Ask the person if he or she has a hearing aid when it appears that hearing is an issue.
- Avoid speaking loudly to the elder as a way to compensate for a perceived hearing deficiency.
- The interviewer should position himself directly in front of the interviewee since he or she may compensate for hearing loss by concentrating on lip movements and facial expressions.
- Establish eye contact with the interviewee prior to speaking.
- Avoid covering your mouth, chewing gum, or smoking during the interview.
- Do not speak too quickly.
- Eliminate background noise as much as possible.
- Use visual aids such as drawings and diagrams when possible.
- Male interviewers may be a preferred option.

Cognitive Limitations

Cognitive impairments vary significantly according to individual conditions. The ability to learn and remember is expected to change as an individual ages. This means older persons may take longer to recall or process information. Memory jogging techniques may enhance the recall for elder victims. Questions such as "Were you eating dinner when he came?" and "What were you watching on television when he came?" are examples. Practice patience by allowing the elder person the time she or he needs to answer a question.

There is a growing amount of contradictory literature looking at the vulnerability of elders to source confusion. *Source confusion* is the difficulty in distinguishing what has been personally witnessed compared to what may have been heard from someone else, or a problem identifying the exact source of the information. The introduction of misinformation has been thought to impair the reliability of statements taken from elders and cause source confusion. Researchers have concluded that no clear evidence exists to suggest an age-related vulnerability to misinformation (Memon, Gabert, & Hope, 2004). Each individual being interviewed must be evaluated independently regarding the reliability of the statement, without age bias. These same researchers suggest that elders frequently recall fewer correct details of an eyewitness event as compared to younger adults. Additionally, elders are consistently more prone to making false identifications from lineups and older adults (60–80) are more likely to "false alarm" to new faces. In other words, they are more likely to falsely recognize a face they had not seen previously. In the eyewitness identification setting, elders may be more prone to making false choices and provide fewer descriptions of the perpetrator (physical, clothing, etc.).

Concerns Due to Dependence

A strong reliance on family and friends for assistance may be the reality for senior citizens preferring to maintain an independent lifestyle. In some cases, but not all situations, loneliness, frailty, and medical conditions may cause the elder to view the perpetrator as their only hope for an improved lifestyle. Since the most common abusers of the elderly are their adult children (National Center on Elder Abuse, 1998), a common risk factor exists when the caretaker is financially dependent on the elder. Dysfunctional family interactions prior to the onset of old age is likely to continue as the members get older unless intervention occurs. Consider the role of the elderly; is the individual one with an overly demanding attitude or one with unrealistic expectations of the caregiver?

When the suspect provides care or services to the elder the exact nature of the care should be determined. An interview with the suspect should document the following circumstances:

◆ Based on the condition of the elder, does it appear that the caregiver has been reluctant to supply the elder with eyeglasses, dental care, medications, or other needed services?

◆ When bedsores or incontinence exist, determine if the care being provided is sufficient to meet the needs of the elder.

◆ Are the services or care provided under a contract with specified payments?

◆ How are these payments made?

◆ Are cash payments provided by the elder or requested by the service provider?

◆ Has the suspect accepted personal gifts from the elder victim? If so, what is the approximate value of those gifts?

◆ Attempt to determine if the caregiver is frustrated or angry due to the responsibilities associated with the providing services to the elder.

Interdisciplinary Interviewing

Increasingly, criminal justice agencies are working with a variety of agencies to identify cases of suspected elder abuse and to gather evidence for prosecution of the perpetrators. The majority of reports concerning elder abuse are made to adult protective services, not the police. The Police Executive Research Forum recommends that investigations should be coordinated with adult protective services personnel or the ombudsman whenever possible to establish cooperative models of intervention (Nerenberg, 1993). Multi-disciplinary teams composed of professionals from law enforcement, adult protective services, mental health agencies, the public guardian's office, and public health agencies are one example. Teams of fiduciary abuse specialists are specially trained to work with bank officials in documenting a paper trail indicative of fiduciary abuse.

Mandatory Elder Abuse Reporting

All 50 states, the District of Columbia, and some U.S. territories require professionals to report suspected abuse or neglect of elders (Teaster, 2003). There is no consistency in the reporting guidelines and definitions. The majority of the states and territories specifically name health care professionals, such as licensed and registered nurses, physicians, and nurse aides, as mandated reporters of elder/adult abuse. Police officers are among those commonly named as mandated reporters of elder abuse.

Crime Perpetrated by Elders

As people get older they commit less crime; this is referred to as *aging out*. This does not mean that old age does not render an individual incapable of committing criminal offenses. In the past, crime committed by seniors was considered insignificant and the perpetrators pathetic rather

---

Been There . . . Done That! 8–4

The largest investigation that I participated in involved the interviewing of over 100 children suspected to have been sexually abused through a multi-generational sex-ring. Working together with the local police department and the Department of Social Services, we identified some of the perpetrators and evidence against them obtained. The sexual crimes against both male and female children were of the worst possible you can imagine. Some were crimes of incest, but these males were indiscriminate pedophiles. The oldest that I arrested was the 72-year-old grandfather. Looking extremely frail and pathetic, he was brought before the court after my arrest of him. The charges were dismissed and the prosecutor admonished me for bringing in an old man! I arrested him again on charges concerning more children that he had raped. Hot and sharp objects had been his tools. The second arrest netted a weekend in jail before an agreement of probation was secured. The man was a monster living among us, just an old one.

than criminal. As the elder population increases in numbers the criminal justice system should be prepared for the probability of the rise in the amount of domestic abuse crime perpetrated by elders. Typically, but not exclusively, this will take the form of abuse against older spouses.

This hidden aspect of old age criminal activity represents a complex social problem. Cloaked under the veil of family secrecy it is impossible to know the extent of domestic abuse committed by the elderly. The National Center on Elder Abuse has reported that an elder spouse was among those likely to perpetrate domestic violence on his or her elderly partner (Tatara, Kuzmeskus, & Duckhorn, 1997). While the majority of perpetrators are the adult children of the senior victim(s), approximately one-third of abusers are believed to be persons aged 60 and above (National Center on Elder Abuse, 1998). According to the 2000 Survey of State Adult Protective Services, the majority of identified perpetrators were a spouse or intimate to the elder victim (Teaster, 2003). The role of criminal justice is the investigation and enforcement of the law, and the protection of the victim, regardless of the perpetrator age, physical condition, or victim participation. Assuming that the victim or the perpetrator is not deserving of intervention will leave near to one-quarter of the population without criminal justice intervention—a dangerous trend for the future!

Conclusions

This chapter introduced a pre-interview step entitled the *conversation-observing approach*. This initial phase of interviewing an elder suggested at this time is used to assess the individual and to learn as much as possible about the conditions under which the elder lives. The phase also provides sufficient information to determine if a specific interviewing format should be considered in the future. Some elderly will present with physical or mental impairments that hinder investigations. Awareness of the signs and symptoms of common afflictions increases the opportunity for successful evidence gathering. Most seniors are capable of providing information to document the criminal event.

The crimes against elderly, however, may be complicated by the family relationship between the victim and the perpetrator. Law enforcement should be guided by existing legal responsibilities, mandates, department policy, and procedures in handling domestic violence cases. For complicated cases requiring special investigations a multidisciplinary team approach is recommended.

Chapter Eight Questions for Review

Short Answer Questions

1. What is a pre-interview and why is it used?

2. What is the most common form of violence against elders?

3. What are the categories of elder abuse?

4. What identifiers should you look for to determine if any of these crimes have been committed?

5. What are the interviewing limitations with this population?

6. Who are the most common abusers of the elderly?

7. What should an interviewer document when interviewing a victim who is dependent on others to take care of them?

8. What are the specific legal protections for elder victims? Find examples in your state code where these exist.

Fill-in Questions

1. In 2030 _____ in _____ Americans will be age 65 or older.

2. Every year an estimated _____ older Americans are victims of physical, psychological, or other forms of abuse and neglect.

3. One method to identify limitations of the interviewee and the nature of the offense among the elderly population is through the _____ .

4. Elders are more susceptible to _____ than younger adults, difficulty in distinguishing what they have witnessed themselves as opposed to what they may have heard from someone else.

5. _____ is the deliberate attempt by a caregiver to inflict injury or emotional stress on an older person.

6. _____ occurs when an older person is tricked, coerced, or under undue influence, signs away money or property.

7. Explained as an invisible epidemic, _____ and _____ misuse is thought to affect 17 percent of older adults.

8. When the elder victim has difficulty recalling information during an interview, _____ might be used to help them in this process.

9. Elders are victimized by consumer fraud at a rate that _____ the victimization of those under 50.

10. In order to build a case, evidence from _____ , _____ and _____ are particularly relevant.

Exercises

1. Elderly interview

   This exercise requires the student to interview a person age 65 or older. The person interviewed can be a relative, a neighbor, or someone that works on campus. The topic of the interview is whether the elder has ever been a victim of crime. If the subject has never been a victim of crime, an alternate topic is whether they have been in a car accident or stopped by the police since turning age 60. Using the steps outlined in the chapter on interviewing elders, conduct a pre-interview then follow each of the steps except for the follow-up. Write a report on the assessment and facts.

2. Explain the role of policing in cases involving abuse to elders. A good source to consider is located at:
   http://www.preventelderabuse.org/professionals/law.html

3. Find out if there is a TRIAD in your city (either where you live permanently or at school). Contact the TRIAD police officer and find out what programs are active in the community.

Reference List

Bonnie, R. J., & Wallace, R. B. (2002). *Elder mistreatment: Abuse, neglect, and exploitation in aging America.* Washington, DC: The National Academies Press.

Boutin, D. (1999). Medical records as investigative tools in elder abuse cases. *Prosecutor's Brief: The California District Attorneys Association's Quarterly Journal,* XXI(2), 9.

Brandl, B. (2000). Power and control: Understanding domestic abuse in later life. *Generations,* 24(2), 39–45.

CDC. (2000). *Profile of the Nation's health: CDC fact book 2000/2001.* Washington DC: Centers for Disease Control and Prevention.

Johnson, K. D. (2003). *Financial crimes against the elderly.* (Report No. 20 Community Oriented Policing Services). Washington, DC: U.S. Department of Justice.

Klaus, P. (2005). *Crimes against persons age 65 or older, 1993–2002.* (Report No. NCJ 206154). Washington, DC: Bureau of Justice Statistics.

Levin, S. M., & Kruger, J. (2000). *Substance abuse among older adults: A guide for treatment providers.* Rockville, MD: U.S. Department of Health and Human Services.

Loue, S. (2001). Elder abuse and neglect in medicine and law: The need for reform. *The Journal of Legal Medicine,* 22, 159–209.

Memon, A., Gabert, F., & Hope, L. (2004). The ageing eyewitness. J. Adler (editor), *Forensic Psychology: Concepts, debates, and practice* (pp. 96–112). Portland, OR: Willan Publishing.

Morris, D. J. (1999). Interviewing cognitively impaired victims. *Prosecutors Brief,* XXI(2), 11–12, 41–45 .

National Center on Elder Abuse. (1998). *The National Elder Abuse Incidence Study.* Washington , DC: The Administration for Children and Families.

National Committee for the Prevention of Elder Abuse. (2003). The basics. Retrieved 2005, from http://www.elderabusecenter.org/default.cfm?p=basics.cfm

National Committee for the Prevention of Elder Abuse. (2005). What is elder abuse? Retrieved 2005, from http://www.preventelderabuse.org/elderabuse/elderabuse.html

Nerenberg, L. (1993). *Improving the police response to domestic elder abuse.* Washington, DC: Police Executive Research Forum.

OVC. (1993). *Improving the police response to domestic elder abuse.* (Report No. NCJ 147558). Washington, DC: Office for Victims of Crime.

Rohn, A. L. (1999). A multi-disciplinary approach to elder abuse prosecution. *California District Attorneys Association: Prosecutor's Brief,* XXI(2), 1–46.

Sajatovic, M., Madhusoodanan, S., & Buckley, P. (2000). Schizophrenia in the elderly: Guidelines for management. *CNS Drugs,* 13(2), 103–115.

Tatara, T., Kuzmeskus, L. M., & Duckhorn, E. (1997). Trends in elder abuse in domestic settings. Retrieved 2005, from http://www.elderabusecenter.org/pdf/basics/fact2.pdf

Teaster, P. (2003). *A response to the abuse of vulnerable adults: The 2000 Survey of State Protective Services.* Washington, DC: National Center on Elder Abuse.

U.S. Department of Health and Human Services. (2000). Our aging population: Promoting empowerment, preventing victimization, and implementing coordinated interventions: A report of proceedings. *OJP Issues and Practices Report,* Vol. NCJ 186256. Washington, DC: Office of Justice Programs.

Zahner, M. (1999). The absent witness in elder abuse cases. *Prosecutor's Brief: The California District Attorneys Association's Quarterly Journal,* XXI(2), 13–15; 44–4

Interviewing Persons with Disabilities or Mental Illness

KEY TERMS

The Americans with Disabilities Act	Appropriate adult
Detailed field evaluation	Distant field evaluation
Facilitated communication	Mental illness
Mental retardation	Personality disorder

CHAPTER OBJECTIVES

After completing this chapter you should be able to:

- ◆ Define how the Americans with Disabilities Act of 1994 applies to criminal justice procedures
- ◆ State appropriate terminology to effectively respond to victims with disabilities
- ◆ Define how Federal Courts are interpreting the term "arrest" for cases that allege violations of the ADA
- ◆ State what effective communication with individuals having disabilities means under ADA
- ◆ Compare and contrast mental retardation with mental illness
- ◆ List the steps involved for interviewing persons with disabilities
- ◆ Describe how to prepare for the interview of a person with a disability
- ◆ Explain the largest impediment to successful interviews of persons with disabilities
- ◆ List ways to determine if a person requires special care

Introduction

This chapter provides an in-depth discussion on issues that affect the practice of interviewing persons with physical, cognitive, and/or communication impairments. Changes in the legal code governing patient rights, affirming the right of persons with mental illness to live in the community, and deinstitutionalization in the 1960's set the stage for increased criminal justice involvement. Approximately 54 million Americans live with a wide variety of physical, cognitive, and emotional disabilities (Tyiska, 1998). In addition to the increased at-large population of developmentally delayed, the community is more vulnerable to victimization.

Impaired adults are at a higher risk for being physically or sexually assaulted at a rate of 4 to 10 times as high as it is for other adults (Sobsey, 1994). Children with disabilities are also victimized more frequently than children without disability. In a study for the Office on Child Abuse and Neglect, authors found that children with disabilities were 2.1 times as likely to endure criminal physical abuse and 1.8 times more likely to experience sexual abuse than children without disabilities (Crosse, Kaye, & Ratnofsky, 1993). Adding to the newly recognized dilemma of protecting those with disabilities are conflicting studies on the incidence of crime perpetrated by persons with mental illness. Sixteen percent of the adult prison population and 20 percent of the juvenile correctional system have a mental illness (Mentally Ill Offender Treatment and Crime Reduction Act of 2004, 2004). According to the National Alliance for the Mentally Ill, up to 40 percent of adults who suffer from a serious mental illness will come into contact with the American criminal justice system at some point in their lives. Research concludes, however, that only a weak association between mental disorder and violence exists; serious violence is perpetrated by a small fraction of the total number (Steadman et al., 1998).

One out of every ten police calls nationally involves someone who is mentally ill, according to Lt. Woody of the Akron Police Department (Gillespie, 2001). Yet recent studies indicate extremely low levels of reporting victimization by persons with developmental disabilities (Petersilia, 2000). When reporting does occur, few cases are successfully prosecuted. In a scathing article one newspaper reported that even when evidence exists of a crime against a disabled person, a mere 5% of investigated cases ends with a conviction (Mishra, 2001). Similar rebukes on the criminal justice response to protecting the disabled have sparked changes, including the development of Crisis Intervention Teams.

The debate regarding the role of the police in dealing with persons having disabilities rages around us. Once again, law enforcement is being tasked with policing social problems that often pose often insurmountable challenges. Still, the duty already has been assigned; it is time to meet it head on. This chapter is intended to aid the criminal justice professional in meeting the increased needs of communicating with the impaired community.

The Americans with Disabilities Act

Given the increasing likelihood of police encounters with persons that are disabled, training on effective communications with persons of the disabled community has taken on greater significance. The *Americans with Disabilities Act* is a legislative mandate to provide equal protections and access of government facilities for persons who have a disability. According to the U.S. Department of Justice, the ADA affects everything that officers and deputies do, for example (U.S. DOJ, 1996):

◆ Receiving citizen complaints;

◆ Interrogating and interviewing witnesses;

◆ Arresting, booking, and holding suspect;

◆ Enforcing laws;

◆ Incarceration.

Title II of the Americans with Disabilities Act (ADA) provides that "no qualified individual with a disability shall, by reason of such disability, be excluded from participation in or be denied the benefits of the services, programs, or activities of a public entity, or be subjected to discrimination by any such entity" (Americans with Disabilities Act, 1994). This mandate of nondiscrimination extends to all state and government services, regardless of whether the person receives federal financial assistance.

Interviewing Accommodations

The ADA requires that government officials attempt effective communication with individuals having disabilities by providing auxiliary devices (Sigmon and Edmunds, 2002). To facilitate the reporting of victimization for the disabled community, it is now imperative that officers make arrangements so that individuals with a disability may feel comfortable reporting to the police. This accommodation may involve the use of an interpreter or other third party to assist. The department may not charge the individual with a disability for the use of any auxiliary aid. Examples of auxiliary aids and services for those with hearing impairments include qualified interpreters, note takers, transcript services, videotext displays, closed caption decoders, and telephones compatible with hearing aids. To assist individuals with visual impairments, qualified readers, taped tests, audio recordings, brailled materials, and large print materials may be required. While the public entities are required to provide alternative auxiliary aids, if available, they are not required to alter the nature of the service, program, or activity when it results in an undue financial or if it causes an administrative burden (Sigmon and Edmunds, Jane, 2002).

Police Liability under ADA

In light of these changes, communications with persons who may be disabled and are suspected to have committed crimes is a critical skill to develop. Sporadic claims against police departments for failure to train officers on handling persons with disabilities have surfaced in Federal Court. Under what is referred to as the *Wrongful-Arrest Theory*, Courts are addressing some of these claims arising from Title II complaints of ADA. The wrongful-arrest situation was addressed by the court in *Jackson* (*Jackson* v. *Town of Sanford*, 1994) when police had arrested a man for drunk driving who was sober; his unsteadiness and slurred speech resulted from a past stroke. In *Lewis* police were held accountable when they beat and arrested a man for resisting law enforcement who was deaf and could not understand their commands (*Lewis* v. *Truitt*, 1997). In their investigation of these claims, the courts are broadly interpreting the term "arrest" to include arrest, pre-arrest investigations, and violent confrontations not technically involving an arrest (*Gohier* v. *Enright*, 1999). The message is clear: law enforcement is expected to be prepared to handle these difficult cases by recognizing situations where a person has a disability.

Avoiding these situations requires an increased awareness on the part of police. Some suggestions include watching for handicapped license

Been There . . . Done That! 9–1

While on patrol one winter evening I noted a person walking in the break-down lane coming towards traffic. From a distance I noticed that this woman was not wearing a coat or shoes and that there was snow on the ground. The nonverbal assessment was that she required special care; she did not appear to be aware of her surroundings. Pulling the cruiser over and slowing approaching I yelled out, "Are you ok?" Oblivious to my presence she kept walking. Calmly and firmly I kept talking as I approached her, making a determination as to the level of danger that she posed. A missing or wanted check showed no warrants. She was then transported to a local mental health clinic that accepted night admissions where she was evaluated the following day.

plates on cars that are stopped; use hand signals or yell to people in a crowd to signal that a person stop running; speak clearly; and use breathalyzers to obtain accurate results of driving under the influence. If while attempting to communicate with a motorist it becomes obvious that the person cannot speak, offer a pen and piece of paper to the operator.

Initial Considerations

The first step to interviewing persons with disabilities is self-confrontation. The lack of familiarity with individuals who have a disability may cause you to feel awkward and uncertain on how to proceed. Negative attitudes may be the largest impediment to successful interviewing of this population. Speak directly to the individual that is being interviewed, even if they are accompanied by another person. Their condition should not cause repulsion, sympathy, or admiration.

COGNITIVE AND COMMUNICATION DISABILITIES					
Intelligence	**Sensory**	**Communication**	**Motor**	**Social**	**Psychiatric**
Amnesia	Deaf	Language processing impairment	Cerebral palsy	Schizophrenia	Personality disorders
Mental retardation	Hearing impaired		Muscular dystrophy	Autism	Psychosis
Learning Disability	Blind	Aphasia	Other Central Nervous System impairments	Personality disorders	Depression
Organic Brain Syndrome	Vision	Cleft Palate			Anxiety
Other brain damage	Deaf-blind	Speech Impairment			Dissociative disorders
	Mute	Autism			

TABLE 9-1. Forms of Disability

A common negative attitude exists regarding people whose physical appearance signals to others that they are different. Individuals with a physical or developmental disability are not "less"of an individual, but do present with different value systems and behavioral expectations. Generally, persons with a developmental disability tend to obey rules and don't want to get anyone in trouble. They may appear overly compliant and initially deny that they have been victimized, or may not realize that what had happened was victimization. These individuals are not less creditable; interviewers must overcome the tendency to treat people with mental retardation as though they are stupid or undeserving of police attention or protection. Don't talk down or treat them as children. People with mental retardation are not stupid, although they may learn and comprehend at a slower rate than others.

Taking the time to become familiar with ways to address persons with a disability will also help to put you at ease. Take care not to label a person according to his or her disability; they are "a man with a disability," and not "a disabled man." While the distinction may seem trivial, to someone who lives with a physical or developmental disability it makes a difference. Prior to any attempt at establishing rapport, the person should be made to feel recognized as an individual, not regarded as an illness. Only ask questions about the disability that pertains to your investigation or to accommodate the individual's needs. Look directly at the person when you speak to him or her, but do not stare at a disfigurement. Treat victims with compassion, dignity, and respect.

Been There . . . Done That! 9–2

Andrew was a 23-year-old male with mental retardation who had been victimized sexually by a 72-year-old man. Andrew did not know that it was not right to have oral sex with another man; therefore it appeared as if he was a willing participant. He was seen having oral sex with the elder man and was called "an animal." It was extremely disturbing to Andrew that he be called that; he did not understand why someone would say bad things about him. He began to have violent outbreaks which had brought this case to the attention of authorities. Andrew was formally diagnosed as having Down Syndrome with the level of understanding to be between 7 and 8 years old. Prior to the incident Andrew was known to be amiable and sought to please adults, which is characteristic of individuals having Down Syndrome. Andrew was able to give me a detailed statement, although understanding his speech was a personal challenge for me.

I arrested the perpetrator and provided his warnings per Miranda, which he waived. Anthony stated that he felt guilty about having sex with the young retarded man and was glad that I had found out about it. He further told me that he had been arrested 40 years earlier for "Unnatural Acts with a Child" and had spent a year in jail for that.

Your goals as an officer are to determine, if possible, whether the contact was consensual. If it is unclear, ask for an evaluation of the individual from a trained professional who has expertise with persons having that particular disability. In this case, it was determined that the victim lacked the capacity to consent and that the suspect sought him out as a victim because of his disability. Taking this case to the logical conclusion of making an arrest served to teach Anthony that he was the victim and the act was illegal. It stopped that perpetrator, and sent a message to the community that these victimizations would be punished.

Identifying When Special Care Is Necessary

Individuals with a mental disorder or physical disability may require special care. Conduct a background check on the individual just as you would with any other individual. A background check may reveal past convictions and information that would provide investigation leads. A background check may also provide information on the level of potential threat the person may pose to the interviewer.

While they usually are able to provide reliable evidence, they may have communication problems that result in misleading statements or inappropriate reactions because of immediate (mis)understanding of the events. The interviewer must watch carefully for signs of disability, since the mental or physical impairment may not be immediately obvious.

Defining disability is a difficult task, since it is not necessarily an immutable or static condition. A person who has a disability cannot be identified by a single common characteristic. Some persons will be readily identifiable as having impairment due to physical effect, obvious mechanisms of assistance, or through inappropriate behaviors. Others with less severe impediments or mental illness may not be recognized as requiring special assistance. These individuals present with psychiatric, social, and intelligence disabilities; these forms represent the most problematic mental illnesses and disorders. Both general categories are protected under the ADA. Individuals with impaired sight or hearing are often assisted in ways that are not immediately noticed.

Persons having a disability do not share even the cause of the disability. Some physical disabilities are caused by brain damage such as cerebral palsy and the impact does not necessary affect intellect or the ability to communicate. Others with cerebral palsy acquired at birth or through traumatic head injury also have speech production impairments and/or mental illness. Most of the physical disabilities do not impair communication or cognition (Baladerian, 1998). Baladerian further cautions that impairments that affect speech production do not necessarily affect intellectual or cognitive abilities.

Most persons being interviewed by the police will be apprehensive; be aware if it appears that the apprehension is excessive and/or an excessive amount of anxiety is evident. A person may require special care if they are incoherent and it is not solely drug or alcohol induced. Some persons with disability may not be able to understand or answer questions; or will exhibit a mood level that is inconsistent with the situation. The individual may have a short attention span, a limited vocabulary, or a speech impediment.

Mental Retardation

Developmental disabilities, sometimes referred to as mental retardation, present different concerns for the interviewer. Persons with *mental retardation* possess less than average ability to process information. Some persons with mental retardation may not be able to understand or answer questions; or will exhibit a mood level that is inconsistent with the situation. Persons with mental retardation are usually arrested for less serious crimes such as public offenses, misdemeanors, and minor felony offenses (Davis, 2000). The individual may have a short attention span, a limited vocabulary, or a speech impediment. Somewhere between two percent to ten percent of the prison population is believed to be made up of persons having mental retardation (Davis, 2000).

Unusual behavior traits or agitation accompanied by physical activity may also become present during an interview. Persons with mental retardation may exhibit inappropriate verbal and nonverbal behaviors such as yelling, biting, hugging, rubbing of genital areas or breasts. Baladerian suggests that the interviewer set limits by asking the person to stop the behavior or by requesting that they put their hands on a desk or table (Baladerian, 1998). The interviewer should take care not to react to unexpected outbursts by laughing or exhibiting anger. Be firm but gentle to direct the interviewee to more appropriate behaviors if they do not comply or act aggressively.

Attention Deficit-Hyperactivity Disorder. Attention deficit-hyperactivity disorder (ADHD) is a developmental neurological disorder that impacts upon learning and behavior (Barkley, 2000). There are three types of ADHD described in DSM-IV: Combined Type, Predominately Inattentive Type, and Hyperactive-Impulsive Type. These terms are often used interchangeably as ADD, ADHD, AD/HD. ADHD is recognized as a disability under federal legislation (ADA,1994). Compared to persons without ADHD, persons having ADHD have greater problems with law enforcement officials. Research is unclear if this is due to greater problems with alcohol and drug abuse rather than the disability itself (Latham, Goldstein, Dickman, Latham, & Quinn, 1995). Once thought to be a disorder afflicting only children, adults are also diagnosed with the disability. Symptoms include hyperactivity, difficulty in deferring gratification or following instructions, greater risk taking, and impulsivity. Coupled with lower self-image and poor self-control, the individuals with ADHD are more likely to come to the attention of law enforcement due to their involvement in automobile accidents, underage drinking, and aggressiveness (Barkley, 2000). Juveniles having ADHD are more 3 times more likely to drive without a valid driver's license. Experts indicate that there is no data that suggests a specific interviewing or interrogation method is necessary for individuals with ADHD, but that recognition of the symptoms is helpful in determining the motivation for criminal behavior (Goldstein, 2003). Goldstein (2003) suggests these questions be asked during an interrogation to determine if the disorder contributed to the individual's behavior:

♦ Do you have difficulty paying attention during conversations, classes, at work, etc.?

♦ Do you feel excessively stressed or overwhelmed?

♦ Do you have difficulty paying attention during conversations, classes, at work, etc., and find that your mind drifts off easily?

♦ Do you become sidetracked easily, leave tasks unfinished, or disrupt tasks in progress to switch to other matters?

♦ Do you become frustrated easily?

♦ Do you forget to complete things that you intended to do?

♦ Do you have sudden outbursts of intense anger?

♦ Do you easily misunderstand directions?

Autism. Autism is a developmental disability whose symptoms may become apparent between 15 to 20 months of age (Autism Society of America, 2006). Autism frequently occurs along with other mental impairments, such as mental retardation, seizure disorders and attention deficit-hyperactivity disorder (Mayers, 2003). Affecting 1 out of every 166 births, there are an estimated 1.5 million Americans with this developmental disorder (Autism Society of America, 2006). It is characterized by impaired social relations and communication deficits which may lead to behavior prohibited by law. This population may become aggressive if interrupted during a preferred activity. Individuals with autism have a high likelihood of victimization (Debbaudt, 1999). During an interrogation there is the possibility of their producing false confessions or providing misleading statements to the police (Debbaudt, 1999). According to the Autism Society of America (2006) persons with autism may exhibit some of these traits which could impact interviews:

♦ They may repeat words or phrases in place of normal responsive language

♦ They may laugh (and/or cry) for no apparent reason

♦ They may have little or no eye contact and appear aloof

♦ They may have no real fear of danger

♦ They may be unresponsive to verbal cues and act as if they are deaf

Mental Illness

Mental illness is defined in the DSM-IV as a clinically significant behavioral or psychological syndrome or pattern that occurs in an individual that is associated with present distress (e.g. a painful symptom) or disability (i.e., impairment in one or more important areas of functioning) or with a significant increased risk of suffering death, pain, disability, or an important loss of freedom (APA, 1994). Several studies conclude that only a weak association between mental disorder and violence exists, suggesting that serious violence is perpetrated by a small fraction of the total number (Steadman et al., 1998). One study concluded that mentally disordered inmates were more likely to have been arrested on less serious charges than non-disabled persons, but that they were significantly more likely to have been carrying a weapon and to be perceived as dangerous at the time of the interaction with the police (Engel & Silver, 2000). Severe mental disorders that are highly represented in the prison inmate population include schizophrenia, bipolar disorder, and serious depression (Fellner, 2003). They may be quick to anger, provocative, and dangerous. Schizophrenia may include disordered thinking or speech, delusions, hallucinations, inappropriate emotions, confusion, and inattention to personal grooming. Bipolar disorder (previously called manic-depressive disorder) is characterized by frequently dramatic mood swings from depressions to mania. During manic phases some people may be psychotic and experience delusions or hallucinations. Persons with bipolar disorder in a manic phase can be disruptive, quick to anger, provocative, and dangerous. Serious depression puts people at an increased risk for suicide and self-mutilation.

Mental Illness	Mental Retardation
Impacts moods and emotions	Decreased ability to learn
Low or High IQ	Low IQ
Occurs at any time	Occurs before age 18
Disability may be noticeable	Unless severe, disability is not often noticeable
May be associated with violent outbursts	
	Persons are not violent

Persons with mental illness and mental retardation disabilities represent disabled persons who are highly represented in the criminal justice system, but these conditions are not the same thing.

Personality Disorders

The most common personality disorders among jail and prison inmates are antisocial personality disorder (ASPD) and borderline personality disorder (Fellner, 2003). The DSM-IV defines a *personality disorder* as an enduring pattern of inner experience and behavior that deviates markedly from the expectations of the individual's culture, is pervasive and inflexible, has an onset in adolescence or early adulthood, is stable over time, and leads to distress or impairment (APA, 1994). Persons with antisocial personality disorder, typically men, can be particularly difficult to manage in a correctional setting. They can be manipulative, volatile, disruptive, and likely to engage in aggressive, impulsive acting out behavior which can include assaults on others, self-mutilation and/or suicide attempts. The essential characteristic is a pervasive pattern of disregard for, and violation of, the rights of others (APA, 1994).

Field Evaluation

An important component of policing is astute observation. The purpose of conducting a field evaluation is to determine an appropriate response to the situation. First responders are often expected to make a quick assessment of the environment with limited information. Two methods of evaluation used to make an assessment in the field are based on distance. A *distant field evaluation* is a nonverbal assessment that is conducted from a distance of over three feet; this is used when a person attracts interest in the field due to one or more of the following conditions:

- ◆ The person may be inappropriately dressed for the weather
- ◆ He or she is in a place where they don't belong and personal danger clearly exists
- ◆ If she or he is stumbling about or appears to be in a confused state
- ◆ When there are inappropriate actions noticed with peers or the opposite sex
- ◆ If the individual appears to be gravely disabled either in judgment or because of substance abuse

A *detailed field evaluation* is an up-close assessment to determine if the subject is mentally disordered or physically handicapped. Its purpose is to determine if there are any needs or problems that must be addressed, or if a situation of mandated reporting exists. The examination should not be conducted in this manner if there is evidence that the individual is armed or dangerous. The officer's first concern should always be towards safety and protection of persons, both for himself and for others. Approach the individual in a non-threatening but controlled manner so as not to agitate or cause distress. Speak firmly and clearly, showing concern through actions and words. "Are you ok?"; "Do you need help?" are examples of introductory statements in the field used when assessing the situation.

Ask for identifying information to determine the level of stress and cognitive awareness of the person. If an individual is not aware of their name or address it may be indicative of impairment. Do not assume that a person failing to answer your questions can hear or understand you. Failure to respond by itself is not indicative of belligerence or of criminal behavior. An indication of alcohol use does not necessarily mean that the individual is drunk; you may be dealing with a person who has a disability that also has an alcoholic beverage!

Most persons with disability present no risk to police. However, subjects with paranoid schizophrenia pose a documented rate of violence to be several times higher than members of the general population with no disorders, unless they are successfully treated (Mohandie & Duffy, 1999). Individuals with this mental disorder may present with anxiety, anger, and aloofness, argumentativeness, along with a superior or patronizing manner. Attempts to defuse a potential violent situation take a show of respect and a calm non-threatening approach of communicating. In addition to the methods already discussed, here are some guidelines that Mohandie and Duffy (1999) suggest when confronted with potentially violent mentally ill individuals:

♦ Assess the REAL risk, does the individual pose a risk, or is it merely threatened?

♦ Make a noticeable attempt to understand the context of the subject's comments.

♦ Avoid arguing about the subject's delusions while attempting to develop reality-based issues.

♦ Use active listening skills such as paraphrasing, emotion labeling, and "I" messages.

♦ Allow the subject to vent frustration.

♦ Do not crowd or violate the subject's personal body space.

♦ Use suggestibility and empathy to attempt a behavioral change.

Been There . . . Done That! 9–3

At the scene of a homicide the victim was found to have been stabbed about 150 times! An adult son that lived with her was on the scene and was also stabbed over 100 times, but lived. My partner went to the hospital to interview the survivor. The interview was audio taped and <u>Miranda</u> warnings were issued since he was a suspect in the killing. The man appeared coherent and his initial behavior was rational. From time to time during this interview the suspect would start "howling" accompanied by blood-curdling screaming and sobbing. He told how the "devil" was present in his TV and transposed to his mother—he could see it through the redness of her eyes (which is why numerous stabbings were to her eyes). He had to rid her of this devil whom he thought had gotten into him, which is why he stabbed himself in every orifice; ears, eyes, and buttocks. The danger was that he believed what he was doing; this goal-directed behavior was organized and premeditated. Officer safety is an important issue with those who are delusional, suffer from hallucinations, and/or present with grossly disorganized or catatonic behaviors.

Interview Considerations

Interviewing the person presenting with a disability involves only a modification of the techniques already discussed throughout this book. Although initially challenging, the interview should be no more difficult than with any other population. Similarly, the interviewer must maintain control, elicit responses, and clarify statements. How this is accomplished obviously differs depending on the unique characteristics of the individual being questioned. It takes patience and a willingness to communicate in the most effective method for the interviewee.

Victims of crime that have a disability may be targeted for criminal activity due to their real or perceived vulnerability; you may be interviewing someone who has been repeatedly victimized. They are targets for abuse and theft from the caregivers that are assigned to care for them. One study has found almost half of the sexual abuse against persons with disabilities was perpetrated by persons who gained access to their victims through disability services (Sobsey, 1994). A cycle of victimization and abuse will make it more difficult to establish rapport and trust from the person being interviewed, another reason to be patient and understanding.

Legal Issues

Prior to the interview with a person that is physically or mentally impaired the interviewer must have a good understanding of the statutes that are specific to protecting disabled persons. Typically the elements of the crime differ for those victimized who have limited cognitive and physical abilities, so it is important to be acquainted with the provisions particular to your jurisdiction before the interview. Numerous distinctions have been made to criminal statutes that provide additional protections for persons with a disability from abandonment, financial exploitation, personal victimization, and neglect. Some examples include:

◆ North Carolina provides that Second Degree Rape (GS14-27.3)(a)(2), against a mentally disabled, mentally incapacitated, or physically helpless person requires a lack of consent, but no force need be established.

◆ The Illinois Criminal Code contains the *Home Repair Fraud Act* (815ILCS 515/5). Aggravated Home Repair Fraud occurs if the contractor commits a home repair fraud against a person who has a permanent physically disabling condition. Aggravated Home Repair Fraud is a Class 2 felony if the contractor is to be paid more than $1,000, and a Class 4 felony if the amount is less than $1,000. The maximum punishment for a Class 4 felony is a term of imprisonment of not less than one year and not more than three years.

◆ The Indiana Criminal Code of Battery (IC 35-42-2-1) provides: (c) it is a Class D felony if a person who knowingly or intentionally touches another person in a rude, insolent, or angry manner commits battery that results in bodily injury to a person of any age who is mentally or physically disabled and is committed by a person having the care of the mentally or physically disabled person, whether the care is assumed voluntarily or because of a legal obligation.

◆ Iowa presents an example where crimes against disabled may be construed as *"Hate crime"* (92 Acts, ch 1157, § 9). It includes one or more of the following public offenses when committed against a person or a person's property because of the person's race, color, religion, ancestry, national origin, political affiliation, sex, sexual orientation, age, or **disability,** or the person's association with a person of a certain race, color, religion, ancestry, national origin, political affiliation, sex, sexual orientation, age, or **disability:**

1. Assault in violation of individual rights under section 708.2C.

2. Violations of individual rights under section 712.9.

3. Criminal mischief in violation of individual rights under section 716.6A.

4. Trespass in violation of individual rights under section 716.8, subsections 3 and 4.

Prepare for the Interview

Prior to the interview determine a location away from the scene that is comfortable and without distractions. Turn off any cell phone or pager that you carry. The best scenario is a one-on-one interview. In some cases it may be advisable to include an appropriate adult. An *appropriate adult* is someone who is able to provide support to the interviewee and to smooth the progress of communication with the police. He or she should have a good understanding or training in dealing with mentally disordered persons, or with the needs or a particular group. He or she should be completely independent of the police and, when possible, the interviewee. As needed the person would act as an interpreter. It is helpful to have developed a relationship with the mental health community that is willing to be called in such a case. An alternative is the development of a team approach for interviewing persons that have a disability. It is not the function of an appropriate adult to advise the person being interviewed whether or how to answer any questions or to object to any

Courtesy of iStockphoto, Inc.

An "appropriate adult" is included in the interview to assist in communication with the police.

questions being asked. It is not appropriate for the helping adult to tell the police that they disapprove of a particular line of questioning or to lead the witness in any way.

In rare cases a controversial method called *facilitated communication* may be used as a form of communication. This is designed for those that do not have the physical ability to use sign language, or the ability to use keyboards, or communication boards on their own. Dr. Baladerian explains that it involves steadying the individual's physical movements which allows for the person to make the communication that they desire (Baladerian, 1998). The method utilizes a keyboard or communication board and the assistance of a trained facilitator. Two separate interviews should be conducted with different facilitators used who have not had prior contact with the victim.

Establish Rapport

Introduce yourself and ask the individual what he or should would like to be called. Referring to someone else by title then calling the interviewee by a first name implies a lack of respect, so be consistent. Avoid touching the person with a disability, since you do not know if it would be perceived as an invasion of personal space or remind them of an attacker. An individual that is "touch toxic" may become upset and unable to continue the interview; the person with mental retardation may not feel able to refuse. Take your cue from the interviewee: if she puts out a hand for a handshake, you should respond. Otherwise, keep your hands to yourself. Don't be afraid to maintain your own personal space. Since it is not professional to hug an individual being interviewed, it is appropriate to firmly and gently avoid personal contact of this kind that is initiated by the interviewee. Kindly tell the interviewee that it makes you feel uncomfortable and you do not want to hug.

Develop rapport with the interviewee by asking if he or she requires physical assistance or that arrangements be made to meet their needs. Explain the process of the interview; explain that you may need to ask questions more than once to make sure that you understand what is being said. Anticipate an adequate length of time for the interview without the need for excessive time. Arrange for support to be available to the person following the interview and let the interviewee know that someone will be there for them.

For persons with physical disabilities, do not jump up and assume that the person needs or wants help. Keep clear of wheelchairs so that the individual can move around or adjust their position;, the "chair" is part of personal space that should not be invaded without specific design. The room should be comfortable without being too large, and absent of child toys.

Conducting the Interview

Use good listening skills; allow the victims to tell the story at first with as few interruptions as possible. Use open-ended questions and avoid overly complicated or technical phrases. Ask the person if they know why they are there to speak with you. It may be helpful to explain that you are someone who speaks with people about difficult subjects, and give them "permission" to talk with you. Give the individual the opportunity to ask questions.

Questions should not be phrased in legal terms; the victim may not know what an "assault" means for example. The primary goal of interviewing victims will be to:

1. determine if a crime has been committed

2. to obtain information to help in the identification of the perpetrator

3. to gather evidence for a successful prosecution

The goal of interviewing witnesses is the corroboration of specific events that substantiates criminal activity. With these goals in mind, the purpose of the interview is to acquire the necessary information.

The criminal justice community has already made great strides in interviewing others with cognitive limitations, children. While care must be taken not to infantilize the person with a disability, we should utilize the lessons learned for effective communication. Remember that the person presenting with a disability does not necessarily have limited cognitive abilities along with a physical or neurological limitation. As much as possible, go into the interview without a pre-conceived notion about the abilities of the interviewee to recount the necessary information.

The cognitive abilities of the individual should be considered when phrasing/asking questions. Be purposeful in your phrasing to avoid miscommunication and misunderstandings. Keep sentences short and to the point. Access the vocabulary of the person being interviewed and attempt consistency in communications. Take extra care not to lead the questioning or to suggest answers. Questions that require a "yes" or "no" response are only helpful for clarification and should be avoided. Encourage the interviewee to express and clarify meanings. All of these considerations must be confined to a relatively short interview period of approximately one-half hour! Persons with a disability may have a short attention span.

Be aware that the vocabulary used by the person being interviewed may have different meanings than you would normally associate with the terms. If the allegation is of sexual abuse, allow the victim to provide not only the words that they use to describe their body parts, but have them to show you on an anatomically correct doll or through drawings what that part of the body is. Encourage the individual to use descriptive terms for what they experienced. Avoid asking the question, "why?"; it is too complicated and can be confusing.

At the end of the interview thank the interviewee for their time and patience. Ask any questions on points that you need clarified. Let him or her know that you may need to speak with them another time, and ask if that would be all right. Be sure to escort the person outside of the interview room to meet with a counselor or other supportive person.

Been There . . . Done That! 9–4

Stemming from an allegation of rape, I interviewed a retarded woman about the event. She was clear in stating that she had been raped. Instructing her that I needed to understand her terms, I asked that she name the body parts. This was done without a problem using an anatomically correct doll that was clothed. Next I asked if she would tell me how it happened. The woman immediately picked up the doll and rubbed her face on the chest area. "See," she stated, "he raped me like this." What she showed was not rape, but it was a sexual assault. She did not want this to happen and said she told him to stop, over and over. The man was charged with an Indecent Assault and Battery on a Disabled Person. The interview had been video-taped. The videotape was shown in the grand jury; the victim also went into the grand jury and, along with the doll, demonstrated what had happened. The fact that her terms were different did not diminish the crime, nor the trauma that resulted from it. The perpetrator was indicted, and he pled guilty to the crime in Superior Court.

Interrogation Considerations

Persons with disabilities do commit crime, and accusations must be investigated similar to allegations against any other perpetrator. There are situations where an officer must interrogate a person suspected of committing a crime where disability is suspected or known. In order to protect the interrogation's results, special care must be taken to preserve the integrity of the case. Most important is strict adherence to the preservation of all Constitutional rights. Taking shortcuts will likely result in a tainted investigation with a statement that is subject to exclusion or worse. Remembering that the purpose of an interrogation is to find the truth, if possible, take pains to make sure that it is the truth that is obtained. Follow any department rules and regulations that may exist relative to interrogating potentially vulnerable persons. Know your state laws relative to the interrogation of juveniles. In all cases, treat the suspect with dignity.

Prior to questioning, make a determination on the level of functioning of the adult suspect. Ask typical questions, such as name, age, and address of the individual. Determine if the suspect can read; if not, be prepared to read and explain individual rights. Ask questions that are non-leading and straightforward. Avoid questions that require a "yes" or "no" answer. Use language that is simple and easy to understand. Your sentences should be short and to the point.

Follow up any statements suggestive of guilt by asking for details of the event. Answers that typically would be considered "admissions" do not take on the same significance when coming from a person with limited cognitive ability. For example, if a man with mental retardation is asked, "When did you kill Mrs. Smith?" and he replies, "Was it Thursday?" without significant evidence that he did in fact commit the homicide, the reply means absolutely nothing! The individual may take your question be about "when" Mrs. Smith was killed and miss the "you" part of the question. Proceed with caution! Justice is not served by arresting the wrong person.

Miranda *Rights*

There is no requirement that *Miranda* rights be given verbatim, or presented to the suspect in written form (*Miranda* v. *Arizona*, 1966) These practices are police procedures developed to assure compliance and consistency. Officers are therefore given the flexibility to explain the rights to the suspect in a manner that allows the person to understand. According to the Arc, people who have mental retardation often do not understand *Miranda* warnings, even if they state that they do understand (The Arc, 1996). The interrogator is not a mental health specialist, and is not responsible for diagnosing a suspect or determining the actual extent of mental limitations. A balance between the need to protect the public through sound investigation practices and recognizing personal limitations must be made.

Persons with mental retardation may incriminate themselves even if they are innocent, in an effort to please the police officer or other interviewer. Persons with retardation are structured throughout their lives to be compliant and submissive. Do not assume that an interrogation with a suspect that is disabled understands without verification.

It is not an ADA requirement that statements be audio- or videotaped (The Arc, 1996). The practice of recording interrogations is recommended, whenever practicable. Preserving the interrogation helps to protect the officer against future claims of using excessive interrogation tactics and the use of heavy-handed methods. It also serves to demonstrate that the individual knowingly and voluntarily waived their rights.

False Confessions

When interrogating persons that have mental retardation false confessions should be a major concern for the interrogator. The individual may be confused about who is responsible for the crime and "confess" even though innocent. He or she may be the last to leave the scene of the crime and the first to be caught. He or she may act very upset at being detained and/or try to run away. Avoid lengthy interrogations; while they may elicit a "confession" it avoids the goal of interrogation, which is to find the truth!

The Court expressed in the *Miranda* decision (id. at 24) some of its concerns regarding persons with low IQ and their subsequent false confessions to police. The Court stated, "Interrogation procedures may even give rise to a false confession." They provided a conspicuous example that occurred in New York, in 1964, when a African American man of limited intelligence confessed to two brutal murders and a rape which he had not committed. The Court in its decision relied upon a similar case, where the defendant was a 19-year-old heroin addict, described as a "near mental defective," who was found guilty of the crime he did not commit; his conviction was subsequently overturned (*Townsend* v. *Sain*, 1963).

Four Maryland cases have been highlighted in the *Washington Post* for police obtaining confessions that later proved to be false (Witt, 2001). Prince George's homicide detectives obtained confessions that put the wrong men behind bars while the killers remained free to commit other crimes. Three of the four false confessions were made by individuals with low IQ; a teenager with learning disabilities who said he stabbed a friend; a high school senior who implicated himself in a triple shooting; and an illiterate janitor who shakily signed a statement a detective wrote for him confessing to slaying a co-worker. The four men were detained in the interrogation room from 11 to more than 38 hours. Three of the four insist that detectives refused to let them speak with a lawyer. In each case, the suspect's alleged statement was virtually the only evidence homicide detectives used to charge him with murder. Without a doubt these officers did not intend to arrest the wrong people. It is very easy to be consumed with finding killers and protecting the public; this is what law enforcement does. Just don't lose sight of the real goal by being overly zealous.

Conclusions

This chapter introduced you to the challenges of interviewing and interrogating persons with disability. Crime against this population is believed to be higher than against the nondisabled community, yet reporting is much lower and still lower are successful prosecutions. Skillful interviewing and careful lay assessments can increase the likelihood of obtaining sufficient information on which to proceed with cases involving this vulnerable community.

In addition to satisfying the needs of criminal justice are the compelling mandates from the Americans with Disabilities Act. Professionals within the field are expected to deal with an increasing number of individuals with developmental, physical, and mental disabilities. If possible, communications with this underserved population is even more important than with others. Generally, they are perceived as easy victims to the predators and monsters that live among us! They need and depend on the criminal justice community to protect them in ways that some are unable to protect themselves. The ADA provides the legal impetus to seek justice for this population, but the moral responsibilities exist within every officer.

Dispelling the myths about this population and dealing with personal prejudices are not easy, but definitely can be achieved. It will take time to develop the needed skills for proficiency in interviewing. It will take patience and good judgment. It takes true professionals to give it a try!

Chapter Nine Questions for Review

Short Answer Questions

1. What does Title II of the ADA refer to and how does it affect policing?

2. Since the ADA affects the job of the police officer on so many levels it is important to understand how the court will define certain actions. According to the Federal Courts, how is the term "arrest" interpreted under ADA?

3. What are the two significant cases involved in wrongful arrest, and what are techniques that can prevent future mistakes?

4. Describe some of the challenges that must be overcome for successful interviewing of this population.

5. What is the difference between someone with a mental illness and a person who is mentally retarded?

6. What are some of the behavioral traits that may occur with individuals with disabilities?

7. In order to assess a situation officer can use a Distant Field Evaluation or a Detailed Field Evaluation. Briefly discuss both.

8. How does the crime rate compare between persons with a disability and the general population?

9. Why would an interviewer use an appropriate adult in an interview with the person who has a disability?

10. During the interview, what concerns should the interviewer have when interviewing a person with a disability?

Fill-in Questions

1. When interrogating persons with mental retardation _____ should be of great concern.

2. According to *Miranda* _____ procedures can lead to false confessions among individuals with a low IQ.

3. Impaired adults are at a _____ risk for being physically or sexually assaulted than other adults.

4. _____ provides that "no qualified individual with a disability shall by reason of such disability, be excluded from participation in or be denied the benefits of the services, programs, or activities of a public entity, or be subjected to discrimination by any such entity."

5. An _____ can be used to help facilitate communication during an interview with a person with a disability.

6. _____ is described by the Federal court under Title II of the ADA as pre-arrest investigations, and violent confrontations not technically involving arrest.

7. The largest impediment to successful interviewing of this population is _____ .

8. Persons who are mentally retarded will have a low IQ, and a person who is mentally is can have an IQ that is

_____ .

9. Mental Retardation usually occurs _____ .

10. Subjects with _____ pose a documented rate of violence to be several times higher than the general population.

Exercises

1. Write an essay on facilitated communication stating the pros and cons of this method. Start your search for information at the Facilitated Communication Institute on the Internet at: http://soeweb.syr.edu/thefci/

2. For this exercise break into pairs. In this mock interview one person will assume the persona of a person with a disability. Determine who will be the interviewer and who will be the interviewee. The interviewee should choose and become familiar with one of the major categories of disability—mental retardation, mental illness, or a personality disorder. The interviewer must become familiar with the cautionary approaches to conducting an interview with a person who has a disability. The purpose of the interview is to determine if the interviewee was sexually assaulted by a neighbor. Take ten minutes for this exercise. Report your experiences to the class.

3. Reverse roles from exercise #2. Take ten minutes for the interviewee to conduct an interview. Report your experiences to the class.

4. Discuss the field evaluation for persons with mental illness and mental retardation in class. Ask students to explain the two methods and give reasons why the evaluation would be beneficial to interviewers. Ask students to list questions that would be helpful when making a field evaluation of a person suspected of having a disability. Write these on the bulletin board.

5. Locate "A police officer's guide when in contact with people who have mental retardation." It is located on the Web at www.thearc.org/publications. Discuss how interrogation with an individual who has mental retardation can affect the process through a written report to the instructor.

Reference List

Americans with Disabilities Act, 42 U.S.C. § 12132 (1994).

APA. (1994). *Diagnostic and statistical manual of mental disorders* (4th ed.). Washington, DC: American Psychiatric Association.

Autism Society of America. (2006). Defining Autism. Retrieved 2006, from http://www.autism-society.org/site/PageServer?pagename=WhatisAutism

Baladerian, N. J. (1998). *Interviewing skills to use with abuse victims who have developmental disabilities.* Washington, DC: National Center on Elder Abuse.

Barkley, R. (2000). *Taking charge of ADHD.* New York, NY: The Guilford Press.

Crosse, S. B., Kaye, E., & Ratnofsky, A. C. (1993). *A report on the maltreatment of children with disabilities.* Washington, DC: Office on Child Abuse and Neglect.

Davis, L. A. (2000). People with mental retardation and the criminal justice system. Retrieved 2005, from http://www.thearc.org/faqs/crimqa.html

Debbaudt, D. (1999). Avoiding unfortunate situations. Retrieved 2006, from http://policeandautism.cjb.net/

Engel, R. S., & Silver, E. (2000). Policing mentally disordered suspects: A reexamination of the criminalization hypothesis. *Criminology, 39*(2), 225–252.

Fellner, J. (2003). *Ill-equipped: U.S. prisons and offenders with mental illness.* New York, NY: Human Rights Watch.

Gillespie, C. (2001). Police training improves safety in dealing with mentally ill. Retrieved 2005, from http://www.taser.com/documents/akronohiomental.doc

Gohier v. *Enright,* 186 F.3rd 1216 (10th Cir.) (1999).

Goldstein, S. (2003). ADHD and implications for the criminal justice system. Retrieved 2006, from http://www.mental-health-matters.com/articles/article.php?artID=682

Jackson v. *Town of Sanford,* 63 U.S.L.W. 2351 (1994).

Latham, P., Goldstein, S., Dickman, E., Latham, P., & Quinn, P. (1995). The criminal justice system and individuals with Attention Deficit Disorder and Learning Disabilities. Retrieved 2006, from http://www.add.org/articles/cjaddld.html

Lewis v. *Truitt,* 960 F. Supp. 175 (S.D. Ind.) (1997).

Mayers, T. (2003). Persons with autism and criminal justice: Core concepts and leading cases. *Journal of Positive Behavior Interventions.*

Mentally Ill Offender Treatment and Crime Reduction Act of 2004, 42 USC 3711 Public Law 108–414 (2004).

Miranda v. *Arizona,* 284 U.S. 436 (1966).

Mishra, R. (2001 June). In attacks on disabled, few verdicts despite evidence, law enforcement drops most cases. *The Boston Globe.*

Mohandie, K., & Duffy, J. (1999). *Understanding subjects with paranoid schizophrenia.* Washington, DC: Federal Bureau of Investigation.

Petersilia, J. (2000). Invisible victims: Violence against persons with developmental disabilities. *Human Rights, 27*(1), 9–13.

Sigmon, J., & Edmunds, J. (2002). Victimization of individuals with disabilities. *National victim assistance academy: Foundations in victimology and victims' rights and services* (Chapter 15). Washington, DC: Office for Victims of Crime.

Sobsey, D. (1994). *Violence and abuse in the lives of people with disabilities.* Baltimore, MD: Paul H. Brookes.

Steadman, H., Mulvey, E., Monahan, J., Robbins, P., Applebaum, P., Grisso, T., Roth, L., & Silver, E. (1998). Violence by people discharged from acute psychiatric inpatient facilities and by others in the same neighborhoods. *Archives of General Psychiatry, 55,* 393–401.

The Arc. (1996). *A police officer's guide when in contact with people who have mental retardation.* Silver Spring, MD: The Arc of the United States.

Townsend v. *Sain,* 372 U.S. 293 (1963).

Tyiska, C. (1998). *Working with victims of crime with disabilities.* Washington, DC: Office for Victims of Crime, U.S. Department of Justice.

U.S. DOJ. (1996). Commonly asked questions about the Americans with Disabilities Act and law enforcement. Retrieved July 19, 2005, from http://www.usdoj.gov/crt/ada/q&a_law.htm

Witt, A. (2001 June). False confessions. *The Washington Post.*Com, p. 1.

PART

IV

Interrogation

In this section of *Smart Talk,* each chapter takes on a different view of the interrogation process. Chapter Ten demonstrates how the law provides guidelines for criminal justice interrogations. While each state may establish procedures and laws that are more restrictive than these federal guidelines, the final authority rests with the Supreme Court. These rules are categorized under the Constitutional provisions that the Courts have identified as applicable to the interrogation process. The four-prong test for lawful interrogations are found within the Fourth, Fifth, Sixth, and Fourteenth Amendments. The *Miranda* standard is a major focus governing interrogation practices. The requirements are clearly outlined for the student. The difference between compelling a suspect to give up protected Constitutional protections and compelling a suspect to give a statement after those rights have been legally relinquished is addressed here. In addition, the difference between the Sixth Amendment right to counsel and the *Miranda* standard is differentiated.

In Chapter Eleven the student will examine the goal of interrogation and methods to reach that goal. The chapter stresses the belief that interrogations should be conducted more frequently than the evidence suggests actually occurs. This position is bolstered by the fact that when police officers do conduct interrogations they are very successful. The chapter introduces the idea that knowledge of the law can be as important as technique for increasing the numbers of interrogations and their successful outcome. Avoiding false confessions and techniques for some case specific criminal interrogations are suggested. Methods for improving interrogations are covered in depth.

Chapter Twelve covers techniques for interrogation. The goal of interrogation is what differentiates the interrogation from an interview. The place and timing are critical but do not define it. The strategies for conducting interrogation in the custodial and noncustodial situations are differentiated. Controlling the interrogation is achieved by a three-phase approach of preparation, assessment, and getting the confession. Steps to accomplish each phase are outlined so that the student can practice and become proficient in the methods. Assessment of the suspect and determining the barriers that inhibit a suspect from making a confession are covered in considerable length. There are numerous confession eliciting models that are outlined in this chapter. It illustrates that there is not a single method that determines how interrogations must take place.

Interrogation Process and Law

KEY TERMS

Custody	Exclusionary rule
Fruit of the poisonous tree doctrine	*Miranda* rights
Power to arrest	Probable cause
Rule of law	*Stare decisis*
State action	Totality of the circumstances

CHAPTER OBJECTIVES

After completing this chapter, you should be able to:

◆ Describe the rule of law
◆ Describe the totality of the circumstances test
◆ Explain the *Miranda* rights
◆ List numerous forms of coercion that would invalidate a confession, even if the suspect's *Miranda* rights were properly waived
◆ Compare and contrast the Constitutional protections from the Fourth, Fifth, and Sixth amendments
◆ Define probable cause
◆ State the protections of the Fourth Amendment and how they apply to interrogation
◆ Define the exclusionary rule
◆ State the purpose of the fruit of the poisonous tree doctrine
◆ List the categories when police officers have the power to arrest

Introduction

The fundamental principle on which the United States legal system rests is the idea that law is created by the people for the purpose of protecting citizens against tyranny and lawlessness, and to protect freedom.

Courtesy of Corbis Images.

The law that guides the system comes from many sources, relying first on the Constitution of the United States as the supreme law of the land. The Bill of Rights and other amendments to the Constitution developed further protections to the rights and freedoms of individuals. State constitutions expand and define the protections within those jurisdictions, but no state can deprive the individual of those rights that are established and guaranteed by the Constitution of the United States.

The *rule of law* provides that those who execute the law must rely on the application of known principles or laws, and those principles must be applied uniformly and fairly to all citizens. This concept is also referred to as the *supremacy of law*. General constitutional principles are the result of judicial decisions determining the rights of individuals in the courts. Supreme Court case law makes up the bulk of what we call constitutional law (Garner, 2004). According to the *rule of stare decis,* judges must make decisions that are guided by previous settled decisions. Many of the decisions that govern interrogation practices by the police are interpretations of the U.S. Constitution, which have evolved since the 1960s. These contemporary interpretations of the Constitution illustrate that the law is a fluid entity; it relies on settled principles to form the basis for contemporary legal standards. The courts are settling issues that could not have been anticipated by the framers of the Constitution, such as the legality of wiretapping or the taking of DNA samples. Still, the old concepts must be applied in a way that is consistent with what the Constitution demands and in a way that is fair to all. The objective application and enforcement of law concerning interrogations by government officials and their agents is established in the law itself and interpreted by the rulings of judges.

The four-prong test for the admissibility of a confession is contained in the Fourth, Fifth, Sixth, and Fourteenth amendments. In the past, confessions that were considered voluntary were admissible in court to be used against the suspect if they passed the Fifth Amendment protections against self-incrimination, regardless of any prior official legality (*Colombe v. Connecticut*, 1961). Since the Fourteenth Amendment requirement of due process was made applicable to state action, the Fourth Amendment has found prominence in the lineup of important considerations.

Fifth Amendment Considerations

The Fifth Amendment of the U.S. Constitution is stated first in this chapter because it contains the earliest example of protections applied to the admissibility of confessions. It protects the right of the suspect against compelled testimonial communication and self-incrimination. It states:

> No person shall be held to answer for a capital, or otherwise infamous crime, unless on a presentment or indictment of a Grand Jury, except in cases arising in the land or naval forces, or in the Militia, when in actual service in time of War or public danger; nor shall any person be subject for the same offence to be twice put in jeopardy of life or limb; nor shall be compelled in any criminal case to be a witness against himself, nor be deprived of life, liberty, or property, without due process of law; nor shall private property be taken for public use, without just compensation.

The Fifth Amendment requires that no person will be incriminated though compelled testimonial communication. *Compel* means to cause or bring about by force, threats, or overwhelming pressure (Garner, 2004). To be *testimonial* a "communication must itself, explicitly or implicitly, relate a factual assertion or disclose information" that is the "expression of the contents of an individual's mind" (*Doe* v. *United States*). The protection against self-incrimination also permits a person to refuse to testify against himself or herself at a criminal trial in which they are a defendant.

The current application of the Fifth Amendment to confession is one that has evolved over time. An admission or confession was allowed to be used in court as evidence of guilt regardless of it being the product of force or duress under early common law. Enforcement officers resorted to torture to extract a confession from the accused during an interrogation rather than conducting an investigation to establish guilt.

Practices of torture as an interrogation method eventually led to the development of rules on the admissibility of confessions in the late eighteenth century. The newer common-law rule excluded coerced confessions from being admitted at trial due to the unreliability of evidence that was the product of torture. During the late 1800s the Court incorporated the common-law rule with the requirement in the Fifth Amendment, which prohibited compelling an individual to give witness against himself, as the standard for judging the admissibility of confessions (*Bram* v. *United States*, 1897).

The common-law rule was later abandoned for the free and voluntary rule during the early 20th century. This rule required that statements must be freely and voluntarily made, without duress, fear, or compulsion and with knowledge of the consequences of the confession (*People* v. *Fox*, 1925). Involuntary confessions were rejected not because of the illegal or deceitful methods used in obtaining them, but because of their unreliability. Torture as a means to extract confessions was expressly denounced in 1937 (*Brown* v. *Mississipi,* 1937). Using a totality of the circumstances test, the Court in Brown concluded that repeated whippings of the suspect produced a coerced statement that could not be used against him in court. A *totality of the circumstances* test is one where the court focuses on all of the circumstances surrounding a situation, rather than any one factor. In 1966 the *Miranda* standard made a distinction between the voluntariness of the statement apart from the validity of the statement (*Miranda* v. *Arizona,* 1966).

The *Miranda* Standard

The Court in *Miranda* said that procedural safeguards to secure the privilege against self-incrimination during custodial interrogations must be used. The Court's reasoning was that the practices of custodial interrogation were inherently coercive (*Miranda,* 1966). Whether the *Miranda* requirements are complied with requires an analysis using the Fifth Amendment. Known as the *Miranda rights,* these procedural safeguards must be stated prior to questioning:

1. the person must be warned that he has a right to remain silent;

2. that any statement he does make may be used as evidence against him;

3. and that he has a right to the presence of an attorney.

4. If he cannot afford an attorney, counsel will be provided at government expense.

Case in Point 10–1

Case in Point: *Miranda* v. *Arizona* (1966)

In 1965, the Supreme Court agreed to hear Miranda's case. At the same time the Court agreed to hear three similar cases: *Vignera* v. *New York; Westover* v. *United States;* and *California* v. *Stewart.* These four cases were combined; since *Miranda* was the first case listed, the decision came to be known by that name.

Ernesto Miranda was a poor Mexican immigrant who was arrested after a crime victim identified him in a police lineup. He was charged with rape and kidnapping and interrogated for two hours while in police custody. As a result of the interrogation, he confessed to the crimes with which he was charged. While his written statement included an acknowledgement that he was aware of his right against self-incrimination, he had never been informed of his rights under the Fifth Amendment or of his Sixth Amendment right to the assistance of an attorney. He was sentenced to 20 to 30 years in prison on each count.

Importance:

1. The Supreme Court in *Miranda* set specific guidelines for police officers on how they must advise suspects of their Constitutional rights and under what circumstances those warnings must be provided.

2. The Supreme Court combined the Sixth Amendment rights to an attorney with the Fifth Amendment right against self-incrimination.

When are the Miranda *warnings* required?

Miranda warnings or their equivalent must be given prior to questioning (direct or indirect) which is initiated BY a state actor AND that person has been taken into police custody or otherwise deprived of his freedom of action by the police in any significant way.

→ State Action

State action is anything that is done by a government, in particular an intrusion on a person's rights by a government entity (Garner, 2004). It exists in interrogation practices when the communication with the suspect is undertaken by federal and state law enforcement officers or their agents. This includes action taken by federal enforcement officers such as the agents of the Federal Bureau of Investigation, Central Intelligence Agency, Drug Enforcement Agency, and Postal Inspectors. State and municipal police officers are governed by these federal standards and may also have additional state laws that restrict their action. It does not cover the actions of private citizens who are not acting under police direction or solicitation.

→ Custody

Custody exists when the suspect is either deprived of his freedom in any significant way or is in formal custody such as an arrest. Custody for *Miranda* purposes is more broadly defined than just the traditional arrest. Custody may be subjective, from the point of the person being questioned, due to a coercive environment. Three factors may be considered in the determination of whether the suspect was in a coercive environment:

1. **Nature of the interview.** Whether the interview is aggressive or informal.

2. **Atmosphere.** Generally the most coercive place is a police station, yet a police station inquiry is not automatically custodial.

3. **Free to leave.** Whether at the time that the incriminating statement is made the suspect is free to end the interview by leaving the place of the interrogation or by asking the interrogator to leave, as evidenced by whether the interview ended with the defendant's arrest.

→ Interrogation

For interrogation to be present a police officer or his agent must subject a suspect to questioning or its functional equivalent which is designed to produce testimonial evidence. The functional equivalent to interrogation includes any words or actions by the police that they should know are reasonably likely to elicit an incriminating response (*Rhode Island* v. *Innis*, 1980).

When is a waiver of Miranda rights valid?

The defendant may waive the *Miranda* rights, provided the waiver is made voluntarily, knowingly and intelligently. If the suspect waives his or her rights, they may refrain from answering questions at any time. The totality of the circumstances test will help the court to determine if the waiver of rights was valid. This means that all of the factors surrounding the waiver will be considered. Three measures of whether the individual has properly waived his or her right to remain silent are:

- That the waiver was made **voluntarily:** The government must prove that the waiver was not the result of coercion or other factors which adversely influenced the defendant's exercise of free will. Torture, threats, promises of leniency, or other inducements may affect the voluntariness of a waiver. If the person is intoxicated to the point that he cannot understand his constitutional rights, the waiver is not valid.

- That the waiver was made **knowingly:** The government must prove that the defendant knew and understood his rights. Providing *Miranda* rights to a person who does not speak English, for example, cannot result in a knowing waiver of those rights. If the defendant is suffering from mental disability that renders him incapable of understanding his constitutional rights, a wavier may not be valid.

- That the waiver was made **intelligently:** The government must establish that the defendant intelligently relinquished those rights, that he understood he was agreeing to answer questions. This requires that the suspect be able to understand the consequences of not invoking the *Miranda* rights. This requirement does not suggest that the suspect is intelligent or have any particular IQ in order to make an intelligent waiver of his rights.

Miranda rights must be waived voluntarily, knowingly, and intelligently in order to constitute a valid waiver.

Voluntary Statements. Statements which are initiated by the defendant are not barred by the *Miranda* decision whether or not the person is in custody. The Court stated that there is no requirement that police stop a person who enters a police station and states that he wishes to confess to a crime, or a person who calls the police to offer a confession or any other statement that he desires to make. Volunteered statements of any kind are not barred by the Fifth Amendment and their admissibility is not affected by the holding in *Miranda*. If a defendant engages in conversation with a police officer and subsequently makes an incriminating statement he does not need to be warned of his rights because there was no interrogation.

If a suspect invokes his right to silence and does not provide a statement to the police he has the right to reinitiate a conversation. The waiver of *Miranda* rights may still be valid if it is clear that it was the suspect who reinitiated the conversation without inducement by the police.

Been There . . . Done That! 10–1

This case involved a man accused of having burned a beloved covered bridge. The case had been investigated and a warrant was issued for his arrest. He fled the area, which is when I became involved. I located the perpetrator in Louisiana; he was arrested on the Massachusetts warrant. Arrangements were made for his rendition.

He was picked up at the Louisiana jail and transported back to Massachusetts by myself and the Sergeant. While he was in a holding cell at the airport I sat outside as his guard. While reading a book I lit up a cigarette and the suspect asked for one. I gave the perpetrator the cigarette without responding and continued to read my book. About a half

hour later the same thing happened. He asked for a cigarette and I gave it to him. Saying nothing, I went back to reading my book. This time the man settled back in contentment and started to talk to get my attention. He said, "You know ma'am, I am not such a bad guy—now my brother-in-law, he is a bad guy! He cheats on his taxes and steals tools from the place he works. All I did was burn down an old bridge!"

I looked over to the Sergeant who was sitting across the room. He said, "Trooper, give that man another cigarette." While the man was in custody, there was no interrogation. His statement of admission was later used in evidence against him in court.

Public Safety Exception. The Supreme Court did not intend for *Miranda* warnings to govern all police interactions with the members of the public. In fact, the vast majority of police and citizen communications do not fall under *Miranda*'s protective umbrella. In situations where there is an immediate or impending danger to the public safety, called the public safety exception, the police may arrest a suspect without informing him or her of their constitutional rights and ask questions to elicit information in order to remove the threat to the public (*New York* v. *Quarles*, 1984). Officers must then provide *Miranda* warnings once the threat is over.

Requiring a person in custody to stand or walk in a police lineup, to speak prescribed words, to model particular clothing, or to give samples of handwriting, fingerprints, or blood does not compel him to incriminate himself within the meaning of the Fifth Amendment (*Schmerber* v. *California*, 1966). The reason why these are not governed under the Fifth Amendment is because are not testimonial in nature.

Right to Counsel under Miranda

The *Miranda* standard includes the right to have an attorney present during a custodial interrogation under its required procedural process. A suspect is entitled to the assistance of counsel during custodial interrogation even though the Constitution does not provide for such assistance (*Davis* v. *U.S.*, 2004). *Miranda* went further than previous case analysis of this right by requiring in cases of custodial interrogation that the suspect expressly be told of his right to an attorney and that he voluntarily waive that right under the same standards as other compelled testimony.

In *Edwards* the Court reiterated and clarified the concerns specified in the *Miranda* decision with respect to the suspect's right to counsel (*Edwards* v. *Arizona*, 1981). The Court held that the waiver of an attorney during custodial interrogation must not only be voluntarily waived, but the knowing and intelligent requirement must be satisfied also. The bright-line, prophylactic *Edwards* rule clearly requires that once a suspect has invoked his right to an attorney per *Miranda*, all questioning must stop. It cannot be reinitiated by the police at any time in the future unless counsel has been made available to the suspect or that the suspect himself initiates further conversations. The request for an attorney must be clearly stated and not be ambiguous for it to be honored, however. In *Davis* (2004) the Court stated that a statement by the suspect, "Maybe I should talk to a lawyer" was not a request for counsel under the requirements of *Miranda*.

If an attorney is made available at the request of the suspect and subsequently leaves, police may not resume interrogation when the attorney is no longer present (*Minnick* v. *Mississippi*, 1990). The police may not simply avoid the suspect's request for an attorney by changing the direction of questioning to a non-related offense (*Arizona* v. *Roberson*, 1988).

♦ **Bright Line: If a suspect in custody and subjected to interrogation requests an attorney ALL QUESTIONING MUST CEASE IMMEDIATELY!**

Sixth Amendment Considerations

Under the Sixth Amendment to the U.S. Constitution the rights of persons accused in criminal prosecution are protected. The remedy for violation of a suspect's Sixth Amendment right to counsel is that the evidence will be not be used in evidence against him. The Sixth Amendment to the U.S. Constitution states:

> In all criminal prosecutions, the accused shall enjoy the right to a speedy and public trial, by an impartial jury of the State and district wherein the crime shall have been committed, which district shall have been previously ascertained by law, and to be informed of the nature and cause of the accusation; to be confronted with the witnesses against him; to have compulsory process for obtaining witnesses in his favor, and to have the Assistance of Counsel for his defense.

The right to counsel under the Sixth Amendment prohibits law enforcement officers from deliberately eliciting incriminating information from a defendant in the absence of counsel after a formal (criminal) charge against the defendant has been filed (*Massiah* v. *U.S.*, 1964). The formal charge refers to the preliminary step to prosecution through a formal accusation of a named suspect (Garner, 2004). Examples of formal charging include an indictment by the Grand Jury and an arrangement.

The Sixth Amendment and the Due Process clause of the Fourteenth Amendment prohibit law enforcement officers from deliberately eliciting incriminating information from a defendant in the absence of counsel after a formal charge against the defendant has been filed, regardless of whether or not the defendant is in custody (*Innis*, 1980). This means that questioning cannot occur by a police officer in any location at any time, whether or not the person is in custody. The suspect cannot be questioned about the crime for which he or she was formally charged even if the police officer inadvertently has contact with the suspect. Examples of inadvertent would be if the police officer sees the suspect on the street, or arrests the suspect on an unrelated crime. However, the right to counsel under the Sixth Amendment is offense specific. It attaches to the suspect for the crimes the he or she was formally charged on only; they can be interrogated on unrelated crimes.

Once formal process has been initiated against the suspect, his or her Sixth Amendment right to counsel is violated by less obvious forms of interrogation, such as bugging, eavesdropping, or contact by an informant (*Massiah*, 1964). No form of interrogation of the suspect is permitted, whether or not the suspect is aware of being questioned by an agent of the government.

Fourteenth Amendment Considerations

The Fourteenth Amendment of the U.S. Constitution affirms the rights, guaranteed privileges, and immunities of citizenship, due process and equal protection. The Supreme Court has interpreted the amendment as restricting the states from denying any citizen the rights that are guaranteed under the U.S. Constitution. Through the Fourteenth Amendment the rules that are constitutionally required apply equally to both Federal and State police action. Section 1, which contains the due process clause and equal protection provision, specifically restrict police action. Throughout this chapter the application of the Fourteenth Amendment to police interrogation procedures will be made evident.

> Section. 1. All persons born or naturalized in the United States and subject to the jurisdiction thereof, are citizens of the United States and of the State wherein they reside. No State shall make or enforce any law which shall abridge the privileges or immunities of citizens of the United States; nor shall any State deprive any person of life, liberty, or property, without due process of law; nor deny to any person within its jurisdiction the equal protection of the laws.

The Exclusionary Rule

The *exclusionary rule* is a remedy that was judicially created to limit the power and authority of government officials and to assist in the enforcement of the U.S. Constitution. The *exclusionary rule* requires that evidence obtained by police in violation of the Fourteenth Amendment's due process clause, the Sixth Amendment's right to counsel provision, the Fifth Amendment's privilege against self-incrimination, or the Fourth Amendment's protection from illegal search and seizure would be excluded from use in trial against the defendant.

In *Weeks* the Court first stated that evidence secured through illegal search and seizure and in violation of the Fourth Amendment would be barred from use in federal prosecutions (*Weeks* v. *U.S.,* 1914). It was not until 1961 that the rule was made applicable to the states through the Fourteenth Amendment's Due Process Clause (*Mapp* v. *Ohio,* 1961). There are several alternatives to the exclusionary rule such as criminal prosecutions against officers who violate suspect rights, but these are extremely rare occurrences. Internal department discipline and prosecutions for civil rights violations in federal courts are other available remedies. Practical considerations, such as the integrity of the suspect, render these options fairly ineffective. As a result, the Court has emphasized the exclusionary rule as the most effective remedy to deter police misconduct.

Case in Point 10-2

Case in Point: *Mapp* v. *Ohio* (1961)

Three Cleveland police officers went to the apartment of Miss Dollree Mapp looking for a person suspected in a bombing. Miss Mapp refused to allow them in without a search warrant. Three hours later and after four more officers arrived the police forcibly gained entry. Miss Mapp demanded to see the search warrant. A paper, claimed to be a warrant, was held up by one of the officers. She grabbed the "warrant" and stuffed it down her blouse. There was a struggle in which the officers recovered the piece of paper, handcuffing her because she had resisted their official rescue of the paper. She was then forcibly taken upstairs to the second floor where officers searched her bedroom, the child's bedroom, the living room, the kitchen and a dinette. In the basement of the building a trunk was found which was also searched. The obscene materials for possession of which she was ultimately convicted were discovered in the course of that search.

At the trial no search warrant was produced by the prosecution, nor was the failure to produce one explained or accounted for. The State said that even if the search were made without authority, it is not prevented from using the unconstitutionally seized evidence at trial, citing *Wolf* v. *Colorado,* 338 U.S. 25 (1949), in which the Court had held "that in a prosecution in a State court for a State crime the Fourteenth Amendment does not forbid the admission of evidence obtained by an unreasonable search and seizure (pg. 33)." The Supreme Court concluded that the Fourth Amendment DOES apply to the states, and evidence obtained in an unreasonable search could not be used against the suspect.

Importance:

1. *Mapp* was the case when the Supreme Court first applied the exclusionary rule to the states.

2. It provides an example of the exclusionary rule applied in a Fourth Amendment context.

Exclusion of evidence that is indirectly obtained when one's rights are violated may also occur under the rule. Sometimes called derivative or secondary evidence, it is the evidence resulting from an illegal search or illegal interrogation. The *fruit of the poisonous tree doctrine* holds that the illegal search or interrogation taints the evidence obtained as well as facts discovered by the processes initiated by the unlawful procedure and that evidence must be suppressed (*Wong Sun* v. *U.S.,* 1963).

The Due Process Clause of the Fourteenth Amendment protects against the admission into evidence of confessions which are involuntary. For example, a suspect may make a valid waiver of *Miranda* rights but the statements may be violating the Fourteenth Amendment based on coercive tactics used by the police to obtain the statement. Statements that are the product of coercion, either physical or psychological, cannot be used as evidence — not because of its unlikely truth but because the methods used to extract them offend the underlying principle in the enforcement of our criminal law: that ours is accusatorial and not an inquisitorial system (*Rogers* v. *Richmond,* 1961).

Confessions are an important component in law enforcement, and any statement given freely and voluntarily without any compelling influences is admissible in evidence (*Innis,* 1980). A statement is inadmissible in court if the accused was coerced into making it. A statement is compelled if it is:

1. the product of either physical or psychological coercion;

2. extracted by any sort of threat or violence;

3. the product of direct or implied promises, or;

4. made as the result of the exertion of any improper influence.

When is a confession coerced? A statement may not be used in court if it was made in an environment that is so coercive as to support the conclusion that it was not freely and voluntarily given (*Colorado* v. *Connelly,* 1986). Typically all of the factors surrounding the incident, or the totality of the circumstances, will determine whether physical or psychological pressures unduly influenced the accused to make a statement.

◆ Generally a promise of leniency will nullify a confession; certain kinds of promises are acceptable, however.

◆ In *Guerrero* (1988) the US Court of Appeals ruled that "it is well settled that police may use small deceptions while interrogating witnesses" (*United States* v. *Guerrero,* 1988).

◆ In *Mendoza-Cecelia* the US Court of Appeals ruled that "Isolated incidents of deception . . . are normally insufficient to preclude free choice" while they "acknowledge that police may use some psychological tactics in interrogating a suspect" (*United States* v. *Mendoza-Cecelia,* 1992).

◆ Threats to arrest members of a suspect's family may cause a confession to be involuntary (*Rogers,* 1961).

These individual factors are among those that the court will look at in determining if the interrogation process was coercive:

Age of the Suspect. The circumstances surrounding the statements from juveniles are more carefully scrutinized because they are more susceptible than adults to coercive forces or intimidation. Courts demand that police officers use caution when questioning juveniles to make sure that they do not confess out of fear. The questioning by several officers at the same time or the absence of a parent may be coercive if the juvenile is young.

Experience of the Suspect. A child's or adult's history of contact with the police and the criminal justice system may be significant to determine whether the statements were voluntary. A person with a history of criminal activity and familiarity with police practice is less likely to feel threatened to the point of being coerced into speaking.

Intelligence or Mental Illness. Someone with a low I.Q. or mental illness may be overly suggestible and subject to intimidation. Persons having mental illness or low intelligence need to be questioned in the same non-coercive atmosphere as a juvenile. Extra care must be taken to assure that the person understands the situation in addition to his or her rights per *Miranda*. The educational level of the suspect should alert the police officer to the possibility that there is a greater susceptibility to coercion.

Alcohol or Drug Intoxication. Although intoxication alone is not enough to negate an otherwise voluntary act, the fact that a statement is given while the suspect is under the influence of alcohol or drugs is relevant to an evaluation of its voluntariness. If the suspect is unduly susceptible to the coercive forces of police questioning due to intoxication it may impact the voluntariness of any statement given.

Physical Condition of the Suspect. An injured or ill suspect or someone who has had little sleep prior to the interrogation may be more susceptible to the coercive forces of an interrogation.

Length of the Interrogation. The Federal Courts have stated a preference that a person under arrest be brought to court for arraignment "without unnecessary delay" in order for a confession to be admissible against him (*McNabb* v. *U.S.*, 1943). This requirement aimed at addressing incommunicado interrogation and coerced confessions is known as the McNabb-Mallory Doctrine. The Court has never imposed the rule on the states nor did it set a specific time after which a confession would be invalid. Congress in 1968 legislated to set a six-hour period for interrogation following arrest before the suspect must be presented to court (Omnibus Crime Control and Safe Streets Act 82 Stat. 210, 18 U.S.C. Sec. 3501(c).) Some states have adopted the rule voluntarily. Known as the "Rosario Rule," Massachusetts requires that the defendant who has been arrested will be brought before a court if then in session, and if not, at its next session (*Commonwealth* v. *Rosario*, 1996).

The exclusionary rule has been controversial and criticized since it was established. Numerous decisions have narrowed its application, most notably the "good faith exception." In 1984 the Court recognized that evidence secured by police officers who rely on a warrant would not be excluded, even if the warrant was later found to be defective (*United States* v. *Leon*, 1984).

Fourth Amendment Considerations

The Fourth Amendment of the U.S. Constitution protects against unreasonable searches and seizures. It states:

> The right of the people to be secure in their persons, houses, papers, and effects, against unreasonable searches and seizures, shall not be violated, and no Warrants shall issue, but upon probable cause, supported by Oath or affirmation, and particularly describing the place to be searched, and the persons or things to be seized.

Since the application of the exclusionary rule to the states, a confession, statement, or admission, which is made by a person who is illegally in custody, may be excluded as evidence obtained as a result of unlawful seizures. The application of the Fourth Amendment as a protection against arbitrary arrests has become established law (*Steagald* v. *U.S.*, 1981). The Fourth Amendment applies to seizures, which may not necessarily mean a formal arrest in order to bring the warrant requirement to bear. An objective justification must validate all seizures of the person, including those that only involve a brief detention.

In order to protect statements and physical evidence that may be acquired from the suspect, attention must be given to the legality of the detention or arrest prior to the interrogation. Under the Fourth Amendment, a seizure is made reasonable by the application for a warrant which is based on probable cause. Probable cause itself may be sufficient to justify the detention or arrest in some situations.

The criminal justice process typically begins when a person is placed under arrest. An arrest occurs when the person is taken into police custody and deprived of his liberty by legal authority, when he or she is no longer free to leave. An arrest may occur when the police officer states that someone is under arrest. The suspect does not have to be placed in handcuffs or restraints nor do the words need to be stated for an arrest to have been made. When the person submits to the authority of the police, either voluntarily or involuntarily they are under arrest. Police have the *power to arrest* in the following circumstances:

◆ **When the police officer personally sees someone commit a crime**

For example, if a police officer is patrolling and sees a man hit another man outside of a bar. The police officer may stop the cruiser and arrest the man for having committed an assault and battery against the other.

◆ **When an arrest warrant has been issued**

The arrest warrant will contain information on the crime that was committed, the identity of the person to be arrested, a location where the person might be found, and the command for the police officer to make that arrest.

♦ **When a police officer has a reasonable belief, based on facts and circumstances, that a person has committed or is about to commit a crime, the officer may arrest that person.**

This is an arrest that is based on probable cause without a warrant. For example, if the police officer receives a radio call that a store has just been robbed along with the description of the suspect, and he or she sees a person matching that description running away from the area, an arrest can be made.

Case in Point 10–3

Case in Point: *Carroll* v. *U.S.* (1925)

Federal prohibition agents developed information that the Carroll brothers were regularly transporting whiskey from Detroit to Grand Rapids, Michigan, a distance of 152 miles. The boys outran the law once and they could not be caught in the act, although they had once agreed to sell three cases of whiskey to an undercover agent. On December 15, 1921 agents saw their Fleet Oldsmobile Roadster and gave chase. The vehicle was stopped and the agents did not see any contraband in the car. Without consent or a warrant one agent concluded that the upholstery was harder than normal and cut open the leather seat. The agents removed 69 quarts of illegal gin and whiskey which had been hidden. George Carroll handed the agent several ten dollar bills and told him to take the liquor and give them one more chance. The defense later said that the bribe offer was a misunderstanding!

Importance:

1. The Supreme Court held that a warrantless search of an automobile stopped by police officers, who had probable cause to believe the vehicle contained contraband was not unreasonable under the Fourth Amendment. This became known as the "automobile exception," where the warrant requirement of the Fourth Amendment did not apply to searches of an automobile.

2. The Supreme Court defined probable cause as existing where the facts and circumstances within the officers' knowledge and of which they had reasonably trustworthy information are sufficient in themselves to warrant a man of reasonable caution in the belief that an offense has been or is being committed.

Probable Cause

The court has acknowledged that an exact definition of probable cause is difficult to express because it depends on the totality of the circumstances (*Brinegar* v. *U.S.,* 1949). The courts determine if probable cause to arrest a person existed by looking at the events leading up to the arrest or detention. However, *probable cause* means more than mere suspicion (*Carroll* v. *U.S.,* 1925).

The court will look at the totality of the circumstances to determine if the police officer had probable cause to make an arrest. Information that was obtained unlawfully, such as statements from an illegal interrogation, cannot be used to establish probable cause for an arrest. An arrest is valid if the police officer had probable cause to make the arrest at that time, even if the person turns out to be innocent. In order to detain or "pick up" and take a suspect to the police station for interrogation,

> ### Case in Point 10–4
>
> *Kaupp* was a 17-year-old man suspected of murder. The case turns on the Fourth Amendment rule that a confession "obtained by exploitation of an illegal arrest" may not be used against a criminal defendant. *Brown* v. *Illinois*, 422 U. S. 590, 603 (1975). After a 14-year-old girl disappeared in January 1999 the Harris County Sheriff's Department learned she had had a sexual relationship with her 19-year-old half brother, who had been in the company of Robert Kaupp on the day of the girl's disappearance. On January 26th, deputy sheriffs questioned the brother and Kaupp at headquarters; Kaupp was cooperative and was permitted to leave, but the brother failed a polygraph examination (his third such failure). Eventually he confessed that he had fatally stabbed his half sister and placed her body in a drainage ditch. He implicated Kaupp in the crime. Detectives immediately tried, but failed to obtain a warrant to question Kaupp due a lack of probable cause.
>
> The police went into his home at 3:00 AM and told him they had to talk. He responded, "ok."
>
> Kaupp was handcuffed and brought to the police station in his underwear and without shoes. Although he was given his rights per *Miranda* prior to an interrogation, the Supreme Court held that the initial detainment was paramount to an arrest without probable cause, causing the confession to be suppressed. His response of "ok" was determined by the Court to be nothing more than submission to lawful authority in a situation where he had no choice but to go with the police officers.
>
> A seizure of the person within the meaning of the Fourth and Fourteenth Amendments occurs when, "taking into account all of the circumstances surrounding the encounter, the police conduct would 'have communicated to a reasonable person that he was not at liberty to ignore the police presence and go about his business.'" *Florida* v. *Bostick*, 501 U. S. 429, 437 (1991) (quoting *Michigan* v. *Chesternut*, 486 U. S. 567, 569 (1988)).

police must have probable cause to make an arrest or a warrant (*Kaupp v. Texas*, 2003). A violation of the Fourth and Fourteenth Amendments can not be remedied by *Miranda* warnings alone (*Taylor v. Alabama*, 1982).

Without probable case for an arrest a suspect can be requested to come for questioning with a full understanding that it is voluntary on the part of the suspect.

Probable cause may be based on personal observations of the officer and through information that is provided from another source:

Courtesy of iStockphoto, Inc.

A valid arrest protects future statements that may be made by the suspect.

♦ Personal observations

If the police officer is legally at the location where he or she observes a criminal act, no further probable cause is needed to make an arrest. This means that the officer cannot make a trespass against the person and use the information to furnish probable cause. For example, a police officer may not go onto someone's property and look through the window to gain information to be used as probable cause.

A suspect's confession or admission that is obtained legally may be used to establish probable cause.

◆ Information provided by others

Police officers may use information that is provided by victims, witnesses, other police officers, and informants to establish probable cause to make an arrest. The reliability of the information must be determined prior to its use. When other police officers provide information it is generally considered reliable and may be used as the basis for probable cause to arrest. For a full discussion on determining the reliability of information from other sources refer to Chapter One.

Conclusions

This chapter outlined some of the legal boundaries for questioning suspects of crimes. The primary source for limiting police action and providing the rights to the accused is the U.S. Constitution. The Court's interpretation of the U.S. Constitution has resulted in numerous procedural rules and requirements. As noted, the U.S. Constitution defines the rights of citizens from government agents, i.e. police officers or someone that is working at their request. It does not apply to protect the rights of citizens from actions taken by other citizens. Since the U.S. Constitution provides the supreme law of the land, the individual state governments cannot infringe on these guaranteed rights.

The Fourth, Fifth, and Sixth amendments of the U.S. Constitution provide very different protections, although they sometimes appear to overlap. The right to an attorney under the Fifth Amendment *Miranda* rule attaches the right to consultation prior to the interrogation stage and is concerned with police custody of the person. This timing is different from the Sixth Amendment right which attaches at the time of any formal court proceeding. The Fourteenth Amendment comes into play for all of these mentioned amendments when the consideration is one of due process, or fundamental fairness.

Chapter Ten Questions for Review

Short Answer Questions

1. What rights of the accused does the Fifth Amendment protect?

2. What rights of the accused does the Sixth Amendment protect?

3. Is the exclusionary rule written in the U.S. Constitution? If not, how did it come to be?

4. Describe the circumstances leading to *Mapp* v. *Ohio*. What significance does this case have regarding the exclusionary rule?

5. Give an example of circumstances where the good faith doctrine would apply.

6. Explain the police officer's "right of arrest." Who can be arrested, where, when and why?

7. What are exigent circumstances? When do they allow seizures normally outside the parameters of the Fourth Amendment?

8. *Miranda* warnings must be issued when custody and interrogation occur simultaneously. For purposes of the *Miranda* ruling, what constitutes custody? What constitutes interrogation?

9. Discuss the differences in the right to counsel under the Fifth Amendment as opposed to the right to counsel under the Sixth Amendment.

10. What rights of the accused does the Fifth Amendment protect? The Sixth Amendment?

Fill-in Questions

1. The _____ provides that those who execute the law must rely on the application of known principles or laws, and those principles must be applied _____ to all citizens.

2. _____ , _____ , _____ , protects citizens from actions of government officials and their agents, and not from other citizens.

3. The exclusionary rule is a remedy that was _____ to limit the power and authority of government officials and to assist in the enforcement of the _____ .

4. The court has acknowledged that an exact definition of _____ is difficult to express because it depends on the _____ .

5. Police officers may be justified in making a _____ of a person based on probable cause that he has committed a felony, a misdemeanor that amounts to a breach of peace in the presence of the officer, or in circumstances where the arrest power is specifically given to police officers.

_____ .

6. The Fifth Amendment of the U.S. Constitution contains many protections, of concern in the area of interrogation is that it protects the right against _____ and

_____ .

7. The defendant may waive the *Miranda* rights, provided the waiver is made _____ ,

_____ and

_____ .

8. The circumstances surrounding the statements from _____ are more carefully scrutinized because they are more susceptible than adults to _____ or _____ .

9. The _____ under the Sixth Amendment and the _____ of the Fourteenth Amendment prohibits law enforcement officers from deliberately eliciting incriminating information from a defendant in the absence of counsel after a formal charge against the defendant has been filed, regardless of whether or not the defendant is in custody.

10. The right to an attorney under the Fifth Amendment *Miranda* rule attaches the right to consultation _____ and is concerned with _____ of the person.

Exercises

1. You be the judge! Using the cases in this chapter, write the opinion for the court relative to the admissibility of this confession. Cite your cases and explain your reasoning as if this were a real case.

John and Jimmy Jones were suspected of a robbery in the liquor store on 5th Avenue where the owner was also shot and killed. They were brought into the police station for questioning and placed in separate rooms. Officer Smith sat in the room with John said nothing to him. After fifteen minutes Officer Fitzpatrick opened the door to the interrogation room and said to Officer Smith, "Jimmy told me everything" (a lie) then left. Officer Smith turned to John and said, we don't need anything from you now. Talk to me if you want because we got the goods on you. Sounds like your brother put the whole thing on you. John gave a full confession. A motion to suppress was brought in court by his attorney.

2. You be the judge! Using the cases in this chapter, write the opinion for the court relative to the admissibility of this confession. Cite your cases and explain your reasoning as if this were a real case.

Cheryl Esposito was arrested for the murder of her boyfriend Jeffrey Tang. Officer Book advised of her rights per *Miranda*, which she waived. During the interrogation Cheryl would not tell who had disposed of the body or why Jeffrey had been killed. Officer Book told Cheryl that her son was seen leaving the house on the night of the murder (a lie) and that he would be arrested for the murder if Cheryl did not talk. Cheryl gave a full confession implicating her new lover Bruce.

Reference List

Arizona v. *Roberson,* 486 U.S. 675 (1988).

Bram v. *United States,* 168 U.S. 532 (1897).

Brinegar v. *U.S.,* 338 U.S. 160 (1949).

Brown v. *Mississipi,* 297 U.S. 278 (1937).

Carroll v. *U.S.,* 267 U.S. 132 (1925).

Colombe v. *Connecticut,* 367 U.S. 568 (1961).

Colorado v. *Connelly,* 479 U.S. 157 (1986).

Commonwealth v. *Rosario,* 422 Mass. 48 (1996).

Davis v. *U.S.,* 114 S.Ct. 2350 (2004).

Doe v. *United States,* 487 U.S. 201

Edwards v. *Arizona,* 451 U.S. 477 (1981).

Garner, B. (2004). *Black's Law Dictionary* (8th ed.). St. Paul, MN: West Publishing Co.

Kaupp v. *Texas,* 538 U.S. 626 (2003).

Mapp v. *Ohio,* 367 U.S. 643 (1961).

Massiah v. *U.S.,* 377 U.S. 201 (1964).

McNabb v. *U.S.,* 318 U.S. 332 (1943).

Minnick v. *Mississippi,* 498 U.S. 146 (1990).

Miranda v. *Arizona,* 384 U.S. 436 (1966).

New York v. *Quarles,* 467 U.S. 649 (1984).

Omnibus Crime Control and Safe Streets Act 82 Stat. 210, 18 U.S.C. Sec. 3501(c).

People v. *Fox,* 319 Ill. 606 (1925).

Rhode Island v. *Innis*, 446 U.S. 291 (1980).

Rogers v. *Richmond*, 365 U.S. 534 (1961).

Schmerber v. *California*, 384 U.S. 757 (1966).

Steagald v. *U.S.*, 451 U.S. 204 (1981).

Taylor v. *Alabama*, 457 U.S. 587 (1982).

United States v. *Guerrero*, 847 F.2d 1363 (1988).

United States v. *Leon*, 468 U.S. 897 (1984).

United States v. *Mendoza-Cecelia*, 963 F.2d 1467 (1992).

Weeks v. *U.S.*, 232 U.S. 383 (1914).

Wong Sun v. *U.S.*, 371 U.S. 471 (1963).

Confessions

Excited utterance	False confession
Frisk	Interrogation
Miscarriage of justice	Question-first technique
Subtle compulsion	Suspect paranoia

CHAPTER OBJECTIVES

After completing this chapter, you should be able to:

◆ Describe the question-first technique and why it is unlawful
◆ Define interrogation according to the Supreme Court
◆ State the three conditions that must be met to obtain a confession legally
◆ Describe the qualities of an interrogator
◆ State the reasons why suspects might confess to the police
◆ Explain the three types of police officers as suggested by Schaefer
◆ List the categories given that are not considered "interrogation"
◆ Describe the three categories of false confessions
◆ Explain the problems of interrogation and how to overcome them
◆ List numerous reasons why miscarriages of justice occur

Introduction

The focus of this chapter is on police and military interrogation and dispelling myths associated with the practice. There are two distinct perspectives concerning interrogations. One view is that false confessions constitute a major problem in our society, despite *Miranda* reforms to curtail coercive police interrogation practices. The other view is that interrogations have become lost since *Miranda*. Fewer interrogations are attempted and the innocent are left vulnerable to unsolved crime because of it.

Courtesy of iStockphoto, Inc.

There exists a balancing act concerning the interrogation which involves providing protections to the guilty without jeopardizing the safety of the innocent. The police in America have become compliant with the rules of *Miranda*. Studies on the efficacy of interrogation suggest that interrogations leading to confession are common and that American police officers are good at it. This is a logical but misleading conclusion since the majority of studies do not take into account those cases where confessions are not attempted by the police. Some case-specific practices to assess guilt as part of the interrogation are provided.

What Is an Interrogation?

Interrogation is a process that is conducted by law enforcement officers and military personnel. Interrogation laws do not protect citizens from a process that is initiated by nongovernment civilians. As stated in Chapter One, the United States Supreme Court has defined *interrogation* as questioning initiated by law enforcement officers after a person has been taken into custody or otherwise deprived of his freedom of action in any significant way (*Miranda* v. *Arizona,* 1966). Interest in interrogation practices is widespread, however. Because practices that government officials use during interrogation are scrutinized by the public, it is useful to study current controversies surrounding the process.

Subsequent to *Miranda* the Court has commented on the opinion to prevent a narrow interpretation of the case. The Court intended to address the "interrogation environment." Concern centered on the police practices that would subjugate the individual to the will of his examiner (*Rhode Island* v. *Innis,* 1980). It is clear therefore that the special procedural safeguards outlined in *Miranda* are required, not where a suspect is simply taken into custody, but rather where a suspect in custody is subjected to interrogation. Interrogation, as conceptualized in the *Miranda* opinion, must reflect a measure of compulsion above and beyond that inherent in custody itself (*Innis*, 1980). The *Miranda* safeguards come into play whenever a person in custody is subjected to either express questioning or its functional equivalent. That is to say, the term "interrogation" under *Miranda* refers not only to express questioning, but also to any words or actions on the part of the police (other than those normally attendant to arrest and custody) that the police should know are reasonably likely to elicit an incriminating response from the suspect.

In order for an interrogation to be conducted lawfully, these three conductions must be met:

1. The opportunity to interrogate a suspect must be lawfully obtained

2. There must be an absence of force, threat of force, or promise of leniency

3. There must be compliance with requirements for warnings of constitutional rights to a custodial suspect

Compliance with the warnings per *Miranda* must be taken seriously. A recent United States Supreme Court strongly denounced the *question-first* techniques sometimes used by police to avoid the requirements of providing the *Miranda* warnings. The *question-first* technique is a deliberate attempt by a police officer to avoid providing a suspect with his or her

Case in Point 11–1

Case in Point: *Missouri* v. *Seibert* (2004)

Patrice Seibert's 12-year-old son Jonathan had cerebral palsy, and when he died in his sleep she feared charges of neglect because of bedsores on his body. In her presence, two of her teenage sons and two of their friends devised a plan to conceal the facts surrounding Jonathan's death by incinerating his body in the course of burning the family's mobile home, in which they planned to leave Donald Rector, a mentally ill teenager living with the family, to avoid any appearance that Jonathan had been unattended. Seibert's son Darian and a friend set the fire, and Donald died.

When a police officer questioned Seibert about Rector's death, the officer intentionally did not read Seibert her *Miranda* rights, hoping to get a confession. During the interrogation, Seibert admitted that she knew that Rector was supposed to die in the fire. After this admission, Seibert was given a 20-minute break from the interrogation; when it resumed the officer

advised Seibert of her *Miranda* rights, which she waived. Seibert then repeated statements she had made prior to receiving a *Miranda* warning. Patrice Seibert was convicted of second-degree murder and sentenced to life in prison for her role in the death of Donald Rector. This midstream reading of warnings after interrogation and unwarned confession could not effectively comply with *Miranda*'s Constitutional requirement. The U.S. Supreme Court held that this interrogation technique rendered both confessions inadmissible.

Importance:

1. In *Seibert* the Court said that the police cannot purposefully avoid providing the warnings per *Miranda* in order to get a confession! In some cases, questioning of a suspect may be the equivalent of custody for the purposes of *Miranda* warnings. Obtaining a confession without the warnings and then giving the warnings a short time later is not acceptable.

rights per *Miranda*. It occurs when the suspect is interrogated first, a short period of time is allowed to elapse, and then the warnings are given and the suspect re-interrogated. The second interrogation is made to document the previous confession made without legal warnings.

Since *Miranda*

The modern confession law in *Miranda* has professionalized interrogation practices and contributed to the declining use of coercion in police practices (Leo, 1996a). Leo found that early studies on the impact of the *Miranda* warnings were mixed: a Yale study concluded that the warnings were largely ignored by police and wholly ineffective; some concluded that its application did not decrease the percentage of felony complaints; others claimed a large decrease in felony cases that reached the grand jury following *Miranda*. He summed up the *Miranda* impact literature up to 1996 with five important findings:

1. After an initial adjustment period American police began to comply regularly with the letter of the *Miranda* requirements.

2. Suspects frequently waived their constitutional rights and chose to speak to detectives.

3. Once the waiver was obtained, police interrogation techniques did not change as a result of *Miranda*.

4. Suspects continued to provide detectives with confessions and incriminating statements, though in some instances at a lower rate than prior to *Miranda*.

5. The clearance and conviction rate did not appear to be significantly affected by *Miranda*, although in some cases it too had dropped.

The evidence suggests that fewer police officers may attempt to interrogate since *Miranda*. As early impact studies indicated, from 1966 to 1969 detectives chose to interrogate fewer suspects (Leo, 1996a). Confessions lost due to procedural handcuffing is a major concern (Cassell, 1999). Clearance rates in some cities dropped significantly post *Miranda* (Leo, 1996a). In almost half of felony cases there may be no attempt by police officers to gain a confession or gather intelligence information (Colaprete, 2002). The evidence is in agreement: police officers are very successful at interrogation when they attempt it (Thomas III, 2004).

Whether police officers follow up with an interrogation or not, they do comply with the mandate to provide the warnings to suspects. A recent study found that the police recite the *Miranda* warnings to suspects most

Been There ... Done That! 11–1

Rarely will a confession be challenged in court if the <u>Miranda</u> warnings are given. Determining if the warnings were given properly is an objective test. Compliance without tricks to overcome the suspect reluctance to waive his or her rights is sufficient to meet the challenge. If anything, police officers are overly compliant with giving these warnings. The Court in <u>Miranda</u> only required that the suspect be provided the warnings once, whereas in many cases a suspect receives them multiple times!

The second part in determining whether the person gave a voluntary statement is found after the waiving of rights. Based on the actions of the police officer during the confession, this test is subjective and can depend on many different factors. In one case where an attorney challenged the admissibility of a confession that I had obtained, he based it on my statement, "I am here to help you," which was repeated a few times during the confession. Do not take this kind of challenge personally when it occurs! It is in the perpetrator's best interests to have a confession suppressed; a defense attorney is only doing their job when they make that claim. In that case the confession was so damming, that the suspect faced heavy prison time if the confession were introduced against him. The challenge was not successful, however.

It is not what you say, but how you say it that matters in these situations. If I had that one to do over I would have suggested that I was there "to help you help yourself." Think before you speak!

of the time; the compliance rate is 95% (Thomas III, 2004). Compliance is further supported in that study, in only 6% of cases do the defendants contest that they received their rights.

Who Are Likely To Conduct Interrogations?

As stated earlier, research indicates that police officers are typically successful when they attempt to interrogate. The problem appears that police officers do not attempt an interrogation in almost half of felony cases. What can explain the large disparity between those highly successful interrogations and the failure to try? No empirical studies have examined the characteristics of a successful interrogator.

A few studies exist that have examined the impact of the police officer gender during an interview. Policing continues to be a male dominated profession. Black males make up a mere 11.8% of the nation's policing workforce (Schmalleger, 2004). Women hold approximately 12.7% of sworn policing positions in the United States (NCWP, 2002).

Research results indicate that the biases and perception of the interviewee have greater impact than the gender of the interviewer (Gelinas, 2005). Neither race nor gender of the officer has been found to have an impact on the outcome of police-citizen encounters (The Committee on Law and Justice, 2004).

Few experts of interrogation address the issue of interrogator characteristics. The ability to use persuasive tactics is often mentioned. The ability to persuade is central to the interrogator who is dealing with the suspect who is unwilling to provide a statement (Rabon, 1992). The police interrogator must possess a high degree of emotional control and feel comfortable using persuasive tactics that may be morally offensive to some investigators (Inbau, Reid, Buckley, & Jayne, 2001).

Others tackle the issue by explaining why interrogations are avoided. Some officers fear the tedious task of memorizing an endless set of rules needed to conduct lawful interrogations (Rutledge, 1994). Another suggestion is that few agencies place sufficient emphasis on the development of needed skills (Hess, 1997). The use of Gestapo tactics and rigid methods is one reason why they are not successful (Yeschke, 2003). Ego can be a undermining influence that causes narrow mindedness on the part of the interrogator (Holmes, 2002).

More to the point, the skills required to successful interrogation are knowledge in the areas of human behavior, psychology, persuasive communication and the law (Buckley & Jayne, 2005). Officers who are most confident in conducting interrogations possess the skills and knowledge to follow through with the difficult task of interrogating. It takes knowledge and skill to conduct a lawful interrogation.

Of the characteristics that have been previously mentioned I believe that those who are most confident in their knowledge of the law will be more willing to conduct interrogations. The educated police officer will follow up his or her knowledge of the law with information that will be beneficial to successfully completing the task. This is not because legalistic officers would be predisposed to enforce the law at any cost. It is because educated police officers have greater initiative, a wiser use of discretion, enhanced communications with the public, more effective job performance, fewer citizen complaints, and a heightened sensitivity to racial and ethnic issues (Carter, Sapp, & Stephens, 1989). Higher education is significantly correlated with better academy performance (Aamodt & Flink, 2001).

Experts have long categorized police officers and their professional performance according to their legal expertise. In his seminal research on police typology, Schaefer suggested that there are three types of police officers based on their knowledge of the legal applicability of *Miranda:* Law Enforcers, Servicers, and Law Enforcers/Servicers (Schaefer, 1971).

Courtesy of iStockphoto, Inc.

The more confident the police officer is about his or her legal knowledge, the more likely they are to routinely conduct interrogations.

- ◆ **Law Enforcers** are officers who score highest in their knowledge of the legal applicability of *Miranda.* These officers feel their role is one of crime control and are most aware of the procedural guarantees that should be extended.
- ◆ **Servicers** are officers perceived their role in criminal justice as primarily aiding the public in any way possible. These officers scored lowest in their knowledge of the legal applicability of *Miranda.*
- ◆ **Law Enforcers/Servicers** is a mixture of the other two classifications. Somewhat familiar with the law, they will interrogate when the department policy requires and in specific cases where they feel comfortable.

Who Are Likely to Waive Their Rights *per* Miranda?

Initially four out of five suspects that are given rights per *Miranda* will waive them and submit to questioning; some change their mind. Ultimately one-fourth of all suspects interrogated invoke one or more rights and refused to talk (Leo & White. W. S., 1999). Police officers know from experience that the ex-felons routinely refuse to waive their rights per *Miranda.* Those individuals are more seasoned criminals who have been exposed to the criminal justice system. Leo confirmed what police officers take for granted; although 78% of suspects will waive their rights per *Miranda,* compared to a suspect with no prior record, a suspect with a prior felony record was four times as likely to invoke his *Miranda* rights. With a misdemeanor record they are three times more likely to refuse to talk with police (Leo, 1996a).

In a study within the Rochester, NY, Police Department identifying the rates of voluntary confessions, attempts to gain voluntary confessions, and the rate of missed opportunities (no attempt to gain confessions) the figures appear much lower (Colaprete, 2002). Voluntary confessions are obtained in the range of 37% of all felony arrests, while no attempt was made to gain a confession or gather intelligence information in 46.22 % of the felony cases.

In a study attempting to replicate the interrogation process, authors found that 58% of all suspects waive their rights, corroborating the tendency of suspects in the police station to act similarly (Kassin and Gudjonsson, 2004). In the Thomas study (2004) the suspects waived *Miranda* 68% of the time. More than 10 times as many suspects waive *Miranda* than those who elect not to answer questions. Summarizing the cases where a confession was elicited, a range between 42% upwards to 70% of suspects waived their rights per *Miranda* and gave statements or confessions (Kassin and Gudjonsson, 2004; Colaprete, 2002).

Why Do People Waive Their Rights?

One reason that might explain the phenomenon is that police use techniques designed to obtain waivers (Kassin & Norwick, 2004). Since obtaining a truthful confession from the perpetrator is the law enforcement goal, the emphasis is on obtaining a voluntary waiver. Establishing rapport with the suspect, offering sympathy and an ally, and minimizing the process as a mere formality are some of the successful approaches that police use when offering a suspect their rights per *Miranda* (Leo, 1996b).

A second possibility of why persons waive their rights per *Miranda* is simply that people are different; they come into the interrogation room with different personalities and experiences (Kassin & Norwick, 2004). As noted earlier, suspects with prior felony records are least likely to waive their rights per *Miranda* and provide a confession to interrogators. Suspects with prior records are at greater risk in the criminal justice system with heightened penalties for second and subsequent offenders as well as mandatory sentencing for a guilty finding for multiple felonies.

Why Do Suspects Confess?

Suspects confess, according to Tousignant, because of *suspect paranoia* (Tousignant, 1991). *Suspect paranoia* is the motivation that suspects have because they are never sure of exactly what information investigators have; they may attempt to give false information to lead investigators in another direction. Their first thought is to escape detection and therefore to find out what the police officers know.

Kassin and Gudjonsson further a number of explanations from the psychological perspective (Kassin and Gudjonsson, 2004). People may confess to overcome feelings of guilt and remorse, as well as the fear of retaliation or of losing love. A suspect becomes entangled in the decision on whether to speak or invoke the rights to silence and an attorney, making those decisions of their perceived probability of the long and short term consequences.

Been There . . . Done That! 11–2

There are two things that the interrogator can do that will give validity
to the voluntariness of the confession
that you have taken. First, when the
statement is being typed make an obvious error on it, something that the
perpetrator will notice. Examples are
the name of his mother or her child
or time of day. Second, allow the
suspect to express his or her feelings
in their own handwriting.

    This is done simply by asking the
perpetrator to read the statement
after it has been typed up and to
make corrections. If he or she does
not read it carefully and misses the
error that was made, call their attention to it and ask if that information is correct. Once it is noticed
ask that they make the correction and
initial the change. This demonstrates

when others are trying to determine if
the confession is forced that you HAVE
given the suspect the opportunity to
read it and object to anything that
is contained in it. Next, ask how he
or she feels, suggesting that they
write "that" at the bottom of the
page. Most people will simple write,
"I'm sorry," or, "I didn't mean to do
it." Others may write more. It is the
only opportunity that the interrogator
has to document the feelings of the
perpetrator AT THE TIME OF THE INTER-
ROGATION, which may be disputed at a
later time. I believe that doing this
has been the reason why none of the
confessions that I have taken were
ever suppressed in court. It is difficult to maintain having been forced
when the evidence says otherwise.

The reasons why suspects confess to crimes are varied and often a combination of factors including the case characteristics, the police behavior, and the personality and experiences of the suspect (Gudjonsson, 2003). In order to overcome the obstacles to obtaining confessions consider the things that make it difficult for people to confess. Gudjonsson (2003) suggests there are five major inhibiting factors:

1. Fear of legal sanctions. This includes the fear of punishment and the consequences of having a criminal record.

2. Concern about reputation. The higher a persons standing in the community, the more likely that person will perceive that he has something to lose. This may be true for relatively minor crimes.

3. Not wanting to admit to oneself. An offender may push the memory out of conscious awareness to protect the psychological well-being and self-esteem.

4. Not wanting one's family and friends to know about the crime. Fear of being rejected by family and friends may inhibit the willingness to confess.

5. Fear of retaliation. An unwillingness to implicate others due to the fear of retaliation may be stronger than the fear of sanctions if convicted.

Does a Waiver Affect the Case?

There was no significant statistical difference between those who waived their rights and those who did not in either subsequent charging or severity of punishment (Leo, 1996a). The only difference was that those who waived their *Miranda* rights were twice as likely to have their case resolved through plea bargaining. The fact that these cases are more likely to be disposed of through plea bargaining provides benefits to the victims of crime who are not called upon to testify in addition to saving time and money on trials that can be avoided. Plea bargaining can actually mean many different things. In some instances a defendant may plead guilty only if the charges are reduced. In other cases, the defendant may plead guilty only if there is an agreement to a lenient sentence. If a plea is negotiated, there will be "something in it" for all the legal parties. It promotes administrative efficiency in the courts:

◆ Saves tax dollars.
◆ Insures prompt correctional measures.
◆ Promotes rehabilitation.
◆ Reduces humiliation and misery to defendants.
◆ Can result in lesser punishment.

False Confessions

Hundreds of people usually come forward to confess to the crime whenever a celebrity, a public official, or a well-known person in the public eye is victimized. They cannot all be the perpetrator. So most, if not all, of the confessions must be false. False confessions do occur in rare circumstances. For example, over two hundred people confessed to kidnapping the Lindberg baby in 1932 and hundreds of people confessed to the 1947 Black Dahlia murder in Los Angeles.

A false confession is a written or oral statement acknowledging guilt, made by one who did not commit the crime.

While there is no concrete estimate on the numbers of persons who have provided false confessions, evidence of the phenomenon does exist. In cases of proven false confessions a common factor was a lengthy interrogation of the suspect, on average 16.3 hours. Psychologists categorize false confessions into three groups (Kassin, 2005):

1. **Voluntary False Confessions**. People may voluntarily give a false confession due to a pathological desire for notoriety; a conscious or unconscious need to relieve guilt over prior wrong-doings; an inability to distinguish fact from fantasy; and a desire to aid and protect the real criminal. Individuals offer voluntary false confessions without any external pressure from the police. These people simply turn themselves in to the authorities, claiming they have committed a crime.

2. **Compliant False Confessions**. In order to escape an aversive situation, avoid an explicit or implied threat, or to gain a promised or implied reward some suspects will confess falsely. Examples of this exist in cases of physical or psychological torture. Coerced-compliant false confessions may result from the pressures during the interrogation process. Since the suspect perceives immediate gains that outweigh the long term consequences this person will confess despite knowing that he did not commit the crime.

3. **Internalized False Confessions.** Some suspects are susceptible to believing during interrogation that they committed the crime, even though they did not. Persons who are particularly vulnerable are those who are young, tired, confused, suggestible, and exposed to false information.

Today the concern is part of a larger problem, miscarriages of justice. A *miscarriage of justice* occurs when a person is wrongfully convicted of a crime. A miscarriage of justice can result from non-disclosure of evidence by police or prosecution, fabrication of evidence, erroneous eyewitness testimony, overestimation of the evidential value of expert testimony, unreliable confessions due to police pressure or psychological instability, ineffective counsel, and misdirection by a judge during trial. Erroneous eyewitness testimony is no doubt is the single greatest cause of wrongful convictions in the U.S. criminal justice system (Warden, 2001). In known cases of wrongful conviction, approximately half from eyewitness misidentification were uncovered when the actual criminal confessed (Cassell, 1999).

Improving Interrogations

Interrogation techniques are called coercive by critics who claim they result in false confessions. The entire criminal justice system is taking a second look at how we might be able to improve procedures to minimize miscarriages of justice. To avoid the problems and pitfalls associated with interrogation techniques federal agents suggest some challenges for police officers and ways to overcome them (Napier & Adams, 2002):

✔ YES: Follow the Facts   **✘ NO:** Reading the Suspect's Behavior

Critics denounce police procedures involving the observation of the behavior of suspects as a way to select someone for more intensive interrogation tactics. Excessive focus on an individual because of a hunch or a lack of eye contact narrows the police vision. Overcome this by following the facts of the case, investigate all leads possible, and interview all suspects, particularly in a major case.

The best use of reading suspect behavior is towards the establishment of rapport. After that point behavioral indicators should be carefully interpreted within the entire context of the interrogation and not as specific indicators of guilt. This is particularly true when interrogating persons with mental illness, retardation, or personality disorders.

✔ YES: Know the Suspect   **✘ NO:** Identifying Personal
                                          Vulnerabilities

Some individuals are particularly susceptible to police interrogation techniques which may lead to a false confession. Examples are youthfulness, low or borderline IQ, mental handicap, psychological inadequacy, recent bereavement, language barrier, alcohol or other drug withdrawal, illiteracy, fatigue, or inexperience with the criminal justice system. Overcome this by doing a thorough background investigation on questionable suspects prior to the interrogation. Place the vulnerability in context at the beginning of the interrogation to get an understanding of whether the suspect understands. Document all efforts to show that a fair interrogation was conducted.

✔ YES: Preserve the Evidence   **✘ NO:** Contaminating
                                              Confessions

Police officers may inadvertently contaminate confessions by relying on questions that contain crime scene data. Using crime scene photos may amplify this flaw and educate the suspect about the crime. Avoid contaminating the admissions by asking for the suspect to describe and explain instead. Use open-ended questions and encourage narrative responses from the suspect.

✔ YES: Use Psychology instead of Coercion   **✘ NO:** Promising
                                                            Benefits

Statements that remaining silent will lead to greater penalties, but confessing will result in a reward are considered coercive. Do not offer the death penalty versus life imprisonment or threaten harm by prosecution of a wife, brother, child or mother. These are as unacceptable as personal threats against the suspect. Instead rely on psychological tools of minimization, rationalization, and projection. Allow the suspect to maintain their personal dignity and self-worth.

What Is Not an Interrogation?

As stated in *Innis* (1980), police words or actions "normally attendant to arrest and custody" do not constitute interrogation. Volunteered statements of any kind, including excited utterances, made to police are not barred by the Fifth Amendment privilege against self-incrimination and are admissible in evidence. An *excited utterance* is a statement made spontaneously by someone while under the stress of excitement caused by the event or condition. It is an exception to the hearsay rule.

Subtle Compulsion

Subtle compulsion is a minimal amount of duress that drives someone to do or say something. It does not amount to an interrogation unless it can also be shown that a suspect's incriminating response is the product of words or actions on the part of police that they should have known were reasonably likely to elicit an incriminating response (*Innis,* 1980). Take for example, a man who has been arrested in the vicinity of a school for handicapped children as a suspect in crimes committed by a man with a shotgun. After having been informed of his *Miranda* rights and telling police that he understood his rights and wanted to speak with a lawyer he is placed in a police car with officers. He is not "interrogated" in violation of his right to remain silent until consulting with a lawyer when, during the course of a ride in the police car by the most direct route to its destination, the car passes by the site of a concealed weapon. The suspect, upon noticing for the first time that the concealed weapon is located near a school for handicapped children, blurts out to the officers that he will show them where the concealed weapon is located. This is subtle compulsion that does not constitute an interrogation.

Traffic Stop

The roadside questioning of a motorist detained pursuant to a routine traffic stop does not constitute "custodial interrogation" for the purposes of the *Miranda* rule (*Innis,* 1980). Although an ordinary traffic stop curtails the "freedom of action" of the detained motorist and imposes some pressures on the detainee to answer questions, such pressures do not sufficiently impair the detainee's exercise of his privilege against self-incrimination to require that he be warned of his constitutional rights. A traffic stop is usually brief, and the motorist expects that, while he may be given a citation, in the end he most likely will be allowed to continue on his way. Moreover, the typical traffic stop is conducted in public, and the atmosphere surrounding it is substantially less "police dominated" than that surrounding the kinds of interrogation at issue in *Miranda* and subsequent cases in which *Miranda* has been applied.

However, if a motorist who has been detained pursuant to a traffic stop thereafter is subjected to treatment that renders him "in custody" for practical purposes, he is entitled to the protections prescribed by *Miranda*. A policeman's unspoken plan has no bearing on the question whether a suspect was "in custody" at a particular time; the only relevant inquiry is how a reasonable man in the suspect's position would have understood his situation.

Sobriety Testing

A suspect for driving under the influence may be compelled to submit to sobriety tests of a nontestimonial nature, including physical tests and a breath analysis, in a Driving while Intoxicated investigation without implicating the right against self-incrimination (*United States* v. *Hubbell*, 2000). The privilege against self-incrimination protects an accused from being forced to give evidence of a "testimonial or communicative nature," but not from being compelled to produce "real or physical evidence (*Pennsylvania* v. *Muniz,* 1990)."

A Stop and Frisk

A police officer may stop a person in order to question them if the officer has a reasonable suspicion that the person is engaged in criminal activity. For self-protection, the officer can at the same time carry out a limited pat-down search for weapons which is called a *"frisk."* This is not a custody situation nor is this considered a search. No *Miranda* rights are required.

In two cases decided in the 2000 term, the U.S. Supreme Court interpreted the "stop and frisk" rule. In one case, the Court ruled that running away from the police is enough of a reason for the police to stop and frisk the defendant (*Illinois* v. *Wardlow*, 2000). In another case the Court ruled that an anonymous tip that a suspect might be armed was insufficient justification for the police to conduct stop and frisk, absent other facts demonstrating the reliability of the tip (*Florida* v. *J.L.*, 2000).

Although a frisk may not turn up a weapon, it may turn up a suspicious package that the officer knows is commonly used to carry illegal drugs or some other illegal substance. This suspicion may turn into sufficient cause for a more intensive search of the person's clothing. A frisk often leads to a search. And if a search produces an illegal substance, it may result in arrests which then require *Miranda* warnings prior to interrogation.

Interrogation Tactics

Police officers may not use any tactic that will coerce an individual to give up his or her rights that are guaranteed by the U.S. Constitution. After a person has voluntarily waived his or her rights, police have some latitude in how to conduct the interrogation. In most cases, officers interrogating use three successful psychological strategies to predispose a suspect to voluntarily waive his or her *Miranda* rights: conditioning, de-emphasizing, and persuasive strategies (Leo, 1996a).

There are a number of citizen-police contacts that do not require that the *Miranda* warnings be given.

- ◆ **Conditioning** is done with the goal of setting up the interrogation so that the suspect will respond favorably to questions. One approach noted was to walk to the jail and meet the suspect, politely introduce oneself to the suspect and apologize for handcuffing him. Inquire about the suspect's physical condition and walk him or her out of the jail to the interrogation room. At the interrogation room the suspect is provided with coffee and possibly a newspaper, politely asking if there is anything else that is needed. The suspect is then left in the room for fifteen to twenty minutes, a strategy to enhance the suspect's desire to talk with the police. Routine booking questions are asked politely when the officer returns. When reading the *Miranda* rights to the suspect, the detective nods his own head up and down to suggest agreement.

- ◆ **De-emphasizing** refers to the strategy of minimizing the potential importance of issuing the *Miranda* rights to the suspect. The detective may blend the rights into the conversation in a way that makes them casual and little more than a procedure that must be followed so that the suspect can speak. Another method of de-emphasizing calls attention to the warnings and implicitly suggests that they are unimportant. The officer may joke about the well-known rights which the subject probably has heard on television many times.

- ◆ **Persuasion** is an explicit attempt to convince the suspect to waive his or her rights per *Miranda,* in a way that is subtle and noncoercive. Telling the suspect that there are two sides to every story and that the suspect's side can only be told if he or she waives his right to silence, adding that the victim's allegations will become the official version of the event unless the suspect speaks.

Some questions in the interrogation format include (Holmes, 2002):

1. Question chronologically to enhance recall

2. Determine the state of mind or the catalyst of the event

3. Ask questions to differentiate between memory recall and fantasy

4. Ask verification questions

5. Evaluate what you have — even if that is only the alibi

6. Ask questions to determine post act behavior

Case Specific Methods of Interrogation

The approach of the interrogator will be slightly different based on the offense that was committed as well as the personality of the interrogator. Generally, perpetrators respond with admissions to a humane interrogation approach. Humane does not suggest friendly or being over-solicitous. Suspect perceptions are extremely important, in particular his or her perceptions on the strength of the evidence will affect their willingness to confess (Kassin and Gudjonsson, 2004). With this in mind, use all available evidence collection methods that are specific to the crime being investigated in order to increase the perception of a strong case.

Have questions ready regarding the things that you want to know don't just listen passively. Ask for detail and explanation of whatever the suspect admits. Be genuinely interested in what the suspect is saying. Credibility that the suspect is telling you the truth will be gained from their answers as to smells, tastes, what they saw, or heard. Ask why a particular victim was chosen; the perpetrator is rarely indiscriminate. Even the one who chooses randomly will provide that as their method of choosing. Why did the suspect steal from *that* car? Assault *that* person? Break into *that* particular house? Kill *that* person? What happened before the event?

In a seminal study on police interviewing, universal problems were identified that have relevance for contemporary interrogations (Fisher, Geiselman, & Raymond, 1987). Interrogators should avoid the following:

♦ Do not excessively interrupt the suspect's description. This will cause the suspect to experience a considerable loss in concentration.

♦ When the suspect describes a recollection of the crime, the interrogator's follow-up questions should be appropriate for the event. Failure to follow-up with sequential questions based on the suspect's recollection will not maximize the suspect's memory. For example, do not interrupt the suspect to ask about weight, height, age, etc.

Sexual offenders and child molesters are among those that may be challenging to the investigator, but offer good rewards if pursued. Be prepared to ask the difficult questions. It can be appalling or disgusting to hear details about sexual crimes against the children or the elderly.

Admissions may cause the investigator to feel anger towards the suspect. Never show emotion or react if the details become disturbing. Any show of emotions from the investigator must be purposeful and self-driven. A few examples of case specific approaches follow.

Child Pornography Cases

Agents suggest that interrogators must respond with compassion and understanding during the interrogation of a child pornography case (Bowling & Resch, 2005). They suggest a two step interrogation process:

Step #1. Make a direct accusation statement that is convincing in its delivery to the suspect, interrupt and dismiss denials.

Step #2. Avoid using judgmental terms and use interrogation themes (RPM's). Theme development offers the suspect a logical reason why they committed the crime by excusing their behavior.

- ◆ **Rationalize the crime.** Example: "I understand your situation; you love kids so much; you never meant to hurt anyone."
- ◆ **Project blame onto others.** Example: "The problem is that parents don't spend enough time with their children."
- ◆ **Minimize the offense.** Example: "We're not talking about hurting children here. We're only talking about a few photographs."

Child Sexual Assault

Comparing violent offenders, rapists, and child molesters, the internal need to confess was greatest among child molesters (Kassin and Gudjonsson, 2004). Child molesters are more likely to respond to a sensitive approach used to overcome their inhibition to confess; most of them will talk to the police. One of the greatest challenges for police officers interrogating a suspect for child sexual assault is in controlling your own emotions. Any expression of anger, disgust or distain toward the suspect will result in his refusal to continue constructively in the interrogation. In many cases obtaining the statement from the perpetrator will be the strongest evidence available.

1. Give the suspect permission to talk

Start off by explaining the investigation that you are concerned with. Tell the offender that you realize he is in a difficult position and are willing to give him the opportunity to talk and give his side of the story. The interview may be difficult. Assure him that you want to hear the reasons for what happened.

Been There . . . Done That! 11-3

When Janet was two years old she began to have many medical problems such as severe urinary tract infections and high fevers. While the child was taken each time to see a doctor they did not find any reason for the urinary tract infections so she was treated for six months on antibiotics. Coincidently the child was changed to a new babysitter after a year and a half. Within a short time the new babysitter noticed that Janet, now four years old, was rubbing herself on a stuffed animal as if masturbating. When asked about it the child said "Hank rugs me." Her mother Susan reported that soon after learning this Janet told her that Hank and she had a secret. The secret was that Hank used to put his "sickoo" on her "gina." Hank was identified as the husband of the woman that had been babysitting Janet during the time that the urinary tract infections were occurring. The infections had stopped after the child was going to a different home for babysitting.

I conducted an interview with Janet. She told me her secret with Hank and drew a picture of him for me. She pointed out on a picture what the "sickoo" and "gina" meant so that I was sure what she was saying. The stick figure of Hank was basically a face with a penis.

Knowing that a trial with a four-year-old victim would be extremely difficult I attempted to obtain a confession from Hank. Something clearly had happened to the child, but was it rape or indecent assault and battery? During the interview with Hank he did admit to fondling Janet over her underwear but denied any penetration. To explain why she drew him naked, Hank said that she had seen him coming out of the shower one day. I was sure that he minimized his assaults on her. There is no doubt that Hank was thinking the whole time that his wife and four kids were going hear about what he had been doing with this little girl. A 4-year-old against a 35-year-old was not good odds, so I sought to strengthen the confession and be sure that there would not be a fight in court. At the end of the statement he wrote that he was really sorry for bringing such hardship on the mother and child and understood that they would be angry. He asked for forgiveness. He thanked me for bringing it forward so that he could get help.

In an investigation by the Department of Social Services, Hank told the investigator that he had never touched the child in a sexual way. He said that he was told by me that if he didn't make a statement he'd be arrested and pulled out of his house in handcuffs! When pressed on that issue he withdrew it and said that "Denise was quite nice during the interview." Funny how things can get turned around when faced with punishment! He further minimized the touching that he had done, saying that he was just kidding around with the child and had accidentally touched her on the inner thigh.

I went with evidence and the perpetrator pled guilty!

2. Don't share any embarrassing secrets to establish rapport.

The suspect who realizes that you are manipulating him will become resentful and you will lose any credibility that you have established.

3. Be prepared to listen.

During the interview with the suspect, investigators should (Pence & Wilson, 1992):

- Display an attitude of confidence in the subject's guilt.
- Point out some, but by no means all, of the circumstantial evidence indicative of the subject's guilt.
- Sympathize with the subject by telling him/her that anyone else might have done the same thing under similar circumstances.
- Reduce the subject's guilt feelings by minimizing the seriousness of the offense. It is also helpful to tell the subject that the interrogator has heard many people tell about sexual activities far worse than any the subject can relate. The conduct itself should be discussed as though it were actually normal.
- Suggest a less revolting and more acceptable motivation or reason for the offense than that which is known or presumed. An offender should always be offered an opportunity to save face by letting him/her base the initial admission of guilt upon a motivation or reason for the act. To secure the initial admission of guilt, the interrogator should suggest such possible reasons, motives, or excuses. The important point is to have the subject place him/herself at the scene or to connect him/herself with the event in some way. Following a partial admission, the interrogator can then point out that the circumstantial evidence negates certain explanations. The inconsistency between the subject's original denial of the crime and his/her present admission will deprive him/her of a possible defense.
- Remember, the main objective of the interview in many instances is to have the subject place him/herself at the scene or in contact with the victim.
- Display understanding and sympathy because it may urge the subject to tell the truth. Urge the subject to tell the truth for the sake of his/her own conscience, mental relief, or moral well-being as well as for the sake of everybody concerned, and also because it is the only decent, honorable thing to do.
- Seek an admission of lying about some incidental aspect of the occurrence. Once a subject has been caught in a lie about some incidental detail, he/she loses a great deal of ground. As he/she tries to convince the interrogator he/she is telling the truth, he/she can always be politely reminded that he/she was not telling the truth just a short while ago.

◆ Ask the subject a question regarding some detail of the offense rather than seek a general admission of guilt; getting an admission on seemingly insignificant details will sometimes lead the accused into a confession.

Offenders will not come right out and state that they sexually assaulted the victim. There may be claims of temptation, accidental touching, an innocent bathing incident. Let him talk. Document the incriminating statements and ask for clarification where needed.

Hate Crimes

The National Center for Hate Crime Prevention suggests that some suspects may assume that officers share their biased opinions (Office for Victims of Crime, 2004). Armed with this knowledge, interrogators can encourage suspects to talk about their feelings toward a particular minority group. Without using hate language, the officer should ask the suspect to express their bias motivations. The Model Hate Crime Protocol suggests these specific questions be asked during an interrogation (2004):

1. How would you like it if someone like the victim moved next door?

2. How do you feel about this victim?

3. What did this person say or do to make you mad?

4. How did the victim provoke you?

5. How do you feel about this person or group?

6. Was this your idea?

7. Has the victim's group hurt you or your friends?

Homicide

If the suspect of the homicide is in custody, the first decision that must be made is whether the subject should be interrogated at the scene of the crime or at the police department. The decision is one that requires flexibility based on the background information that is available to the investigator at that point. If the suspect is talkative or wants to tell his story at the scene, do not delay. Advise the suspect of his or her *Miranda* rights and let them talk. Some important observations that should be noted include:

> I'm sorry whats been happening, I don't know I do what I do but I know I need help bad. I'm scared for me and mostly my family.
> I'm sorry if I hurt any body, I didn't mean any harm.
>
> Mark a.

The perpetrator should always be given the opportunity to read and make corrections to their statement. Ask the person if they have anything else to say. The majority will apologize. Have them put it in their own writing at the bottom of the confession.

◆ Does the suspect speak rationally or irrationally?

- Is the response to questioning intelligent or confused?
- Is there any evidence of intoxication or doe the suspect appear to be under the influence of any drugs?
- Does the suspect give any reasons for his or her actions?

Transporting the suspect is a critical point in the investigation. If the suspect's attitude hardens against the victim or the police it could result in an unwillingness to cooperate with the investigating officer. It can also be the period of time when the suspect develops remorse for crime. It is imperative that the transporting officers do nothing that would cause the suspect to resist subsequent investigative efforts. The following are recommended during the transportation of a homicide suspect (Naramore, 1988):

1. If the suspect becomes talkative, officers should listen, remember, and later make notes of statements. It is not the duty of the transporting officers to provide *Miranda* rights or attempt to elicit information from the suspect.

2. Do not discuss the case with the suspect.

3. Do not engage the suspect in friendly conversation.

4. Do not use gestures or language that could be interpreted as hostile by the suspect.

5. Do not insult or berate the suspect.

Questions concerning homicide are generally organized around four phases of the murder. These phases are: the pre-crime phase, the murder event, the disposal of the body, and the post-crime phase. In addition to obtaining information about the crime these categories will establish the suspect's motive and opportunity to have committed the act.

Pre-crime Phase. Determine if the murderer had a conscious or unconscious intent for the act. Murderers with conscious intent are able to describe what triggered the murder. Those without conscious motive typically do not remember why they kill but are able to describe their feelings prior to the murder. Ask what the offender did the day prior to the murder and their thoughts and feelings prior to encountering the victim.

The Murder Event. Questions should concentrate on important aspects of the crime, such as how the suspect gained access to the victim. Conversation and behavior involving the victim, transporting the victim from one location to another, and specifics on methods of torture before or after the victim's death are central to the interrogation. If there is any indication of sexual contact the interrogator should focus on what was done prior to and after the victim's death.

Disposal of the Body. Determine through questioning what was done with the body, how the offender left the scene, and whether anything was taken from the body. The interrogator should explore the thoughts and feelings of the murderer during this phase.

Post-crime Phase. The behaviors that occur after the murder are extremely important to the interrogator. What did the offender do right after the murder? Did he wash, go out with friends, go to sleep, or eat? Did he return to the crime scene or attend the funeral? Include questions about the recovery of the body. Did the offender assist police in the recovery?

When a suspect denies guilt of a homicide, it may be useful to use a third party strategy. This involves asking why someone (else) would have committed that crime. This technique may uncover the motive of the homicide and facilitate further discussion surrounding the incident.

Sexual Assault Cases

Sex offenders generally tend to confess more frequently than other suspects because of a strong internal need to confess, despite their feelings of shame (Kassin and Gudjonsson, 2004). Offer the suspect a viable alternative by suggesting that the woman told him she was older than she really was, or ask if she wanted to do it or did he make her.

When the offender identification is made within a reasonable period of time, the collection of evidence from the suspect's body and clothing contributes to a successful interrogation and aids in solving the sexual assault crime. Evidence such as pubic and head hair samples, body fluids (dried and wet), and articles of clothing can be used as comparative or reference samples with hair, fibers, and fluids found on the victim. Photographing scratches or bruising on the perpetrator may be indicative of victim resistance in addition to notifying the suspect of your knowledge. Proper collection, conducted under all legal requirements, aids in the establishment of status for the interrogator. In addition it provides possible physical evidence. Accurately record any alibi statements or utterances made by the suspect prior to the actual interrogation during the process of collection.

Evidence of sexual assault may be collected from the body of the suspect without a warrant if the suspect has been arrested and probable cause exists for the seizure of the suspect's clothing and documenting of injuries as a search incident to arrest due to exigent circumstances. A standard "rape kit" may be used to gather evidence from the suspect and maintain the chain of custody, while some states use a suspect specific evidence kit (Gaensslen & Lee, 2001).

Truth and Consequences

Many people have erroneous ideas on what a police officer can or cannot legally do. Before you believe these statements, consider the consequences of your actions. Here are some of the most common examples:

1. What really happens if the police fail to read a suspect his rights or use coercion to extract information from a suspect?

Many people believe that if they are arrested and not "read their rights," they can escape punishment. Not true. But if the police fail to read a suspect his or her rights, they can't use anything the suspect says as evidence against the suspect at trial. The prosecution may use the statements to impeach the defendant if he or she decides to take the stand in court. The individual may still be tried in court if sufficient evidence exists that is not related to the illegally gained evidence. All other evidence may be used if it was not gained in connection with the statement.

2. Police officers interrogate suspects in most felony arrests.

Wrong, officers may not even attempt interrogations in almost half of all felony arrests (Colaprete, 2002). Why? The variables are experience, motivation, training, and most importantly the randomness of case assignment. Heavy caseload and time are other important factors that influence whether an interrogation would take place.

3. Does an undercover police officer have to admit who they are if a person asks?

Many people believe that if they ask someone if they are an undercover police officer, and the person denies being a police officer, they are safe to sell or share drugs with that person. Not true. Police officers are not required to reveal their undercover identity. There is no entrapment because the officer is not forcing someone to buy or use drugs. The person has shown a willingness to buy or sell drugs—the courts call it predisposition.

4. If you haven't been arrested and a police officer wants to question you about a crime, you must answer the questions.

Refusing to answer a police officer's questions is not a crime. Of course, people often voluntarily assist the police by supplying information that might help the police make an arrest. A police officer generally cannot arrest a person simply for failure to respond to questions. This means that unless a police officer has "probable cause" to make an arrest or a "reasonable suspicion" to conduct a "stop and frisk," a person approached by the police officer has the legal right to walk away. But the fact that there may be a legal right to walk away doesn't mean this is a wise move.

This is because there is no real way to tell what information the officer is using as a basis for his or her actions. In fact, the officer may have information that gives him or her valid legal basis to make an arrest or to conduct a "stop and frisk," even if the individual is, in truth, innocent of any wrongdoing. While there may be grounds for arrests, no one can ever be arrested purely because they declined to speak to the police officer.

5. There is no law against lying to the police.

Wrong. It is a five year felony to lie to a Federal police officer (Title 18, Part I, Chapter 47, §Sec. 1001). Remember Martha Stewart! Some, but not all, states have similar laws.

Conclusions

Confessions have been the primary focus of this chapter. The question, "why would a guilty person confess?" can be just as difficult to answer as "why would an innocent person confess?". The purpose of the intervening laws restricting interrogation practices is for the protection of the suspect, whether that individual is innocent or guilty. There are no shortcuts or magic words to induce a confession. It takes hard work and self-control; even then, obtaining a confession is never assured. The confession is only part of the investigation process and should never by itself be the basis for a prosecution.

It is not surprising that suspects with prior criminal records may be the most hesitant to waive their rights and provide statements. They are the most hardened against the system and typically have a lot more to lose. It is interesting to note that the police are very good at obtaining voluntary confessions from persons who commit crime, but that attempts at interrogation are relatively low. Enhancing professionalism translates into reducing the possibility of false confessions; these techniques are the hallmark of the future of contemporary interrogation.

Chapter Eleven Questions for Review

Short Answer Questions

1. Explain the early impact *Miranda* warnings had on police interrogation.

2. Explain the three types of police officer depicted in Schaefer's studies circa 1971.

3. Discuss plea bargaining. What are the potential benefits for the suspect? What are the potential benefits for the state?

4. What are the three major categories of false confessions? Explain each.

5. Subtle compulsion, traffic stops, sobriety testing and stop and frisk are not considered interrogation. Why not?

6. In most cases, officers interrogating use three successful psychological strategies to predispose a suspect to voluntarily waive his or her Miranda rights. What are they? What do police officers hope to achieve in each instance?

7. Outline the proper approach for interrogating suspects associated with child pornography. How does this differ from other interrogation styles?

8. Outline the proper approach for interrogating suspects associated with child sexual assault. How does this work toward securing admissions from a suspect?

9. Explain the Model Hate Crime Protocol used to interrogate individuals suspected of committing hate crimes.

10. Why is the timely identification of the offender especially important in sexual assault cases? How does this affect the gathering of evidence?

Fill-in Questions

1. There exists a balancing act concerning the interrogation which involves providing _____ to the guilty without jeopardizing the _____ of the innocent.

2. The *Miranda* safeguards come into play whenever a person in custody is subjected to either express questioning or its _____ _____ .

3. The police interrogator must possess a high degree of emotional _____ and feel comfortable using persuasive tactics that may be morally offensive to some investigators.

4. There is no significant statistical difference between those who waive their rights per *Miranda* and those who did not, in either subsequent _____ or _____ _____ .

5. In cases of proven false confessions a common factor was a _____ _____ of the suspect.

6. Police officers may inadvertently _____ confessions by relying on questions that contain crime scene data.

7. The approach of the interrogator will be slightly different based on the _____ as well as the personality of the interrogator.

8. Child molesters are more likely to respond to a _____ approach used to overcome their inhibition to confess, most of them will talk to the police.

9. Sex offenders generally tend to _____ than other suspects because of a strong internal need to confess, despite their feelings of shame.

10. Evidence of sexual assault may be collected from the body of the suspect without a warrant if the suspect has been arrested and probable cause exists for the seizure of the suspects clothing and documenting of injuries as a search _____ _____ due to exigent circumstances.

Exercises

1. What's my lie?

In this exercise a panel of three people must be assigned by your teacher to leave the room. Outside of the room the panel is prepared. Something about one of the individuals is selected as the "story" (Example: I did white water rafting through the Grand Canyon). The details of the story are shared with the other two panelists. The panel returns to the room and each person states the story. They are then "interrogated" by the class. Which two are lying? Can you tell? Why?

2. What's my lie?

The class breaks into pairs. One person is the interrogator and the other is the "suspect." The suspect comes up with a story of something he or she did. The interrogator now determines if the person is telling a lie or not. (Example: I make great cappuccino!)

Reference List

Aamodt, M., & Flink, W. (2001). Relationship between education level and cadet performance in a police academy. *Applied HRM Research, 6*(1), 75–76.

Bowling, R., & Resch, D. (2005). Child pornography cases: Obtaining confessions with an effective interview strategy. *FBI Law Enforcement Bulletin,* 1–7.

Buckley, D., & Jayne, B. (2005). *Electronic recording of interrogations.* Chicago, IL: John E. Reid & Associates.

Carter, D., Sapp, A., & Stephens, D. (1989). *The state of police education: Policy direction for the twenty-first century.* Washington, DC: Police Executive Research Forum.

Cassell, P. G. (1999). The guilty and the "'innocent": An examination of alleged cases of wrongful conviction from false confessions. *Harvard Journal of Law and Public Policy.* 22, pg. 523–597. Available: http://www.prodeathpenalty.com/guilt.htm.

Colaprete, F. A. (2002). Managing change in the investigative process: A process-centered approach to professional development and change management. *Police Chief, 69*(10), 121–126.

Fisher, R., Geiselman, E., & Raymond, D. (1987). Critical analysis of police interview techniques. *Journal of Police Science and Administration, 15*(3), 177–185.

Florida v. *J.L.,* 529 US 266 (2000).

Gaensslen, R. E., & Lee, H. C. (2001). *Sexual assault evidence: National assessment and guidebook* (2nd ed.). University of New Haven: West Haven, CT.

Gelinas, A. (2005). Effects of interviewer gender on interviewee response. Unpublished report: Western New England College.

Gudjonsson, G. H. (2003). *The psychology of interrogations and confessions: A handbook.* Hoboken, NJ: Wiley & Sons Inc.

Hess, J. (1997). *Interviewing and interrogation for law enforcement.* Cincinnati, OH: Anderson Publishing.

Holmes, W. (2002). *Criminal interrogation: A modern format for interrogating criminal suspects based on the intellectual approach.* Springfield, IL: LTD.

Illinois v. *Wardlow,* 528 U.S. 119 (2000).

Inbau, F. E., Reid, J. E., Buckley, J. P., & Jayne, B. C. (2001). *Criminal interrogation and confessions* (4th ed.). Gaithersburg, MD: Aspen Publishers, Inc.

Kassin, S., & Norwick, R. (2004). Why people waive their *Miranda* rights: The power of innocence. *Law and Human Behavior, 28*(2), 211–221.

Kassin, S. M. (2005). True crimes false confessions. *Scientific American Mind, 16*(2), 24–32.

Kassin, S. M., & Gudjonsson, G. H. (2004). The psychology of confessions: A review of the literature and issues. Psychological Science in the Public Interest. 5, 67. Available: http://www.psychologicalscience.org/pdf/pspi/pspi5_2.pdf.

Leo, R. A., & White. W. S. (1999). Adapting to *Miranda:* Modern interrogators' strategies for dealing with the obstacles posed. *Minnesota Law Review,* 84, 397–472.

Leo, R. A. (1996a). The impact of *Miranda* revisited. *Journal of Criminal Law & Criminology.* 86, pg. 621. Available: http://www.lexisnexis.com/universe.

Leo, R. A. (1996b). Inside the interrogation room. *Journal of Criminal Law and Criminology.* 86, pgs. 266-303. Available: http://www.lexisnexis.com//universe.

Miranda v. *Arizona,* 384 U.S. 436 (1966).

Napier, M., & Adams, S. (2002). Criminal confessions: Overcoming the challenges. *FBI Law Enforcement Bulletin,* 71(11), 9–15.

Naramore, D. (1988). Psychology of interviewing. *NESPAC: Homicide School* unpublished.

NCWP. (2002). The status of women in policing: 2001. Retrieved 2006, from http://www.womenandpolicing.org/PDF/2002_Status_Report.pdf

Office for Victims of Crime. (2004). Responding to hate crime: A multidisciplinary Curriculum for law enforcement and victim assistance professionals. Retrieved 2005, from http://www.ojp.usdoj.gov/ovc/publications/infores/responding/welcome.html

Pence, D., & Wilson, C. (1992). *The role of law enforcement in the response to child abuse and neglect.* Washington, DC: National Center on Child Abuse and Neglect.

Pennsylvania v. *Muniz,* 496 U.S. 582 (1990).

Rabon, D. (1992). *Interviewing and interrogation.* Durham, NC: Carolina Academic Press.

Rhode Island v. *Innis,* 446 U.S. 291 (1980).

Rutledge, D. (1994). *Criminal Interrogation: Law and Tactics* (3rd ed.). Pacerville, CA: Copperhouse Publishing Company.

Schaefer, R. C. (1971). Patrolman perspectives on Miranda. *Law and the Social Order,* 81, 81–101.

Schmalleger, F. (2004). *Criminal Justice.* Upper Saddle River, NJ: Prentice Hall.

The Committee on Law and Justice. (2004). Fairness and effectiveness in policing: The evidence. Available: http://www.nap.edu/books/0309084334/html.

Thomas III, G. C. (2004). Stories about *Miranda. Michigan Law Review,* 102(1959), 1959–2001.

Tousignant, D. (1991). Why suspects confess. Retrieved 2005, from http://www.crimeandclues.com/91ar002.htm

United States v. *Hubbell,* 530 U.S. 27 (2000).

Warden, R. (2001). How mistaken and perjured eyewitness testimony put 46 innocent Americans on death row. Retrieved June, 2005, from http://www.law.northwestern.edu/depts/clinic/wrongful/Causes/eyewitnessstudy01.htm

Yeschke, C. (2003). *The art of investigative interviewing* (2nd ed.). Boston, MA: Butterworth-Heinemann.

Techniques for Interrogation

KEY TERMS

Admission	Apathetic offender
Confession	Complementary principle
Custodial interrogation approach	Guilt-ridden offender
Inculpatory evidence	*Modus operandi*
Non-custodial interrogation approach	Slam-dunk approach

CHAPTER OBJECTIVES

After completing this chapter, you should be able to:

- Describe the complementary principle
- Explain the difference between a confession and an admission
- Explain why an interrogation is only one part of an investigation
- Describe a slam-dunk approach to interrogation
- Explain the term *modus operandi*
- Explain the difference between a noncustodial and custodial interrogation
- Describe the three phases of an interrogation
- List the top ten interrogation tactics use by police
- Develop outcome-based tactics for interrogation

Introduction

Many of the techniques for interrogation in this chapter rely on an attempt by the interrogator to understand the behavior of the suspect and his or her resistance to the interrogation process. The interactions between the interrogator and the suspect are critical themes throughout. Understanding the interpersonal relations of the interrogator and of the suspect provides a good starting point for using interrogation techniques. A useful explanation of interpersonal relationships is found within the complementary principle of interpersonal psychology. The *complementary principle* is the idea that individual behaviors are based on interpersonal reactions. It states that from a relationship there exists the predictability of a set of reactions in response to certain actions. The complementary principle involves two major assumptions: first, interpersonal behaviors invite reciprocal behaviors and second, over time these lend to a repetitive pattern of relating (Gurtman, 2001).

What does this mean to the potential interrogator? First, complementary principle suggests that the interpersonal style of one individual can influence the reaction of the other, bringing an expected set of responses. Potentially, the astute interrogator can persuade the suspect through knowledge of the expected parings that occur during human interactions.

Secondly, the primary interactions between humans which will occur are friendliness and dominance (Sadler & Woody, 2003). The interrogator can purposefully determine which relationship pairing will work best with a particular suspect. When a relationship or connection develops, the suspect will respond to the interrogator in a way that is similar. This pairing is seen when rapport is established between the interviewer and interviewee. A connection between two people brings about corresponding levels of friendliness. This connection may be achieved if the suspect feels that the interrogator understands him or treats him with respect. A friendly relationship would encourage a friendly response; a cooperative relationship is likely to have a corresponding cooperative effect.

Pairings of expected behaviors to specific responses are somewhat predictable when the suspect grants status to the interrogator. Status may be achieved when the suspect respects the interrogator due to his status as a police officer or acknowledges inwardly that the interrogator has sufficient evidence to prove his guilt. When granting of status occurs, what results is an opposite or negative complementary response. A negative complementary response is dominant to submissive behavior. For example, the suspect may take the role of being submissive in response to a dominant interrogator. The suspect may become cooperative in order to overcome a distrustful interrogator. Another possibility is that the suspect becomes friendly to the hostile interrogator in an effort to please him or her.

The interrogator should determine if the approach to the interrogation is best made by establishing a status role or connecting through a rapport relationship. An overriding consideration is that once the interrogator has taken on a hostile role with the suspect it is impossible to go back and later develop rapport!

Purpose of the Interrogation

The interrogation is an important part of a criminal investigation. The Supreme Court has recognized that the suspect's own confession may be the most damaging evidence that can be admitted against him (*Bruton* v. *U.S.*, 1968). The primary purpose of the interrogation is to obtain a statement from the suspect that acknowledges or indicates the guilt of that person. The best statement is one that provides the interrogator with the truth. If the suspect will not give the truth, then document the lies, a secondary purpose! Success is achieved with either a confession or an admission.

- ◆ The confession is a statement in which a person admits to his or her role in committing a crime in a way that excludes the possibility that the crime was committed by someone else.
- ◆ The admission is any statement that that ties the suspect to the crime, to the victim, or to the place of the offense, which may be used to infer guilt.

Both confessions and admissions are known as *inculpatory evidence*. Inculpatory evidence tends to show one's involvement in a crime (Garner, 2004). They are generally treated the same under constitutional analysis. This means that that the methods used to obtain the statement will be judged under the same constitutional standards that were outlined in Chapter Ten. Either the confession or an admission can be valuable for use against the suspect. In criminal cases the prosecution must prove the case beyond a reasonable doubt and juries may have difficulty in reaching guilty verdicts when a case is based on circumstantial evidence or on witness testimony which has been impeached by defense counsel.

A confession or admission from the defendant properly admitted at trial can secure a conviction in these cases.

While the interrogation is an important part of an investigation, it should not be considered as the primary method of gathering evidence. As stated earlier in this text, interviews of the victim and other witnesses are critical to obtaining evidence for an investigation. A medical examination when warranted and search warrants properly executed are other methods of gathering critical information. Conducting a background check on the suspects constitute another valuable piece of the investigative process.

The investigation process becomes compromised when the investigator puts all energy into obtaining a confession rather than collecting evidence. This single-mindedness may mean that evidence exonerating the suspect is overlooked or that extreme measures are taken to obtain the confession. Neither are acceptable alternatives to a full and fair investigation. Another reason to be concerned about a strong reliance on interrogations is that in the absence of corroborating evidence, the case is lost if the confession is not admitted (for any number of reasons). A third reason to avoid strong reliance on interrogations is the common view that a confession alone is not enough to prove a person guilty (*Commonwealth* v. *Forde*, 1984).

It is against the self-interest of a suspect to admit guilt, yet this is the purpose of the interrogation. In order to obtain a confession the interrogator must obtain the cooperation of the suspect. Cooperation may be based on either part of the complementary principle, through granting of status or through a connection. Either way, this is no easy task. Some will confess to relieve guilt, some due to the interrogator's persuasion, and others confess because of belief that they are caught.

The interrogation should take place when the guilt of the suspect is fairly certain. It should not be an attempt to gather information. That purpose is achieved through the interview.

Interrogation Approach

There are conflicting opinions about the best way to conduct an interrogation. That is because it is a complicated process. Gordon and Fleisher suggest that the assertion of force plus the weight of evidence will result in a confession (Gordon & Fleisher, 2002). These authors suggest that the interrogator must forcefully claim that the suspect is guilty and not allow him to deny. This *slam-dunk approach* is too simplistic and should not be used until the interrogator makes the assessment on whether the suspect is cooperative, mentally ill, or emotional. If an interrogator begins the process by being argumentative and angry it may cause some perpetrators to be fearful of making statements and they will not talk at all. It does not take into account the offense type, which may necessitate a different initial approach. For example, the person who illegally dumped trash should not be interrogated in the same manner as one suspected of murder. Neither does this approach recognize that the offenders themselves are different. For example, interrogating a 60-year-old man for strangling his wife does not require the same approach as the 21-year-old gang member who shot a rival, or a 25-year-old woman who suffocated her child. All of these are crimes are murder, yet require different approaches during interrogation of the suspect. The slam-dunk style is not useful as a method to begin an interrogation.

Awareness of the differences between offenders is recognized by Inbau and colleagues in the Reid Technique (Inbau, Reid, Buckley, & Jayne, 2001). These authors classify offenders as emotional or nonemotional (pg. 209–210). In making clear that offenders differ considerably based on the level of guilt they experience, it is obvious that the interrogator must change tactics in order to be successful in moving the suspect to confess. The Reid Technique is a highly structured nine step interrogation approach which is excellent for the advanced student of interrogation. For those who do not take the time to thoroughly understand the method it gives

Been There . . . Done That! 12–1

In one case there were three children who told their mother that their grandfather had been touching them. The interviews with these children were particularly difficult and the allegations were indecent touching, situations where little physical evidence would be possible. I made the decision to interview the perpetrator in his home rather than to interrogate him at the police station. This proved to be the best move that could have been made. There was no custody and no Miranda rights were necessary in order to speak with the suspect. He confirmed that he had been the only person with access to each of the children in the incidents that they had described to me as being sexual. He also tried to convince me that these incidents were not sexual and gave some reasons why the children might be saying that he had touched them. In all cases he had admitted to taking down the underpants of these children. These admissions were not a confession, but they were the information that ultimately led a jury to believe the children's explanation over his for what had happened. He was found guilty and spent ten years in jail for these assaults. Why is this an interrogation rather than an interview?

the interrogator a false sense of security. It is more than just follow the steps and the interrogation will be complete! Unless the interrogator is thoroughly familiar with all of the steps and can recite them in order and explain the reasons for each step, AND follow each step in order, he or she may find it difficult to justify the approach when testifying in court.

A somewhat different interrogation approach involves an assessment of the suspect, strategizing the relationship between the suspect and interrogator, and documenting the proof obtained through the confession (Rutledge, 1994). The assessment is a process of finding the strengths and weaknesses that would help in convincing the suspect to provide a confession. Indications of guilt, remorse, or entitlement are all examples of personal emotions that the interrogator can use. If the perpetrator is a man who severely beat his girlfriend, suggestions from the interrogator that she "deserved it" is an example of entitlement that might be used by the suspect to justify his crime. If a similar identity is perceived, then the suspect imagines a relationship with the interrogator and trusts enough to talk. The relationship with the suspect is an important consideration for the interrogator. Since it is in a person's best interest not to give information against himself, then he may most likely waive his rights if there is the perception that it IS in his best interest to talk. If the suspect believes that the interrogator can be convinced of his innocence, then the suspect is also likely to talk. Understating the position and rank of the interrogator is better than demanding respect due to status. Offenders are generally more interested in themselves than with the police officer, so don't bother trying to impress him in order to obtain a confession!

Another approach to interrogation requires a person to focus on the purpose of the interrogation rather than the place. Typically the interrogation is pictured as a room designed for that purpose in a police station. The goal of an interrogation is to obtain a statement from the suspect that he or she is guilty of a crime. An admission will provide information which may suggest guilt. Most examples of interrogation involve major crimes such as homicide or rape. The importance of confessions and admissions should not be overlooked as part of the investigatory process for all crimes, even the minor ones. It is limiting to the interrogator to think of statements taken in the interrogation room as an interrogation and all other encounters as interviews. If you put the picture of the interrogation room aside for a moment the possibilities become endless. An interrogation may take place at the home of the suspect, at some other neutral setting, or at the police station. The offender can be called on the phone and asked questions that are designed to elicit incriminating information. An interrogation can be conducted whether the suspect is in custody or not.

One major advantage to conducting non-custodial interrogations is that it typically introduces a strong element of surprise. Getting the suspect talking is a critical element of obtaining a confession. Remember that an interrogation is not an option after the individual has been arraigned in court on the crimes under investigation or asks to speak to an attorney regardless of custody. Both the non-custodial and the custodial interrogation situation are described in the next section.

Non-Custodial Interrogation Situation

Prior to attempting an interrogation, the approach should be based on whether the questioning will be custodial or non-custodial. A *non-custodial interrogation* situation occurs when the suspect is not in police custody or under arrest. The suspect must be fully aware that he or she is free to leave at any time. This awareness may be based in part on the location of the interrogation, the attitude of the interrogator, and follow-through by not arresting the suspect at that time. As you learned in Chapter Ten, *Miranda* warnings are not required when the suspect is not in custody. If the situation changes to custodial during the interrogation however, they must be provided. The decision not to arrest the suspect unless it is absolutely necessary must be made in advance.

The non-custodial interrogation is not as threatening to the suspect. In some cases they may feel freer to talk, thereby incriminating themselves through admissions. The non-custodial interrogation is less formal, allowing the interrogator to understate his or her position as well as giving the impression that statements are less damming to the suspect.

An interrogation is defined not by where it takes place, but why it is conducted.

Conduct a non-custodial interrogation by introducing yourself to the suspect as a police officer investigating the crime, whatever that might be. If the suspect is willing to go to the station or office to talk, then ask if they would like to follow in their own car or have a friend accompany them in the cruiser. This reinforces that the suspect is voluntarily involving himself in the process. If the suspect invites you into his or her home to talk, accept any offer for coffee or tea. When the interrogation has ended, thank the suspect for cooperating and suggest that you may want to talk to them again in the future.

*Custodial
Interrogation
Situation*

The custodial interrogation occurs when the suspect is under arrest or is not free to leave because arrest is impending. The *Miranda* warnings are necessary prior to questioning the suspect in custody. The offender must understand his or her rights and voluntarily waive them. For a full discussion on the *Miranda* warnings refer to Chapter Ten. A knowing waiver of rights is compromised if the individual has a mental disability, cannot read or write, or is under the influence of alcohol or drugs. It is the responsibility of the investigator to assess the ability of the suspect to understand his or her rights and make a voluntary waiver. An individual may not be coerced or forced to give up his or her rights. The spirit as well as the letter of the law must be adhered to.

Once an individual has made a knowing and voluntary waiver of his *Miranda* rights it is not necessary to repeat them over and over until the person wonders why they ever agreed to speak in the first place! Department policy dictates if the individual must waive his or her rights in writing. *Miranda* does not require this. Neither does *Miranda* require that an individual be given his or her rights verbatim.

Remember, if the individual asks for an attorney the interrogation must stop. The request for an attorney is not an unequivocal mention of an attorney or a question asked to the interrogator about the need for an attorney. The interrogator is under no requirement to give advice to the suspect. However, it is good practice to follow up even a vague mention of an attorney.

The waiver of rights against self-incrimination can be revoked by the suspect at any time. Even when the person agrees to speak with the interrogator, the right to stop speaking can take place at the discretion of the suspect. The right against self-incrimination belongs to the suspect. No one can take it from them; neither can one insist on it for another. For example, an attorney may ask to speak with his client and the suspect must be informed that an attorney is available for them. If the suspect wants to continue to talk with the police without that attorney, the right is his. Do not interpret this as a providing a way to deny individual rights! Tell the suspect that they have the right to continue speaking with authorities and let him or her make the decision.

Confession Eliciting Models

There are numerous techniques for eliciting confessions. Each method slants the approach to interrogation from a different perspective.

Gudjonsson suggests that custodial interrogation perspectives fall into five confession-producing theoretical models, the Reid Model, a Decision-Making Model, a Psychoanalytic Model, An Interaction Process Model, and a Cognitive-Behavioral Model (Gudjonsson, 2003). Review these confession eliciting models and look for them later in the chapter. You should notice that they are incorporated into the interrogation phases.

1. The Reid Model approach relies on decreasing the suspect's perception of the consequences of confession. The interrogator uses rationalization to help the offender avoid full responsibility and projection to distort the account of what really happened. At the same time, the suspect's internal anxiety associated with his deception is increased by the interrogator, making the confession a more likely event. Manipulating the suspect's anxiety is achieved by exasperating normal feelings of guilt and shame.

2. The Decision Making Model is a hedonistic calculation by the perpetrator on the options available and the consequences of choosing. In this pain versus pleasure analysis the suspect will choose to confess or not based on the factors that pressure the suspect in one direction. The pressures include social, psychological, and environmental considerations that make confession the better choice. The interrogator facilitates the process by reinforcing the pressures to confess.

3. The Psychoanalytic Models rest on the assumption that there is a psychological need to confess based on guilt and the desire for self-punishment. Highly controversial, this approach relies heavily on Freud's concept of the id, ego, and superego. Only after confessing will the suspect begin to release the pressure of guilt. According to this model the two driving forces are the fear of losing love and fear of retaliation. The anxiety which the suspect endures due to guilt is exploited to elicit the confession during an interrogation.

4. The Interaction Process Model views the interrogation as a three prong process that influences the outcome. The characteristics of the offender and his offense, the strength of the evidence, and the interrogator's technique are believed to affect the suspect's decision. The model stresses the interplay of influences during the interrogation process. In order to achieve a confession the interrogator considers the background characteristics of the suspect such as age and gender in addition to the type of offense that was committed. Strength of the evidence is the second most important consideration. The third influence is the technique used by the interrogator. Interrogation success depends on whether the interrogator correctly accessed the suspect and

responded with appropriate methods to overcome resistance to providing an interrogation.

5. Gudjonsson (2003) argues that confessions occur through the existence of a relationship between the suspect, the environment, and the interrogator in his Cognitive-Behavioural Model. In his perspective, suspects are motivated to confess due to the social, emotional, cognitive pressures of isolation, police pressure, distress, and belief that the police know he did it. Additional factors that influence the likelihood of a confession are situational, such as the presence of an attorney or familiarity with police procedures.

Interrogation Phase I: Preparation

Regardless of the type of interrogation, the approach is formal and systematic. That means that it is necessary to prepare and plan for an interrogation. It is intentionally accusatory with the interrogator dominating a great deal of the conversation. As stated earlier, the suspect can be interrogated while in custody or not — it depends on the type of case and goals of the interrogation. The systematic nature of the interrogation is notable throughout the process. Success is enhanced when the interrogator is well-rested and confident about the case. It takes tremendous energy to conduct an interrogation. The interrogator must be one step ahead of the suspect in every way, from anticipating excuses to confronting denials. The interrogation may be as short as an hour but may be several hours. As you will see, the preparation for an interrogation begins in the same manner as the interview. The interrogator who starts the interrogation must be prepared to follow through to the end.

The five steps that are outlined in this preparation phase include: know the case, determine the prior record, view the scene, establish the timing, and determine who will interrogate.

Step 1: Know the Case

The interrogator should be thoroughly familiar with the case that the suspect is thought to be involved in. Statements of victims should be reviewed, particularly if the interrogator did not interview victims or witnesses. If the investigation involves a major felony there may be more than one person involved in the investigation. The interrogator should speak with each person, in a group meeting if possible. It is not unusual for facts of the case to be known to one investigator and unknown to the others. Take the time to contact the individuals who have been involved with the case or similar cases that may be linked.

Prior to conducting an interrogation the officer should review the statutes concerning the crimes that may have already been charged and those that may be considered in the future. Be familiar with the elements of each law that must be satisfied in order to obtain a court conviction. During the interrogation it is imperative that evidence concerning the violation of the specific elements be addressed. For example, if the charge is "rape" then the proof of penetration by any object must be established. A lesser crime would be an attempted rape or sexual assault. Did the suspect undress himself or unzip the fly on his pants? This alone could be used to substantiate the intent to rape. "Breaking and entering with the intent to commit a felony" requires proof of both the "break" and of "intent."

Reviewing the offense to determine an interrogation approach includes an understanding of the case that would provide numerous different ways in which the suspect could be charged. Knowing your legal options provides leverage that can be used throughout the interrogation. Reviewing the case goes beyond merely knowing the category of crime that the suspect is thought to have committed. For example, what are the ways in which the perpetrator has been identified? Examples could include the suspect's voice inflections or the types of words that were used during the crime. It could include an identifying mark on the suspect or even the way the suspect smells. Information on the specific words or gestures used by the perpetrator provides tools that the interrogator will be able to use. Ideally the interrogator should be the investigator in the case who has interviewed the victims and witnesses.

Step 2: Determine the Prior Record

A background check should be done on each individual prior to an interrogation. Determine if the suspect has been prosecuted and found guilty for crimes in the past. A suspect may be concerned if he or she has a violent felony record from past convictions. For jurisdictions with three strikes or mandatory sentencing laws the suspect may have an additional fear that will impact the interrogation. Under three strikes and mandatory, a felon will face long periods of mandated imprisonments for a third conviction.

Check to see if there are any outstanding warrants which may be used to hold the suspect in custody if necessary. Also of value is to find out if they have any suspended sentences.

Step 3: View the Scene

Conducting a search for evidence is as important as the interrogation. Viewing the scene may produce undisputable facts which could be brought

Been There . . . Done That! 12–2

An officer from the Vermont Sheriff's office contacted the Massachusetts State Police. He had arrested a man who was passing phony prescriptions to obtain drugs. A search of the subject revealed evidence of scripts being passed in Northampton, MA. I was assigned the investigation and learned that Mr. T had gone on a four-day spree to obtain narcotics fraudulently. His modus operandi was to phone a pharmacy and order a prescription for a Schedule II narcotic while his wife waited inside the pharmacy to see if the police were called. Modus operandi is a term used by criminal investigators to describe the particular method that a suspect uses to commit the crime. In this case, Mrs. T would come outside and warn her husband if the police were called so that they could flee. Mr. T had also

gone to a local doctor complaining of pain, requesting Diliuid (a Schedule II narcotic). At the time of his arrest he had numerous labels from prescriptions for Codeine issued by a pharmacy from MA. He had used the prescribing doctor's name for the phony scripts.

Subsequently I recovered nine prescriptions for Mr. T which had been filled for Schedule II and III narcotics. These had been phoned in by a "doctor" and were found to be fraudulent. Mr. T and his wife had also stolen script pads from legitimate doctors and had written their own fraudulent prescriptions. The doctors were interviewed and gave statements that they had not issued the medication prescriptions. Mr. T had used at least two alias names in the scheme. An arrest warrant was issued.

into the interrogation itself. Faced with physical evidence that points to his guilt the perpetrator may be less likely to deny the charges.

In order to determine if the suspect is linked with other similar crimes, it is necessary to find out how the individual committed the crime. Referred to as the *Modus Operandi*, or method of operation, these are the usual things that the suspect does during the commission of a particular crime. In a house break for example, what type of neighborhood did the suspect invade? Was entry gained at the front door or the back door? Was a tool used or glass broken? Was there a significant difference in the type of item stolen, such as jewelry, electronics, or guns and ammunition? These particulars can later be compared to crimes of similar a nature to determine if the suspect could have been involved in other house breaks.

Step 4: Establish the Timing

Generally the suspect should be confronted as soon as practical, ideally before they learn about the investigation. This provides an opportunity to lock the suspect into a story or alibi. The less time the he or she has to make up an alibi or justify the offense, the better. In cases where evidence may be found on the body of the individual, speed is of the essence. Whatever timing is chosen it is the prerogative of the interrogator to determine the best opportunity. The officer must then assess whether or not it is safe to proceed.

Courtesy of iStockphoto, Inc.

An interrogation room should be free of distractions.

While speed and surprise are the general rule to an interrogation, there are times when purposeful delay is the best approach. Situations that may cause delay to the interrogation include:

♦ Passage of time since the crime
♦ Multiple victims
♦ Previous relationship between the offender and officer
♦ Execution of a search warrant

It is generally accepted that the passage of time makes it more difficult to solve the crime. Leads dry up and evidence can be difficult to generate. The investigation that continues after the case is cold requires an approach that is slow and steady. Talk to the suspects; take the time to review the files.

With the possibility of multiple victims comes a sense of urgency in solving the case. It is an impulse that is best held back. When multiple victims are linked to a single possible suspect, the investigator has an additional responsibility of learning the details of all cases. Failure to take the time can result in details that are overlooked. There may be only be one opportunity to conduct an interrogation; be careful not to go too fast and miss the opportunity to be thorough.

A previous relationship or newly cultivated relationship with the offender can be used to the benefit of the investigation process. If the offender is used to seeing the officer and some respect has been established, a major barrier against disclosing is broken down prior to the interrogation itself. It can be a sense of relief for the suspect when the time comes for the case to be discussed. It is possible to have the suspect anticipate the day of the interrogation.

Been There . . . Done That! 12-3

This investigation started with a phone call from the Department of Social Services. The social worker told me that she had investigated the death of an infant a few days earlier. She had originally thought that the child had died from fractures due to brittle bone disease (osteogenesis imperfecta). Brittle bone disease is a genetic disorder that is characterized by having bones that break easily for no apparent reason. The genetic disorder is present at birth, but the individual may not show symptoms for years. In this case, the child had been diagnosed with the disease at the time of birth and had suffered fractures prior to her death.

The reason that the social worker was having second thoughts about the cause of death was because a second child of the same parent had just been taken to the hospital with severe injuries that were indicative of abuse. It was unknown at that time if the second child was going to live or not. When the social worker gave me the name of the child's mother I immediately knew who it was. The family was known to be very violent. I had arrested her brother a year prior for homicide. There was no evidence that the mother had killed her sick baby, but I had a sinking feeling that was exactly what had happened.

Going to her apartment, I introduced myself and explained that I was investigating what had happened to her two children. The mother allowed me in to the apartment to look at the room while she described what had happened. Her explanation of the situation did not fit the scene. For example, she said that she had picked up the sick baby who was crying and had woken up her sleeping boyfriend. She brought the child into the kitchen and had tripped on a toy which was on the floor. The child fell. At my request she drew a picture of the place she had "tripped" and where the baby had fallen. I took pictures of the apartment. But there were no toys in the apartment! Not one. It was a two-room, one bedroom apartment. The two children slept in the same room with the mother and her boyfriend. The child did not fall straight down (as falling objects tend to do). The child came to rest at the opposite side of the kitchen. From the position of the objects in the kitchen, it appeared as though the child was forcibly thrown against the side of the stove and had landed far to the left of it.

After reviewing the case I made the decision to interrogate the mother during a non-custodial interrogation. I asked her if she would be willing for me to write down her statement at my office—and was there anyone she would like to come with her? She asked if I would pick up her mother on the way. I did. Her mom stayed outside of the room during the actual statement. The above facts were incorporated into the statement, along with the fact that her boyfriend was very angry when the baby started crying. She in turn became angry at the children and had "probably thrown" them both. The second child did not die, but he would be brain damaged for the rest of his life . . . this was no accident. This was not an interview; persuasion was needed to extract the statement. The goal was to have her admit to causing the death and injury to her children. She did admit it and signed the confession before I brought her and her mother home. She was later indicted and pled guilty.

Step 5: Determine Who Will Interrogate

Many officers have conducted interrogations during a one-on-one interrogation. The primary consideration is whether the suspect might be a threat to the safety of the officer. The seriousness of the case is not necessarily the determining factor; the decision to delay a confession should be on whether the officer is outnumbered, if the suspect is mentally ill, if the suspect is a member of the opposite sex, or if there is a violent history involved. It is dangerous and unnecessary to assume that the size or strength of the interrogator determines the place or timing. The bottom line is that the interrogator has complete control over the questioning and should not be forced into conducting the interrogation in a time or place that is not desired.

Ideally two persons should be in the room with the suspect during the interrogation, but one should do the majority of the questioning. There are several reasons for this arrangement. The primary reason is for officer safety. Secondly, having two persons in the room allows for flexibility in the interrogation. If the suspect is not responding to the primary questioning officer, they can switch roles. It is not uncommon for a suspect to turn anger on one of the officers without reason, having a switch person available continues the flow of the questioning. It is the responsibility of the interrogator to determine when his or her effectiveness is lacking and be willing to step back and allow another to continue the interrogation. Another reason is that the second interrogator can take detailed notes, freeing the primary interrogator from that responsibility. The note-taker should seat him or herself behind the suspect and slightly to one side, within sight of the primary interrogator but outside the line of vision of the suspect. This is done so as not to distract the suspect during the interrogation. An alternate arrangement is that a second interrogator monitor the interrogation from behind a two-way mirror.

When preparing for an interrogation, the most important aspect of the case is the preservation of the constitutional protections of the accused. Know the federal and state mandates before attempting to conduct an interrogation. For this reason it is typically a seasoned investigator who is the best choice for conducting interrogations. Denial of the suspect's rights does nothing but jeopardize the case. Evidence may later be excluded from the trial if an improper interrogation takes place. Obtaining the confession is only worthwhile if it is obtained correctly. Confession admissibility is guided by the Fourth, Fifth, Sixth, and Fourteenth amendments of the U.S. Constitution, case law, federal law, and state law. It must be established that a suspect's incriminating response was not the product of words or actions on the part of the police in violation of these provisions.

The place that is chosen for an interrogation should be quiet and free of distractions. There should not be any telephone, radio, clock, or other electronic devices. The officers in the room should turn off any pagers or cell phones they carry when entering the room. In the best of situations the room would have a two-way mirror for observation.

Suspects may be interrogated in their own home or any other place where privacy can be assured. The location should encourage suspects to feel willing to release the burden of guilt in an atmosphere that is private and safe. An absence of judgment from the interrogator adds to the feeling that the suspect has nothing to fear about opening up.

Interrogation Phase II: Develop Outcome-Based Tactics

Prior to beginning the interrogation an investigator develops outcome-based tactics that are used to persuade the suspect to cooperate. These are persuasive arguments that are designed to overcome the resistance of a suspect to confess. Certain approaches are generally accepted as valuable in conducting successful interrogations. These include minimizing the crime, blaming the victim, decreasing the shamefulness of the crime, increasing guilt, and appealing to the suspect's hope for a better outcome. The experienced interrogator will develop many more approaches than are mentioned here! The characteristics of the suspect such as age, level of education, and marital status will complicate the interrogation process. The suspect's employment, community status, or life style will also impact the approach used to persuade.

To get to the point of a confession the interrogator considers the many reasons why the suspect would not want to confess and which persuasive arguments would overcome that resistance for the crime that is under investigation. The interrogator must defeat the fears that plague the suspect. Fears may cause resistance to the interrogation and inhibit the suspect from admitting his guilt. Identifying the fears that affect that particular individual is an important part of developing persuasive arguments. Following are the top ten interrogation tactics (Leo, 1996), suspect fears, and suggested methods for interrogation. The fears that are highlighted may be used with different tactics for overcoming resistance. These are just a few examples for illustrative purposes.

Tactic #1.
An appeal to the suspect's self-interest

The most frequent interrogation tactic involves this appeal to the suspect's self-interest. This can also be stated as appealing to the hope of a better outcome to the case. A common impulse is to suggest that the suspect would be "better off" if they give a confession. Care must be taken because a promise of leniency violates the suspect's right to due process and may cause legal challenges to any confession that might be obtained. There are other ways to appeal to the self-interest of the suspect. One approach would be to suggest that they would "feel better" if they talked about the act. Encourage the suspect to "get it off his chest" or "tell his version of what happened." When you ask someone to do something and they perceive you as a person that has their best interests in mind, and/or would like you to have their best interests in mind, they are strongly motivated to fill the request.

When a person is emotionally involved and has a stake in the outcome of the situation, logical reasoning is not enough to persuade them to provide a statement. The interrogator may choose to face the suspect with the reality of their situation by asking, "What would I have to tell you in order to convince you that talking to me is in your best interest?"

   ♦ **Fear of Retaliation** — The suspect's fear for his safety or the safety of his family member can be difficult to overcome. This fear is particularly relevant in drug cases and with gang involvement.

Consider telling the suspect that you are concerned with their safety because of their associations. Ask what you can do to help them. Empathize with the dilemma that the suspect faces. Be firm in stating that the suspect has more to fear from the gang or drug dealer than from the police. Tell them that they are not safer by not giving a statement; their presence at the station will already be known by the people they fear. Their best option is to cooperate with the police.

Tactic #2.
Confronting the suspect with existing evidence of guilt

Another very common approach to persuade the suspect is to confront him or her with the evidence of their guilt. This may involve telling the suspect about physical evidence that demonstrates they committed the crime. Recognize that they may be trying to turn the focus of the investigation in another direction for fear they will be discovered as the guilty person. This can cause him or her to act as if they are helping the police.

♦ *Paranoia*—Suspects may fear that the police are looking in their direction as a suspect and may volunteer information to police that is designed to send the investigation in another direction. Suspects have been known to offer a diversion so that the police will not focus on them. They don't know how much information the police have, so they take the role of a compliant witness who may be helpful to the police. A suspect may even offer the identification of a fictitious perpetrator, or give evidence that would appear to exonerate them.

Use any evidence that has been obtained which could indicate the person's guilt. For example: point to a failed polygraph test as providing evidence that they are guilty. If the person passed the polygraph test explain that the test is not an exact science which is why it is not allowed as evidence in many states. Suggest that even guilty individuals can pass the polygraph.

Use the relationship that the individual had to the victim in case of personal violence, housebreaks, or even arson. Provide reasons why the individual would want to "get back" at the victim for some perceived wrong. Use the suspect's knowledge of the geographic area as an indication that the suspect had access to the place where the crime was committed. Consider the access the suspect had to property or money at their place of employment for crimes that have been committed at work.

Tactic #3.
Undermining the
suspect's confidence
in his or her denials

If the suspect does not think that you have sufficient evidence to arrest, they may be reluctant to provide that information during an interrogation. This can work in the favor of the interrogator. This suspect may agree to talk in order to convince the interrogator that they are innocent. Another approach is simply not to allow denials. Stop the individual from denying and assert firmly that there is sufficient evidence that they are lying. Present them with your firm belief of their guilt.

♦ **Fear of Arrest**—The fear of being arrested is equally high for those that have had little contact with the police as those who have been arrested before. Suspects that have prior arrests may fear the laws that mandate jail for multiple arrests. Those with no previous contact with the police fear the consequences of arrest.

There are two options for overcoming the suspect's fear of arrest. The first is to decide that you will not arrest that individual when the interrogation is over. With this decision the suspect is told, "You will not be arrested TODAY, I will consider everything you have to say and make that determination at another time." Add, "This is your chance to tell me everything you want to say, it will be your only chance to do this." Having taken this position, you must follow through and not make the arrest at that time!

The second option for overcoming the resistance to arrest is to state that they are already under arrest; nothing is going to change that (when in fact they have already been arrested). Or, "regardless of what you say, the facts of the case speak for themselves, you only have the option of cooperating at this point."

Tactic #4. Identifying contradictions in the suspect's alibi or story

The term "because" has been identified as a powerful persuasive word (Hogan, 2002). Use it liberally during an interrogation to make your point. Tell the suspect that he or she committed the crime BECAUSE . . . Examples: "You did the robbery because you wanted the money, plain and simple." Or, "Your alibi does not make sense because there was plenty of time for you to have committed the burglary before . . . or after . . ." Or, "Because I think you did not mean to keep that money I want you to tell me what really happened." Consider in financial crimes that the person might be more concerned with returning the money or property or making restitution. Identifying contradictions the suspect's story is one of the most successful interrogation tactics for obtaining a confession (Leo, 1996).

◆ **Fear of financial repercussions** — The officer should act in a manner that is nonjudgmental. The perpetrator may have committed the crime because it seemed like the only alternative at the time. Afterwards the fear sets in and they may be torn on what to do about it.

Faced with evidence that the suspect stole money or properties consider that there may be reasons that the suspect justified the theft at the time, but feels remorseful. Attempt to engage the suspect with why they committed the crime. "Were you late in paying your bills?" Or, "Do have a drug or alcohol problem?" Or, "Do you feel underpaid and undervalued by your employer?" Minimize the crime and offer justifications that would encourage the suspect to talk about their "reasons" for committing the act.

Tactic #5.
Asking specific "behavioral analysis" interview questions

The suspect may make an emotional or rational choice to confess having committed a crime. Determine if your suspect is a guilt-ridden offender or an apathetic offender in order to present an emotional argument or a rational argument. A *guilt-ridden offender* would be expected to experience a higher level of remorse, be sensitive about the effects of the offense, and be concerned what others think about him or her. The *apathetic offender* is one who does not experience remorse, considers himself justified in having committed the crime, and is most concerned with avoiding punishment.

Offenders with a guilty conscience would react to the words of the interrogator, may appear to have a more relaxed body posture, and an unwillingness to look the interrogator in the eyes (Inbau et al., 2001). This offender type may show signs of nervousness such as sweating or frequent licking of lips and wiping of eyebrows. A guilt-ridden offender may stutter and verbally trip over their words during conversation.

The apathetic offender appears not to care about his or her situation as the suspect of a crime. This offender may lack remorse due to mental illnesses such as antisocial personality. The offender will look the interrogator in the eye with defiance and deny participation in the crime.

Refer back to Chapter Six for additional behavioral techniques that would be useful for determining the types of questions that might be asked and some expected responses to guilt. Use behavioral indicators of guilt as a means of confronting the suspect. Point out that they may be able to hide their emotions, but not their facial expressions! Look at their body posture and determine if they are generally truthful or evasive. Use this information as a part of the argument to overcome resistance to providing a statement.

Tactic #6.
Appealing to the importance of cooperation

- ◆ **Loss of Job** — If the individual has status in the community or a well paying job, they may fear losing that employment job as a result of being arrested. Fear that admitting guilt will have financial repercussions is a real concern.

During the assessment questions on employment status are common. Use this information to springboard to a statement like, "What do you think will happen to your job because of this?" This allows the interrogator to firmly but kindly state, yes, you are guilty and there are repercussions. Face them with the suspect in order to overcome denial. Suggest starting over when this is behind him or her. A new start in the future will be their choice. If the suspect expresses concern about a family, be compassionate and minimize the repercussions.

Tactic #7. Offering moral justifications and face-saving excuses

Minimize the crime and never refer to it by its legal term. Encourage the suspect to express guilt, remorse, or anger towards the victim. In sensitive or potentially embarrassing cases the suspect can be told that you the interrogator will not contact the press and give out details of the acts. The media may report the crime, suggests the interrogator, but the information will not come from this discussion. Consider the fears that may contribute to the resistance in an effort to better use this tactic.

- ◆ **Shame** — The suspect's fear may be related to the category of crime that the suspect is accused of committing. The concern for the suspect is that in divulging the particulars of the crime they will lose respect, shock family or friends, or suffer embarrassment. The person that was victimized was likely known to the perpetrator; guilt is likely high.

Use empathy to overcome shame. Ask the suspect why he or she did what they did! Abusers of children often speak about their love for the child and how the relationship benefited the child. If the suspect knew the victim, don't circumvent that relationship, put it right out into the open. Ask if there had been an argument, or something that caused him or her to commit the crime. Offering moral justifications or excuses to the suspect is one of the most successful tactics for obtaining a confession (Leo, 1996).

Tactic #8. Confronting the suspect with false evidence of guilt

There are a variety of situations when confront the suspect with false evidence of guilt makes sense. This is particularly true when there are more than one persons involved in the crime. The suspects should be interrogated separately. Information that is provided by one partner can be embellished on and presented as fact to the other person. The weakness of one can be presented to substantiate that their partner provided information. Suggest that the suspect has been named as the ringleader, the one who pulled the trigger, or the person who planned the crime.

  ◆ **Fear of blame**—the suspect who played a minor part in the crime will be fearful of taking blame for the crime. The concern for this suspect is that he or she will be punished disproportionately to the role they had in the act. The thought that someone else will get away with the crime and they will be imprisoned seems unfair to the suspect.

Overcome this fear by pointing out that he or she will take all of the blame unless they provide information on who actually planned and executed the act. Suggest that "You don't seem like the type of person that would kill an old lady, steal from the blind, break into the liquor store (whatever the crime was)."

Tactic #9. Praising or flattering the suspect

There are some personalities that exhibit signs of insecurity and self-doubt while others appear to thrive on attention and praise. Look for evidence that the suspect may be one who is insecure. Considerations include whether the crime committed was without apparent cause. This might suggest that the perpetrator committed the crime because it made him or her feel good. Did the suspect appear to take pleasure in the crime based on evidence that was left behind? Is there any indication that the suspect took an article of clothing, jewelry, or other keepsake from the crime scene?

  ◆ **Fear of Insignificance**—the suspect may feel powerless and insecure about his or her personal identity. Being powerful over a person or situation compensates for that fear of insignificance.

Overcoming a person's fear of insignificance requires acknowledgment from the interrogator of a "job well done." Praise and supportive statements convey a positive judgment to the suspect. This can be accomplished without supporting the act itself, but stating the obvious about what the suspect did. For example: "You did a pretty good job at cleaning up the scene." Or, "You have been successful at avoiding being caught for a long time." Or, "I noticed that you covered up the suspect. That was very considerate." Generally people will respond to praise. Flattery or praise is one of the most successful tactics in terms of obtaining a confession (Leo, 1996).

Tactic #10.
Appealing to the
detective's expertise
and authority

This last tactic refers to the display of an overconfidence by the interrogator. It is used to place emphasis on the ability of the interrogator as an investigator. It is meant to overcome resistance through status. This entails statements to the suspect that downplay their ability to "get away" with committing the crime. It might be used with the suspect who himself appears overly confident. The tactic allows the interrogator to take charge of an interrogation by suggesting that he or she is much smarter than the suspect. Break down the confidence of the suspect through negative statements on the crime, how it was accomplished, and what will result because of it.

Remember these tactics are goal oriented. They are considered prior to the interrogation and planned to meet the goals of the interrogation. Failure to consider a plan is like appearing a play without having rehearsed your lines!

Interrogation Phase III: Getting the Confession

Don't be overly solicitous or friendly; establish yourself as a professional. Always minimize the crime when speaking to the suspect. Do not use legal terminology or police jargon. Speak with the person firmly but with respect. While maintaining control over the interrogation, don't verbally back the suspect into a corner. Once the suspect feels there is no way out, they will stop talking. So give the suspect an out from the very beginning. Instead of focusing on the crime, start with what motivated the suspect to commit the crime. Don't invite a denial, ask for an explanation.

Step 1:
Make the claim

Suspects should feel that the interrogator is one who will listen. In order to actually begin the interrogation, an accusation must be made by the interrogator. There are a number of ways to do this. It is my experience that honesty works best. The interrogator's sincerity will be apparent to all but the hardest of criminals. Use their first name and do not shout. Anger should never become involved; it indicates weakness to the suspect. At all times the interrogator must be in complete control of her or his emotions and reactions.

There is one thing that an innocent man has in common with a guilty man: they will both deny having committed the crime!

When the moment arrives that the claim is to be made, the interrogator should be sitting in close proximity to the perpetrator. There should not be any tables or furniture between them. Lean towards the perpetrator slightly and say it! Firmly tell the suspect that you know he or she is guilty. Say that there is no doubt in your mind based on the investigation, that they did it. An innocent person will more likely to have a quick and strong denial along with anger at having been accused. They may jump right out of the chair and begin yelling. A guilty person is also likely to deny, but it will be slower or there will be weak protest.

Step 2: Lock it in

Once the claim has been made, there can be no further discussion on innocence. Having already considered the outcome-based tactics that can be used, this is the time to use persuasion. Tell the suspect that they need to move on, understand why it happened, or to get their version of the story. Present an excuse for the suspect, minimize their culpability in the crime, or suggest that he or she was tormented and that there was no other choice. No one likes to be caught with their hand in the cookie jar! It is predictable that people do not like being confronted with something they have done wrong. Give them good intentions; suggest that you understand that they did not mean to hurt the person, meant to return the money, or whatever fits with the crime that was committed. This will allow the suspect to maintain face.

The more a person denies something, the more they begin to believe in their own innocence. Prevent this from happening by interrupting the suspect. Encourage the person to continue in a way that is going to move forward and figure out what to do next. The situation is not going to go away, tell the suspect, they have an opportunity to have their side of the story included when it does come out. Allow the suspect to maintain their personal dignity.

There will be times when the interrogator senses an anger or disrespect from the perpetrator that would be difficult to overcome. It is perfectly acceptable to recognize that the likelihood of your obtaining a confession is low. If there is another individual that can continue the interrogation with better chances at being successful, step back and allow that individual to take over.

Been There . . . Done That! 12–4

Jane Doe was a 23-year-old female. She told me during an interview that she had left her home around 6:30 AM to go jogging. She was wearing a pair of running shorts, shirt, sneakers with socks. As she began running she noticed a commercial truck with old faded red letters on the side and back of it parked by the side of the road. It later drove past her. As she was running down a country road she saw a man running towards her. He was screaming, "ARAHAHH." He tackled her to the ground and she fell into a cornfield. She hit him in the groin and stomach. He got on top of her and she was on her back. She asked what he was doing and he replied, "I don't know." He grabbed her on the left side of her shirt and touched her left breast. Jane said she was very much in fear and kept trying to hit him. She thought her life was in danger and she kept swearing and hitting him. At one point she was able to roll him off of her and she ran to a house nearby.

She described the man as having a high voice for a man. He was a white man in his 20s, wearing a bright red shirt (pullover type) with a round neck. He was wearing tight black biker pants that came to his mid thigh. He had blonde curly hair (not tight curls) with bangs that half covered his ears.

What are crimes (if any) that you would charge this suspect? What is your assessment of him? What approach would you use to interrogate? Look for the exercise at the end of this chapter.

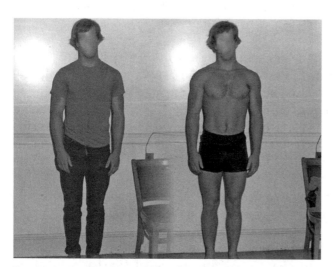

FIG. 12-1. Practice your skills! This is the suspect for the exercise at the end of this chapter. Refer back to this photo as needed.

FIG. 12-2. At the time of his arrest, your suspect was operating this truck.

Conclusions

Based on the complementary principle the interrogator can influence the suspect responses. Persuading the suspect can occur through the primary interactions of friendliness and dominance. This concept sets the stage for the interrogator to take charge of the interrogation. The interrogation is different than an interview because it presupposes the guilt of the person being questioned. Therefore, the purpose of an interrogation is to obtain a confession or an admission. Obtaining either is a successful conclusion to the interrogation process. The same legal standards that were explained in Chapter Ten govern the admissibility of the confession pertain to the admission.

The chapter covers different interrogation approaches and confession eliciting models. This should impress on the student that there is no one way to conduct an interrogation. The process is complicated. Three phases have been suggested for an outline to the interrogation process. The first phase is a preparation that should look very familiar! The first three steps are the same as the preparation for an interview. Since the guilt of the suspect is fairly certain when the interrogation takes place, additional preparation involves the timing and interrogator determination. Phase II is an important step in persuading the suspect to confess. It is suggested that the interrogator go into the process after having already considered the possible tactics that might be used to overcome resistance to providing a confession. Central to the development of outcome-based tactics is the understanding of fears that the suspect has to the interrogation. Suggestions have been made on how to overcome the listed fears, but by no means is this an exhaustive list of possibilities.

Chapter Twelve Questions for Review

Short Answer Questions

1. Explain what the complementary principle might mean to the potential interrogator.

2. Explain the difference between a confession and an admission.

3. What are the three reasons why the interrogation process becomes compromised when the investigator puts all energy into obtaining a confession rather than collecting evidence?

4. Discuss the concept of having two people conduct an interrogation. Why should one person do most of the interrogating? What should the other person focus on?

5. Explain why the non-custodial and custodial interrogations differ for the purposes of *Miranda* warnings.

6. State two reasons why the interrogator should know the case prior to conducting the interrogation.

7. What is the value of conducting a background check on the suspect prior to the interrogation?

8. What can be gained from the interrogator viewing the scene of the crime prior to the interrogation?

9. What are some of the factors that might influence the timing of the interrogation?

10. List three fears that cause resistance to interrogation.

11. Explain at least three of the tactics that have been identified as frequently used by police.

Fill in Questions

1. According to_____ , humans interact within the two boundaries of dominance and friendliness.

2. The primary purpose of the interrogation is to _____ from the suspect that acknowledges or indicates the guilt of that person.

3. An _____ is a statement of guilty conduct, containing only facts from which guilt may be inferred.

4. The interrogation should take place when _____ .

5. An interrogation is not an option after the individual _____ on the crimes under investigation or asks to speak to an attorney.

6. It is necessary to _____ and plan for an interrogation.

7. The interrogation is intentionally

_____ .

8. Develop _____ tactics prior to conducting an interrogation.

9. One thing that an innocent man has in common with a guilty man is that they will both

_____ .

Exercises

1. Non-custodial *vs.* Custodial Interrogation

   ◆ List the differences between a non-custodial and custodial interrogation for purposes of *Miranda* warnings.

   ◆ Provide three non-custodial situations. Are *Miranda* warnings required for these situations? Why or why not?

   ◆ Provide three custodial situations. Are *Miranda* warnings required in these situations? Why or why not?

   The victim statement for the following exercises is located in Been There . . . Done That 12-4. You can refer to figures 12–1 and 12–2 as the evidence for this exercise.

2. Complete each step of Interrogation Phase I : Preparation. Describe in writing what you have done for each step, justify any decisions that you make. For step 3 go to the law library or online and find the statute that defines all of the possible crimes for your state regarding this case. Write down the information on all of the possible crimes. This is a great place to look for the criminal code in your jurisdiction: http://straylight.law.cornell.edu/topics/state_statutes2.html#criminal_code

3. Complete Interrogation Phase II : Develop Outcome-Based Tactics. Consider the obstacles that may be present in this case scenario. How might they be overcome? What tactics would be beneficial to persuade the suspect to provide a confession? What fears might the suspect have about what he did?

4. Without actually questioning anyone, determine the approach for making the claim and locking the suspect in on the guilt. Explain your reasoning.

Reference List

Bruton v. *U.S.,* 391 US 123, 139 (1968).

Commonwealth v. *Forde,* 392 Mass. 453 (1984).

Garner, B. (2004). *Black's Law Dictionary* (8th ed.). St. Paul, MN: West Publishing Co.

Gordon, N. J., & Fleisher, W. L. (2002). *Effective interviewing & interrogation techniques.* San Diego, CA: Academic Press.

Gudjonsson, G. H. (2003). *The psychology of interrogations and confessions: A handbook.* Hoboken, NJ: Wiley & Sons Inc.

Gurtman, M. B. (2001). Interpersonal complementarity: Integrating interpersonal measurement with interpersonal models. *Journal of Counseling Psychology,* 48(1), 97–110.

Hogan, K. (2002). *The psychology of persuasion.* Gretna, LA: Pelican Publishing.

Inbau, F. E., Reid, J. E., Buckley, J. P., & Jayne, B. C. (2001). *Criminal interrogation and confessions* (4th ed.). Gaithersburg, MD: Aspen Publishers, Inc.

Leo, R. A. (1996). Inside the interrogation room. *Journal of Criminal Law and Criminology.* 86, pgs. 266–303. Available: http://www.lexisnexis.com//universe.

Rutledge, D. (1994). *Criminal Interrogation: Law and Tactics* (3rd ed.). Pacerville, CA: Copperhouse Publishing Company.

Sadler, P., & Woody, E. (2003). Is who you are who you're talking to? Interpersonal style and complementarity in mixed-sex interactions. *Journal of Personality and Social Psychology,* 84(1), 80–96.

Juvenile Rights and Police Responsibilities

CHAPTER
OBJECTIVES

After completing this chapter, you should be able to:

- Describe the difference between the status offense and juvenile delinquency
- Define the term "juvenile"
- State the significance of *In re Gault*
- Explain the U.S. Constitutional rights that apply to juveniles
- Explain the infancy rule
- Compare and contrast firesetting with fireplay
- List the categories of juvenile encounter that do not involve custody
- Describe the method to interview a juvenile sexual offender
- Explain the circumstances under which a child may be taken into temporary custody
- List numerous factors considered for the juvenile waiver of rights to be valid

Introduction

The treatment of juveniles by society has varied over time. Christian beliefs stressed their innocence, while the eighteenth-century viewed children as potential little devils. During the English feudal system the notion of *parens patriae* was established. *Parens Patriae* is the power of the State to act on behalf of the child and provide care and protection equivalent to that of a parent, sometimes over the objection of the parent. In America children soon became creatures to exploit as an important part of economic life.

Courtesy of iStockphoto, Inc.

Children were treated as adults in criminal matters, absent the due process rights enjoyed by adults. They were sentenced in adult courts and taken to adult jails. It was not until 1889 that Illinois enacted the first juvenile law to regulate the treatment and control of dependant, neglected, and delinquent children. Since that time children could be picked up by the police with little reason, held and questioned for long periods of time without notifying the parents, and placed in institutions with no recourse by the parents. Under the notion of *parens patriae* the power of the state over children is absolute and juvenile rights provided at the whim of the court. Juveniles are not adults; as such they do not automatically have constitutional protection. The rights that are applicable to juveniles have been expressly granted by the courts and through legislative action.

What Is a Juvenile?

A *juvenile* defined under federal law is a person who has not attained his eighteenth birthday (U.S. Code 18 U.S.C. § 5031 (1994). A person over eighteen but less than twenty-one years of age is also accorded juvenile treatment if the act of juvenile delinquency occurred prior to his eighteenth birthday. All states specify by statute the maximum age for an individual to be considered a juvenile, typically 17 or 18 years old. Some states specify a younger age; in Georgia for example, a minor remains a juvenile until age 16 (The National Center for Juvenile Justice, 2004). A juvenile in Connecticut, New York, and North Carolina is a person 15 years and younger (Sickmund, 2003).

The distinction between juvenile and adult is becoming more important for the police interrogator as states move towards trying juveniles in court as adults for major crimes. This imposes a responsibility on the interrogator to ensure greater personal protections equivalent to those afforded to adults in addition to special considerations afforded to a minor.

Age of Criminal Responsibility

Children under the age of 7 are presumed to be without the ability to form criminal intent under common law. Referred to as the *infancy rule*, it is the minimum age at which a child may be charged with a criminal act. Many states have made some change in the age of criminal responsibility by statute. The age varies from state to state, and in some cases there is no minimum age. Massachusetts, for example, relies on the common law rule of age 7 to determine juvenile court jurisdiction; the Colorado delinquency age is 10; and Arizona has no lower age specified (The National Center for Juvenile Justice, 2004).

Juvenile Offending

The vast majority of juvenile offenders enter the juvenile justice system through law enforcement agencies. Approximately seven out of ten arrested juveniles are referred to juvenile court (Sickmund, 2003). There are two different categories of wrongdoing that apply to juveniles: the status offense and the delinquent offense.

A *status offense* is an act that would not be a crime if it was committed by an adult; it is illegal only because the child is under age. If the act were committed by an adult, it would not be criminal. Examples include truancy, runaway, and curfew violations. Some states treat status offenders differently from delinquents. In other states, the distinction as a status offender can have relatively little effect on the child's treatment. Many states view these behaviors as indicators that the child is in need of services; then the matter is handled though social services. Many states retain juvenile court jurisdiction for status offenses, abuse, neglect, or dependency through age 20 (Sickmund, 2003).

Juvenile delinquency is the violation of a law of the United States committed by a person prior to his eighteenth birthday which would have been a crime if committed by an adult (U.S. Code 18 U.S.C. § 5031 (1994).) The age for a minor to be adjudicated under the jurisdiction of the juvenile court will vary from state to state depending on its definition of juvenile. The juvenile court authority may extend as late as age 24 in California, Montana, Oregon, and Wisconsin, yet most states end jurisdiction in delinquency cases at age 21 (Sickmund, 2003). Age and offense together provide another way of determining juvenile delinquency. Some state statutes exclude types of juvenile offenders from juvenile court jurisdiction, mandating that the case originate in criminal court.

Been There . . . Done That! 13–1

Like other typical seven-year-old boys, Michael and Stephen frequently took turns spending the night at each other's house. I interviewed the boys to determine who had been victimized by whom. Michael and Stephen, I learned, performed anal and oral sex on each other. This had occurred on at least a dozen occasions.

It was Michael who had initiated the sex; he had been doing it with his step-brother every night for about a year. Jerry was sixteen years old and had come to live with Michael and his parents at that time. They shared a room with bunk beds and Jerry would come down from his bunk bed at night to have sex with Michael. Jerry was a special education student who had both physical and learning disabilities.

Who is the perpetrator here? Are there more than one? Is the perpetrator a juvenile or adult?

Juvenile Delinquency

The juvenile arrest rate grew substantially during the late 1980s and peaked in 1994. Decreasing steadily since its peak, by 2002 the arrest rate of persons under the age of 18 was nearly half its 1994 level (Snyder, 2004). While this is encouraging, juvenile crime remains a significant problem with an estimated 2.3 million arrests in 2002. According to the Federal Bureau of Investigation (FBI), juveniles accounted for 17% of all arrests and 15% of all violent crime arrests in 2002. Females represent an increasing proportion of juvenile arrests. Approximately 85% of delinquency cases referred to juvenile court in the United States originates from police officers.

Due Process and the Juvenile

In 1966 the Supreme Court of the United States responded to the problem of nonstandardized procedures and a general lack of juvenile protection with one of the first cases concerning juvenile rights. Although the *Kent* decision was confined solely to the issue of waiver proceedings in the juvenile court, its expression of disenchantment with juvenile justice has had a wide ramification in the entire juvenile justice system (*Kent* v. *United States*, 1966).

The most important case in the history of juvenile justice is the *Gault* decision, an attack on the *parens patriae* doctrine (*In re Gault,* 1967). This one case is almost solely responsible for changing the juvenile system into an adversarial process, bringing it closer to resembling the adult system. The Supreme Court stated that due process and the Fourteenth Amendment of the U.S. Constitution apply to juveniles when the juvenile faces possible commitment.

Case in Point 13–1

Case in Point: *In re Gault* (1967)

The case of *In re Gault* started when 15-year-old Gerald Gault and his friend made lewd telephone calls to a neighbor. After a complaint by that neighbor, Gault was arrested and detained by police. His parents worried that their son was not at home that day, they were never notified of his arrest and only found out later through a friend of Gault's. The complainant, Mrs. Cook, never testified about the phone calls. No one was sworn in and the trial was not recorded. After proceedings before a juvenile court judge, Gault was committed to the State Industrial School for six years, until he reached the age of 21. An adult charged with the same crime would have received a maximum of a 50-dollar fine and two months in jail.

The U.S. Supreme Court decided that the proceedings for juveniles had to comply with the requirements of the Fourteenth Amendment. These requirements included adequate notice of charges, notification of both the parents and the child of the juvenile's right to counsel, opportunity for confrontation and cross-examination at the hearings, and adequate safeguards against self-incrimination. The Court found that the procedures used in Gault's case met none of these requirements.

Importance:

1. *In re Gault* is the most significant case in juvenile justice history. The Court established that juveniles do have certain due process rights. This changed the adjudication procedure into an adversarial process and opened up the flood gates for juveniles to be treated more formally and increasingly more like adults within the criminal justice system.

Initiated in 1971, the Juvenile Justice Standards Project developed a set of standards for juvenile justice after the *Gault* decision (Flicker, 2005). Rejecting the conventional medical model based on a need for treatment as the reason for the court's involvement, it adopted a due process model governed by equity and fairness. Several principles developed, including a greater accountability of the juvenile justice system with the rights and responsibilities of agencies clearly stated and enforced. According to Flicker (2005) ten basic principles emerged; known as the IJA-ABA Juvenile Justice Standards:

1. Sanctions should be proportionate to the seriousness of the offense.

2. Sentences should be fixed by the court rather than indeterminate sentence determined by correctional authorities.

3. The least restrictive alternative should be required at every stage of proceedings.

4. Status offenses should be removed from juvenile court jurisdiction.

5. Limitations should be imposed on interventions prior to adjudication.

6. Open court proceedings should replace closed sessions.

7. The juvenile delinquent should have part in the decision making process.

8. Parental roles in the process should be redefined.

9. There should be a right to counsel at all crucial stages and unwaivable right to counsel for juveniles.

10. Strict criteria should be established for waiver for juvenile court jurisdiction to regulate the transfer of juveniles to adult court.

This due process approach dominates the juvenile justice system today. Rather than providing consistency, however, the approach means that we now have a different juvenile justice system in every state in the nation. Increasingly the juvenile system more resembles the adult system, but there is no uniform approach that has been adopted. Generally, the due process model favors accountability and punishment, with less focus on juvenile rehabilitation.

The current legal trend is toward the punishment of juveniles as adults for felony crimes; the extent varies from state to state. In specific circumstances, juveniles in every state may be prosecuted as adults. In order to prosecute a juvenile in adult court, the vast majority of states authorize juvenile court judges to waive jurisdiction, and prosecutors in fifteen states have that authority (Griffin, 2004). In at least 29 states, juveniles who commit specific major crimes must be tried in adult court if they had attained the minimum statutory age requirement (Griffin, 2004). Greater access to juvenile records mean that subsequent adults sentences may be enhanced under three-strikes laws or pursuant to sentencing guidelines in both the federal and state criminal justice system (Shepherd, nd).

At the same time, an increasing concern over the vulnerability of juveniles has surfaced. Studies indicate that juveniles are in the category of those particularly susceptible to police interrogation techniques which may lead to a false confession (Napier & Adams, 2002). Examples of at risk persons include youthfulness, low or borderline IQ, mental handicap, psychological inadequacy, illiteracy, fatigue, or inexperience with the criminal justice system. The questioning approach for juveniles requires not only a due process orientation in addition to the recognition that juveniles require special protections as children.

Questioning a Juvenile NOT in Custody

Juveniles can be approached informally and asked questions without parent present or *Miranda* warnings given (*Miranda* v. *Arizona,* 1966). It should not be overlooked that every police encounter is not adversarial or accusatory. In the investigation of crime, it is legitimate to seek witnesses of any age. It should be standard procedure that when a police officer responds to a home, particularly for domestic disputes, that each child in the home be interviewed separately at the scene. The primary reason is to assess the safety of the child in addition to obtaining information on the crimes under investigation.

Juveniles may also be questioned in relation to a complaint. There is a great amount of police discretion on how the matter will be resolved. Approximately one-quarter of all juveniles arrested are handled within the police department and then released (Sickmund, 2003). To settle the complaint, a police officer will likely speak to the juvenile in an encounter. Two general types of police encounters are common in complaints concerning juveniles (Cicourel, 2005):

- ◆ **Field Examination.** Police officers may be called to the scene or they may be passing a situation that appears to be suspicious.
- ◆ **Station Investigation.** Police officers conduct an investigation into a crime that may involve a juvenile offender.

In the field examination encounter there are usually people around that can provide information about what happened. Examples include situations when a juvenile is accused of stealing, or a fight broke out, or the school called reporting a student that did not attend. The police officer asks people what happened, including the juvenile who was involved, and the matter may quickly be resolved if it is a minor violation or a status offense. Possible resolutions include having a parent or guardian called to pick up the child along with a warning or a school sanction. If the event was serious, or the juvenile is a repeat offender, then a juvenile probation officer might also be contacted. A summons to juvenile court would be requested by the police officer or school official if court involvement is warranted.

The station investigation would occur when the offense is of a serious nature or the juveniles would not give information about their involvement towards the resolution of the complaint. The juvenile may be detained for a short period of time until the matter is resolved or a legal guardian is available to come to the station to pick the minor up. The station investigation allows the officer the opportunity to get background information on the juvenile and collect evidence if warranted. The officer would have experience in dealing with juvenile offenders and be aware of the possible dispositions that are available in that jurisdiction.

Been There . . . Done That! 13–2

In an otherwise quiet neighborhood an unexpected homicide occurred. A fifteen-year-old girl was bludgeoned to death in the woods on her way to school one day. There was no apparent sexual offending, although her skirt had been left raised up to her waist.

The investigation pointed towards a fifteen-year-old boy who had recently fallen for the girl, but had been rebuked. Going to the home of the boy, his mother admitted the police into the house. She gave permission for a search of her son's bedroom. A parent can give consent for a search of his or her home and the space that is occupied by a minor in most situations. Only when the child has a heightened expectation of privacy due to age, payment of rent, or a lock on the door that does not allow access by the other family members do the parents lose their standing to consent to a search. These conditions vary from state to state. A sneaker was found which appeared to have a blood stain; it was confiscated.

At the time the law specified that a child in my state could not be tried as an adult unless it could be shown that he was not "amenable to treatment." In other words, the prosecution had to show that the minor had been in treatment prior to the offense and could not be rehabilitated. This killer had never been arrested before, not even for shoplifting. He was tried as juvenile and found delinquent. At age 18 he would be released.

Interrogation Methods

The location for questioning the juvenile should be private and free of distraction. Avoid interviewing the juvenile in a public place where they can be seen; they are more liable to be embarrassed or angered. A juvenile interviewed on the street is ever mindful that someone may be watching which may cause the child to be overly cautious of what is said. Give the juvenile some privacy; even stepping inside a store or around a corner may be of benefit. A sign that this is a problem is evident when the juvenile keeps looking around rather than focusing on the police officer.

Interrogating at his or her home should be avoided if the juvenile is suspected of wrongdoing. It is not unusual for a juvenile to be fearful of how a parent will react to bad behavior or criminal involvement. Avoid contacting them at school and only remove the child from school as a last resort. Be sure that the parents are notified if the child is removed from school. Involving the school tends to stigmatize the juvenile, regardless of the outcome of an interview.

The officer conducting the questioning should have a general understanding of the developmental stages of children. More importantly, the police officer should feel comfortable with children, willing to speak on whatever level is necessary to put the child at ease. Be mindful that an interrogation without custody means NO custody. The suspect must be fully aware that he or she is free to go and is not under arrest. The atmosphere should not be adversarial or lead the suspect to believe that they are no longer free to stop the questioning. Factors that might affect the issue of custody include:

♦ Early morning or late evening demands to report to the police station
♦ An interrogation where the juvenile is not appropriately clothed, is denied food, or water
♦ The absence of any offer to take a "break"
♦ Promises to let the suspect go only if a confession is provided

If possible, a parent or guardian should be contacted and requested to bring the juvenile to the place of questioning. The situation should not be discussed on the telephone, necessitating the personal interview with the child and parent or guardian. Providing the juvenile his or her rights per *Miranda* occurs under the same conditions as with adults; custody and interrogation remain the controlling factors. There are no special inter-

Case in Point 13–2

Case in Point: *Yarborough* v. *Alvarado* (2004)

Michael Alvarado was 17 years old when he was questioned by police about his crime involvement. His parents brought him to the station and waited in the lobby during the interview. Alvarado was interviewed by one officer for two hours; he was not given a warning under *Miranda,* nor was he arrested. During the interview, Alvarado confessed involvement in an attempted carjacking and death of the vehicle's owner. He was twice asked if he needed a break, and when the interview was over his parents drove him home. In part based on these statements Alvarado was convicted of second-degree murder and attempted robbery. After conviction his case was appealed, resulting in a reversal of the conviction. The Ninth Circuit held that the state court erred in failing to account for Alvarado's youth and inexperience when evaluating whether a reasonable person in his position would have felt free to leave the interview.

The U.S. Supreme Court disagreed. Justice Kennedy delivered the majority opinion in a 5–4 decision that reversed the Ninth Circuit. The majority found that the state criminal court that convicted Alvarado had reached a reasonable conclusion that the minor was not in custody for *Miranda* purposes when he was

interviewed. The Court cited a number of factors that indicated that Alvarado was not in custody at the time he was questioned, including the fact that he went to the station voluntarily, was never told he could not leave, was not threatened by authorities, was told the interview would be brief, and was allowed to return home afterwards. According to the Court, *Miranda* can be distinguished from other cases that require special consideration of age for juvenile offenders.

The majority also stressed the importance of a clear rule for police to apply. Allowing different standards for juveniles would make it more difficult for police to determine when *Miranda* warnings are necessary.

Importance:

1. This case answered an important question: when deciding whether a suspect is "in custody" and therefore entitled to his *Miranda* warnings, must a police officer consider the suspect's age and previous history with law enforcement? The U.S. Supreme Court ruled "NO" to the question. The *Miranda* test was an objective rule with objective criterion that the police officer must consider when determining custody. Age and other subjective individual characteristics do not need to be considered in that determination.

rogation rules or requirements for juveniles that differ from adults (*Yarborough, Warden* v. *Alvarado,* 2004).

In order to obtain a complete and accurate report from the juvenile avoid alienating him. Do not lose your temper and avoid a tough guy attitude. Coercive practices may push an innocent but frightened or emotionally troubled child to confess.

Questioning a Juvenile IN Custody

When the purpose of the interview is to elicit information that may incriminate the juvenile in criminal activity, and the juvenile might be considered to be in custody, he or she must be provided his rights per *Miranda.* If a juvenile has been arrested on probable cause, the parent or guardian must be contacted along with any other person required by statute in the state. The questioning of juvenile suspects raises legal issues which could have a bearing on the admissibility of any confession made by a juvenile in custody. In addition to federal doctrine, each state has set the standards for a juvenile waiver to be considered valid. A legal determination of voluntariness does not depend upon youthfulness alone, but is considered a factor.

There is a national movement towards the requirement of recording confessions for both adult and juvenile offenders. In the state of New Jersey, for example the recording by video or audio of the suspect's final statement is required for juveniles facing adult charges as of January 2006 (Caher, 2004). All interrogations of juvenile offenders must be documented in writing or through recording.

Temporary Custody and Juveniles

A police officer may take a child into protective or *temporary custody,* typically for 48 hours, without a warrant if there is an emergency or if the officer has reason to believe that leaving the child in the present situation would subject the child to further abuse or harm (Hess & Drowns, 2004). Temporary custody without hearing is allowed under state welfare regulations and codes. Child maltreatment, abandonment, the child's inability to self-protect, or needed medical care refused by the parent are among the reasons why police might take a juvenile into custody which would not be considered an arrest.

In many cases concerning delinquency the police make an initial determination to detain the juvenile following an arrest. A detention hearing is conducted after 24 or 48 hours as specified state statute. Unlike the adult criminal justice system, in the juvenile system bail release is uncommon if it is permitted at all. Release of the juvenile is determined based on whether the minor is a flight risk or a danger to self or others.

Fourth Amendment Considerations

The Fourth Amendment to the Constitution of the United States protects citizens from an unreasonable search and seizure. The exclusionary rule that prohibits the use in court of any evidence that was seized illegally was applied to the states in 1961 (*Mapp* v. *Ohio,* 1961). This same protection against unreasonable search and seizure, as well as the remedy of exclusion, applies to police action involving juveniles.

The landmark Supreme Court cases that focus on unreasonable search and seizure issues of juveniles settle disputes on the actions of school officials but expressly include police conduct. For example, in *New Jersey* v. *T.L.O.* the Court stated:

> The Fourth Amendment's prohibition on unreasonable searches and seizures applies to searches conducted by public school officials **and is not limited to searches carried out by law enforcement officers.** Nor are school officials exempt from the Amendment's dictates by virtue of the special nature of their authority over school-children. In carrying out searches and other functions pursuant to disciplinary policies mandated by state statutes, school officials act as representatives of the State, not merely as surrogates for the parents of students, and they cannot claim the parents' immunity from the Fourth Amendment's strictures (*New Jersey* v. *T.L.O,* 1985).

The language in state courts has made the specific application of Fourth Amendment protections to juvenile cases a bit clearer. In New Jersey a Superior Court held:

> Is not more outrageous for the police to treat children more harshly than adult offenders, especially when such is violative of due process and fair treatment? Can a court countenance a system, where, as here, an adult may suppress evidence with the usual effect of having the charges dropped for lack of proof, and on the other hand, a juvenile can be institutionalized for "rehabilitative" purposes because the Fourth Amendment right is unavailable to him? (*State* v. *Lowry,* 1967).

Fifth Amendment Considerations

A juvenile suspected of committing a crime has the a privilege against self-incrimination (*Gault,* 1967). A juvenile may waive his or her Fifth

Amendment rights and consent to interrogation (*Fare* v. *Michael C.*, 1979). A voluntary relinquishment of a right occurs when the relinquishment is the product of a free and deliberate choice rather than intimidation, coercion, or deception (*Moran* v. *Burbine*, 1986). A determination on whether the juvenile's waiver is voluntary and knowing is one to be resolved on the totality of the circumstances surrounding the interrogation.

The court must determine not only that the statements were not coerced or suggested, but also that they were not the products of ignorance of rights or of adolescent fantasy, fright, or despair. A juvenile's waiver of *Miranda* rights will always be suspect if given without the advice of a parent or adult guardian. The presence of a parent or guardian is not required for a voluntary waiver under the federal standard, although it is a factor to be considered. Some states do require a waiver be made by an interested adult for the juvenile waiver to be valid. Among the factors that are considered will be:

- ◆ The juvenile's age;
- ◆ experience with the criminal justice system;
- ◆ level of education;
- ◆ background;
- ◆ intelligence;
- ◆ whether he has the capacity to understand the warning given to him;
- ◆ the nature of his Fifth Amendment rights;
- ◆ and the consequences of waiving them.

The Right to Counsel

The difference between the Fifth and Sixth Amendment rights to counsel deserves emphasis. The Fifth Amendment right attaches during all custodial interrogation. The Sixth Amendment right is not triggered by custody but by the initiation of adversary judicial proceedings. These begin when a formal charge is filed (*Rhode Island* v. *Innis,* 1980).

With the landmark case *In re Gault,* the right to counsel for juveniles was firmly documented during custodial interrogation (*Gault,* 1967). That right does not refer to a probation officer, parent, or other interested adult. A waiver of the assistance of counsel in a majority of states is required by both the juvenile and a parent when the suspect being interrogation is under age 14. States may require consultation with an adult in order for a waiver of counsel to be valid. The "opportunity" for consultation with an adult after age 14 is the requirement in other states; whether or not that consultation actually occurs is immaterial. Several states prohibit or limit waiver of counsel by juveniles; those that permit it require proof that the juvenile understands the meaning and consequences of waiver, or grant waiver only after a juvenile consults with parents or guardians.

The Sixth Amendment of the U. S. Constitution protects children's rights to assistance of defense counsel (*Gideon* v. *Wainwright*, 1963). The Sixth Amendment right attaches only "at or after the initiation of adversary judicial criminal proceedings"(*Kirby* v. *Illinois*, 1972). Once adversary proceedings have begun, a defendant may not be interrogated in the absence of counsel, nor be induced into making incriminating statements, unless he initiates further interrogation and freely waives his Fifth and Sixth Amendment rights. After the Sixth Amendment right to counsel attaches and is invoked, any statements obtained from the accused during subsequent *police-initiated* custodial questioning regarding the charge at issue (even if the accused purports to waive his rights) are inadmissible. Police officers are not prohibited from interrogating a juvenile about uncharged crimes following his valid waiver under *Miranda* of his right to counsel just because he previously appeared with an attorney at a judicial proceeding on an unrelated offense.

The right to effective assistance of counsel has been acknowledged to apply to juvenile justice (*Stickland* v. *Washington*, 1984). Some, but not all state statutes require appointment of counsel at all stages of the juvenile proceedings (Jones, 2004).

Juvenile Confession Admissibility

In addition to voluntariness, the courts also have considered the statutory requirement of prompt presentment in connection with the admissibility of confessions. Below is the federal provision; state codes provide similar requirements. Title 18 U.S.C. § 5033 provides, in part:

> **The juvenile shall be taken before a magistrate forthwith. In no event shall the juvenile be detained for longer than a reasonable period of time before being brought before a magistrate.**

Similar to the McNabb/Mallory rule for adults, some courts have held inadmissible those confessions obtained during a delay in presenting the juvenile before the court. Factors used in deciding when the federal provision has been violated include a focus on the "forthwith" language and some courts rely on the "reasonable period of time" language.

What is considered a reasonable time to bring a juvenile before the court for arraignment after an arrest? The Second Circuit held a delay between a 10:15 a.m. arrest and a 3:00 p.m. presentment to be reasonable under the circumstances (*U.S.* v. *Smith*, 1978). The Ninth Circuit

Been There . . . Done That! 13–3

Fifteen-year-old Alice had vanished from her home one afternoon. No one knew what happened to her, until her body washed up on the bank of the river a week later with something tied around her neck. A canvass of the neighborhood brought no information until two 12-year-old boys claimed they knew what had happened. I was called in to interview the boys before their statements could be contaminated.

Each boy claimed that he had seen Alice get into a really "hot car" with two boys. She was not forced into the car, but got into the front seat between the driver and the passenger. They had seen the boys around, but neither boy knew who they were. The boys did not really look at the two males and could not describe them in any detail. What they did notice was the CAR! Armed with my drawing equipment, I asked each boy to draw me a picture of the car and explain to me why it was so hot! What came out of that was a very specific car with custom dual tailpipes. From their description we found the car and identified the driver.

The driver of the car was a 17-year-old white male and his passenger was a 16-year-old Hispanic male. They confessed to me and two other interrogators that they had taken their friend Alice for a ride and wanted sex on the riverbank. She said no. Angry, the 17-year-old took off his sock and tied it around her neck. She was kicking and scratching at them as they took her by the arms and legs and threw her into the river alive. They told me that they were her friends.

has held that a valid waiver of *Miranda* rights also constitutes a waiver of prompt presentment rights (*U.S.* v. *Indian Boy X*, 1978). Because of the different approaches to this issue, it is essential to consult the law of your circuit and the requirements under your state law.

Specific Crime Categories

Generally, juveniles tend to victimize other juveniles. The majority of victims of juvenile violence are juveniles; more than half of juvenile violent crime victims faced a juvenile offender (McCurley & Snyder, 2004). Almost half of the victims of nonfatal violent crimes are juvenile acquaintances of the offender.

Juvenile Firesetting

Arson is the crime most frequently committed by juveniles; untreated, the probability that the child will set another fire is over 80% (Liscio, 1999). The problem of juvenile arson is staggering. Approximately half of all arrests for arson involve a juvenile (Snyder, 2004). Fires set by juveniles claim the lives of approximately 300 people and destroy more than $300 million worth of property each year (Putnam & Kirkpatrick, 2005).

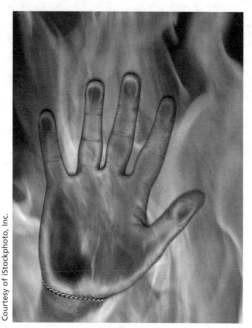

Arson is the crime most frequently committed by juveniles.

The authors make a distinction between fireplay and fire-setting, behaviors with different degrees of damage and intent. *Fireplay* is a curiosity and fascination of fire, most common among children and adolescents; damage caused is not maliciously inspired but is related to expression. Expressive fireplay suggests unresolved trauma or psychopathology. For example, a young victim of sexual abuse may intentionally set her bed on fire as an expressive means to control a situation in which she feels powerless. *Firesetting* is willful action with a higher level of intent to use fire as a weapon and an instrument of power; its setting is to achieve a goal.

An effective interview of the suspected juvenile may make the difference between an unsolved fire and one with the cause clearly established and the offender arrested (Zipper & Wilcox, 2005). Authors Zipper and Wilcox (2005) suggest that there is give-and-take between the juvenile and the investigator where the suspect tests to find out if the real cause has been determined. The interrogator must go into the interview fully prepared with information from early witness interviews. Similar to other interview techniques the investigator must first introduce him/herself and the purpose for the interview; rapport is then established during which time an analysis of the suspects living conditions can be determined. Allow the juvenile to give a complete narrative without interruption, using the information to determine follow-up questions. Closure occurs with a statement that there may be a need for a future interview.

Questions to consider during an interrogation of the juvenile firesetter include:

- What did you use to start this fire?
- Where did you get these lighters or matches?
- What did you set on fire?
- What did you do after you used the lighter or matches to get the fire started?
- How many others were involved? Who were they?
- How did you feel after you started the fire?
- Has anything happened lately that really bothers you?
- What have you set on fire in the past?

Sexual Offending

Sexual offenses committed by juveniles represent a serious problem. Indications are that one half of adult sexual offenders began their sexually abusive behavior as a juvenile. Almost one third of arrests for sex offenses involves youth under the age of 18 (Righthand & Welch, 2001). Studies indicate that males are the most frequent sexual offenders; however the rate of girls who commit sex offenses is believed to be highly underreported (Barnett, Miller-Perrin, and Perrin, 1997). Preadolescent children, as young as 3 and 4, have been identified as being sexually aggressive, although the common age of onset appears to be between ages 6 and 9 (Righthand & Welch, 2001). Early intervention stands as the most successful approach to rehabilitation for sexual offenders; criminal justice plays an important role.

Polygraph tests may be an appropriate method to facilitate more complete disclosures of sexually abusive behaviors by juveniles (Righthand & Welch, 2001). Juvenile sexual offenders are often victims as well; structuring the interrogation or interrogation requires extreme sensitivity to that possibility. Getting ready for the interview is the similar whether the juvenile is a victim or a known sexual abuse offender. Preparation includes:

- ◆ Obtain background information on the offense under investigation.
- ◆ Obtain a through background on the juvenile being questioned. Determine if the child had ever been arrested or accused of a similar offense, for example.
- ◆ What are the living arrangements of the juvenile, where and with whom does he live? Who is the legal or custodial guardian?
- ◆ What is the age and grade level of the juvenile? Determine if this child is one who has a learning disability or low functioning level.
- ◆ If the child is suspect of sexual offending, is he a known victim?

If any of these preparation questions cannot be answered prior to the interview, the child should be asked directly. In some states the interview of the juvenile will be conducted by social service workers as part of the criminal investigation and sometimes prior to police involvement. Sit with the parent or guardian and explain the juvenile's *Miranda* rights and ask for a waiver of these rights. It is not advisable to interview or interrogate a juvenile on sexual offending in the presence of a parent or guardian. If a voluntary waiver is obtained, then ask the adult to allow the questioning to proceed in private, if the juvenile is willing. Explain that it is difficult to speak about these issues and they would benefit from the privacy. Here are six stages to interviewing a suspected juvenile sexual offender:

Step #1 Introduction. Explain to the juvenile who you are and why you are speaking with him or her. Establish creditability with the child by telling him or her that you frequently talk with people about things that have happened with children and families.

Step #2 Rapport building. This is an important step for the juvenile interrogation as well as an interview. Provide the juvenile with reasons why he or she might speak with you. Include the statement that the purpose of the interview is to learn the truth.

Step #3 Background. Explore information about the juvenile including family composition, criminal history, and employment history. During this phase the interrogator is gaining information about the functioning level of the juvenile. Determine the general educational level, linguistic comprehensive, comprehension about the process, and the presence of mental health issues. Verify the relationship of the victim to the offender and the circumstances under which access was gained to that child. Obtain an understanding of the typical eye contact and body language of the juvenile when discussing general topics.

Step #4 Allegation. Explain the allegation in very general terms; do not use legal language or speak above the level of understanding for the juvenile.

Step #5 Questioning. Ask the juvenile to explain the criminal acts that are under investigation. Move from general questions about specific topics to abuse focused questions. Note the changes in body language and eye contact that may occur in response to specific questions or areas of inquiry. Note consistencies and inconsistencies with what is already known about the allegation.

Explore the rationalizations for the behaviors. A juvenile may have difficulty providing reasons for sexual offending, so do not ask, "why did you . . . ?" Reasons for sexual offending may be as simple as it was done to them or that it felt good. Do not make judgments on the child but explore who had offended against him or her in a similar way. Always ask who else they have touched in a similar way; multiple offending is common.

For each event, ask where and when the act took place. Determine if there was anyone else present. Ask for specific details about each event. If the juvenile says that he had sex, for example, ask what that means. Juveniles use language for sexual acts and sexual parts that may not mean the same thing to an adult; clarification is necessary. An additional reason for specific detail is to determine that the juvenile really committed the act under investigation.

Answer questions that the juvenile may have as honestly and completely as possible.

Step #6 Closure. End the interrogation as you would an interview. Assure the juvenile that you appreciate their honesty even though the subject is difficult to talk about. Leave it open that you may want to speak with him or her again. Provide the supporting parent or guardian information without going into detailed sexual behaviors. Take the time to answer questions for the parent or guardian.

Police officers have an additional legal responsibility in cases of sexual abuse, even when the perpetrator is a juvenile. In all states and DC a report must be filed with the appropriate social services agency on suspected child victims of abuse or neglect. Mandated reporters file with the names and addresses of all victims discovered through a sexual abuse investigation.

Conclusions

It should be apparent by the end of this chapter that there are variations from state to state on the age that qualifies a person under the jurisdiction of the juvenile court in addition to differences on how juvenile offenders will be handled by the system. The consistent baseline is those rights that have been afforded to juveniles by the Supreme Court of the United States. No state can infringe on these rights. The basic Fourth, Fifth, Sixth and Fourteenth amendment rights as outlined in this chapter are applicable, and probable cause remains the standard of proof required. For the interrogator it is important to investigate the state differences on the conditions under which a juvenile can knowingly and voluntarily waive those rights. Age and crime may be factors, in addition to the presence or opportunity for the juvenile to consult with a parent or other interested adult.

Chapter Thirteen Questions for Review

Short Answer Questions

1. Compare the absolute rights afforded an adult versus those afforded a juvenile. Why is there a difference?

2. Explain the difference between status offenses and delinquency.

3. Explain the effect the *Kent* decision had on juvenile procedural.

4. Explain the effect *In re Gault,* 1967 had on the doctrine of *Parens Patriae.*

5. When is a juvenile considered to be in custody relevant to questioning? What should happen when this point is reached?

6. Under what conditions may police officers take juveniles into temporary custody? How long can the juvenile be held under these conditions?

7. Explain the rights to counsel under the Fifth and Sixth Amendments. What are the differences?

8. Discuss the scope of juvenile fire setting/arson. How does it compare to other juvenile delinquency?

9. List the steps taken to interview a suspected juvenile sex offender. What role could social services play?

10. How does the baseline of juvenile rights outlined by Supreme Court decisions help to mitigate the vast differences in juvenile law from state to state?

Fill-in Questions

1. _____ _____ is the power of the State to act in behalf of the child and provide care and protection equivalent to that of a parent.

2. The distinction between _____ is becoming more important for the police interrogator as states move towards trying juveniles in court as adults for major crimes.

3. Children under the age of 7 are presumed to be without the ability to form _____ _____ under common law.

4. Initiated in 1971, the _____ developed a set of standards for juvenile justice after the *Gault* decision.

5. Greater access to juvenile records mean that subsequent adults sentences may be _____ under three-strikes laws or pursuant to sentencing guidelines in both the federal and state criminal justice system.

6. The _____ investigation allows the officer the opportunity to get background information on the juvenile and collect evidence if warranted.

7. A voluntary relinquishment of a right occurs when the relinquishment is the product of a free and deliberate choice rather than _____ , _____ , or _____ .

8. Almost half of the victims of nonfatal violent crimes are juvenile _____ of the offender.

9. Indications are that one half of adult _____ _____ began their sexually abusive behavior as a juvenile.

10. The law requires that _____ _____ make a report to the specified agency of the names and addresses of all victims discovered through an abuse investigation.

Exercises

Who Is a Juvenile?

Directions: Decide whether or not each of the following persons is a juvenile and answer the questions below each case or hypothetical. Go to http://www.ncjj.org/stateprofiles/ to research juvenile law and procedure in YOUR home state.

1. Angela is 15 years old. She and her 18-year-old brother, Daniel, go to the shopping mall together. Daniel convinces Angela to shoplift a part he needs to repair his car; she puts it in her vest. They are both caught.

   a) Can Angela be tried in juvenile court? Why or why not?

   b) Can Daniel be tried in juvenile court? Why or why not?

2. Richard and his friend Jill are both 17 years old. They are caught driving a car they took without permission. Richard turns 18 one week after his arraignment. Jill is found guilty at her adjudicatory hearing (trial) and, based on her prior adjudications, the court orders that she spend 20 weeks in confinement. After Jill has spent 8 weeks in confinement, she turns 18.

a) Can Richard's adjudicatory hearing (trial) take place in juvenile court?

b) Will Jill be transferred from the facility operated by the Department of Social and Health Services at the time she turns 18?

Reference List

Barnett, O. W., Miller-Perrin, C. L., & Perrin, R. D. (1997). *Family violence across the lifespan: An introduction.* Thousand Oaks, CA: Sage.

Caher, J. (2004). NJ Attorney General to expand policy of taping suspects' confessions. *The Legal Intelligencer,* 231(121), 4.

Cicourel, A. V. (2005). Process and structure in juvenile justice. D. L. Parry (editor), *Essential readings in juvenile justice* (pp. 136–140). Upper Saddle River, NJ: Prentice Hall.

Fare v. *Michael C.,* 442 U.S. 707, 725 (1979).

Flicker, B. (2005). Introduction to the IJA-ABA juvenile justice standards. D. Parry (editor), *Essential readings in juvenile justice* (pp. 120–124). Upper Saddle River, NJ: Prentice Hall.

Gideon v. *Wainwright,* 372 U.S. 355 (1963).

Griffin, P. (2004). National overviews. *Juvenile Justice Profiles.* Available: http://www.ncjj.org/stateprofiles.

Hess, K., & Drowns, R. (2004). *Juvenile justice* (4th ed.). Belmont, CA: Wadsworth/Thompson Learning.

In re Gault, 387 U.S. 1 (1967).

Jones, J. B. (2004). *Access to counsel.* (Report No. NCJ 204063). Washington, DC: Office of Juvenile Justice and Delinquency Prevention.

Kent v. *United States,* 383 U.S. 541 (1966).

Kirby v. *Illinois,* 406 U.S. 682 (1972).

Liscio, D. (1999). Juvenile fire-setters. *Firehouse,* 42–46.

Mapp v. *Ohio,* 367 U.S. 643 (1961).

McCurley, C., & Snyder, H. (2004). *Victims of violent juvenile crime.* (Report No. NCJ 201628). Washington, DC: Office of Juvenile Justice and Delinquency Prevention.

Miranda v. *Arizona,* 384 U.S. 436 (1966).

Moran v. *Burbine,* 475 U.S. 412 (1986).

Napier, M., & Adams, S. (2002). Criminal confessions: Overcoming the challenges. *FBI Law Enforcement Bulletin,* 71(11), 9–15.

New Jersey v. *T.L.O,* 469 U.S. 325 (1985).

Putnam, C., & Kirkpatrick, J. (2005). *Juvenile firesetting: A research overview.* (Report No. NCJ 207606). Washington, DC: Office of Juvenile Justice and Delinquency Prevention .

Rhode Island v. *Innis,* 446 U.S. 291 (1980).

Righthand, S., & Welch, C. (2001). *Juveniles who have sexually offended.* (Report No. NCJ 184739). Washington, DC: Office of Juvenile Justice and Delinquency Prevention.

Shepherd, R. Jr. (nd). Rebirth of the infancy defense. Juvenile Justice Articles.

Sickmund, M. (2003). *Juveniles in court.* (Report No. NCJ 195420). Washington, DC: Office of Juvenile Justice and Delinquency Prevention.

Snyder, H. (2004). *Juvenile arrests 2002.* (Report No. NCJ 204608). Washington, DC: Office of Juvenile Justice and Delinquency Prevention.

State v. *Lowry,* 230 A.2d 907 (1967).

Stickland v. *Washington,* 466 U.S. 668 (1984).

The National Center for Juvenile Justice. (2004). State juvenile justice profiles. Retrieved July, 2005, from **http://www.ncjj.org/stateprofiles/**

U.S. Code 18 U.S.C. § 5031 (1994).

U.S. v. *Indian Boy X,* 656 F.2d 585, 9th Cir. (1978).

U.S. v. *Smith,* 574 F.2d 707, 2d Cir. (1978).

Yarborough, Warden v. *Alvarado,* 539 U.S. 986 (2004).

Zipper, P., & Wilcox, D. (2005). Juvenile arson: The importance of early intervention. *FBI Law Enforcement Bulletin,* 74(4), 1–9.

Index